Swimming Upstream

SWIMMING UPSTREAM

*Parenting Girls for Resilience in
a Toxic Culture*

Laura H. Choate

OXFORD
UNIVERSITY PRESS

OXFORD
UNIVERSITY PRESS

Oxford University Press is a department of the University of
Oxford. It furthers the University's objective of excellence in research,
scholarship, and education by publishing worldwide.

Oxford New York
Auckland Cape Town Dar es Salaam Hong Kong Karachi
Kuala Lumpur Madrid Melbourne Mexico City Nairobi
New Delhi Shanghai Taipei Toronto

With offices in
Argentina Austria Brazil Chile Czech Republic France Greece
Guatemala Hungary Italy Japan Poland Portugal Singapore
South Korea Switzerland Thailand Turkey Ukraine Vietnam

Oxford is a registered trademark of Oxford University Press
in the UK and certain other countries.

Published in the United States of America by
Oxford University Press
198 Madison Avenue, New York, NY 10016

Cataloging-in-Publication data is on file at the Library of Congress
ISBN 978-0-19-939113-4

Dedicated to my daughter, Abby. May you continue
to stay strong and resilient!

CONTENTS

ACKNOWLEDGMENTS

First, as always, I would like to recognize the continued love and support of my husband Michael and my children Benjamin (age 12) and Abby (age 10) as they encouraged me to complete this book. I also thank my parents, Lloyd and Judy Hensley, who offered many prayers, meals, and hours of child care during my long writing days over the past year. I am also deeply grateful for the support of Petra Hendry and Jackie Bach, my writing group members at Louisiana State University (LSU). They encouraged me to write the book in the first place, read early drafts of the manuscript, and gave me invaluable feedback at every step along the way. In addition, I could have never completed the book without the help of the LSU Counselor Education graduate assistants, especially Shannon Smith, Helen Wilson, Merritt Guercio, Alexandra Ambeau, and Erin Savoy. They didn't blink an eye when I asked them to conduct massive literature searches or handed them reference lists to create. I was continually impressed with their excellent work and positive attitudes. Finally I would like to thank Dana Bliss and his team at Oxford University Press for their incredible support of this book. I so appreciate both their enthusiasm and professionalism during the publication process. I am fortunate and grateful to have had the opportunity to work with an editor who believed in the book from the outset and has remained committed to its successful publication.

INTRODUCTION

If you were drawn to the topic of this book, it is likely that you are like many parents, concerned about your daughter but not quite sure of what to do about it. You look around, often shocked by what you see in current culture that is being directed toward your daughter. Every day you notice how cultural pressures encourage girls to look "hot and sexy" when they are too young even to know what this means. You walk down the toy aisles and see Monster High and Bratzilla dolls with their fishnet stockings, stiletto heels, and feather boas. You go to the girls' clothing department and notice string bikinis with pushup tops for girls barely out of diapers. Then, as girls reach the preteen and early adolescent years, you see how they are pressured to be thin and beautiful and to look much older than they actually are. You browse the Internet and see girls posting provocative pictures in order to gain attention and fame online. You read about how sexting is on the rise in middle school and how common girl-fighting videos have become on YouTube. You see TV reality shows that portray young women as backstabbing "frenemies" who view one another not as friends but as competitors for male attention. And on top of all of this you observe that a girl is expected to accumulate a long list of accomplishments—to do it all—in order to be deemed a success. You worry that this means top grades and at least ten extracurriculars if she is to compete for a spot in a top college. Oh, and girls can't look as though they're trying too hard; it should all come effortlessly. As you observe all this, you may wonder how today's girls can survive without collapsing from exhaustion! How will they ever feel that they are *enough*? How will they ever meet these unrealistic expectations?

You know that these messages aren't good for your daughter, but they are pervasive; everywhere she turns, she hears that these are standards that she must meet if she is to be a success. You feel as if the culture is pushing hard against you and your family, and you may even feel that you are the only one who is struggling with these issues. Maybe you are wondering if there is anything you can do besides just tread water or to try not to drown in these trends. First, I am here to tell you that no, you are not the only one who feels this way. You are not alone. In my experience as a parent of two children, licensed counselor, faculty member in counselor education, workshop presenter, and author of three books on girls' and women's issues, I have seen first hand that many of today's parents are confused, not knowing what to do to raise a healthy daughter in such a complex cultural climate. Many parents are struggling as they feel the culture pushing them one way while their instincts lead them in another. I too am alarmed as I raise my own daughter, who will soon be ten years old. It seems that every day I have to make difficult decisions about what to say and do. *Is that outfit she wants to wear appropriate? Is this toy or game okay to purchase even though all her friends have it? Do I let her watch this movie or listen to that song? Do I allow her to sign up for an activity when our family is already too busy? What do I tell her about the commercials she is seeing on television? Where do I draw the line on her Internet use?* Even when I do know the right answers, following through with my decisions is never easy for me or for anyone else.

I wrote my first book, *Girls and Women's Wellness*, when I was pregnant with my daughter; as I noted in the preface to that book, given the sociocultural climate for girls, I felt concerned even then about my daughter's future. Now, almost ten years later, things have not improved and in some ways have worsened. Current troubling trends for girls are not just going away. Parents, including myself, need help and support to know how to best protect and guide our daughters who are immersed in such a toxic culture.

Therefore the central point of this book is to give you some good news: there *is* an alternative to floating with or even drowning in the culture. You don't have to go on autopilot, just accepting that these trends are the norm for you and your daughter. If you know that chasing after these demanding expectations can be harmful to girls, you can start to question them and decide for *yourself* what will be most empowering for your daughter. You can choose to opt in or out of current trends and to be intentionally countercultural in your choices. What I hope to do in this book is to help you to step back and reflect on what is happening in our culture—both for girls and for parents—and then recognize that these messages are not mandates for us. They are cultural expectations that are newly evolving, are not founded on research, and do not generally reflect what most parents want for their daughters. My hope is that as you read the book you will start to recognize that you have more options and choices than you might have realized.

As I emphasize repeatedly, making a different choice is hard work. Sometimes you will have to decide to go against the cultural grain and make an extra effort not to waste your energies comparing yourself with other parents. You will have to make a commitment to what you want in the long term for your daughter instead of what might be popular in the moment. You will need resolve to swim upstream in your parenting decisions in order to help your daughter swim upstream against cultural expectations.

In the book I refer to this process as *building your inner core*. Your inner core is your parenting foundation: you know who you are as a parent, what you want for your daughter, and what you think is best for her both now and in the future. For you to build your inner core as a parent in today's culture, I believe you need three things: (1) information about the culture and your daughter's development, (2) opportunities to clarify your parenting values, and (3) effective parenting strategies that encourage resilience. So, first, you need information. You need to be aware of the pressures floating around you and your family and take the time to step back and evaluate them. This book will offer you the resources and research you need in order to do this. You should also be aware that *you* will be the buffer between your daughter and these popular cultural messages that tell her she is not enough as she is. Your influence will make a significant difference in how likely she is to be affected by these messages.

Once you have the necessary information, you will be in a position to clarify your values and make conscious decisions about what you really want to do. Given current cultural expectations, are these the values that make sense to you as a parent? Are these the values that you want your daughter to accept and live by? Finally, in order to help you carry out these decisions, you need effective skills and strategies that will support you in your parenting efforts. This book is designed to help you through this process—gaining information, clarifying values based on what you know, and developing effective strategies that emanate from these values.

This book is also intended to support your efforts to help your daughter through the same process. You can help her gain awareness of cultural pressures, learn to question them, and recognize that there are alternatives to these values. She can learn that she has options other than buying into what the culture is telling her about her own worth. As her parent, you play an instrumental role in helping her see that her worth does not have to be based only on her attractiveness, her ability to gain attention, or the variety of her accomplishments. Through the ideas you gather from this book, you will be able to teach her that she is worth so much more than her ability to reach a thin-beautiful-hot-sexy ideal. She can learn that she is much more than her ability to gain thousands of so-called friends or followers on social media. She can know that she is not just a collection of numbers—her GPA, SAT, or her running list of extracurricular activities.

Just as you need to build your inner core as a parent, your daughter will also benefit from developing an inner core in the form of an *authentic identity*, which comprises who she really is and what she wants for herself *apart from what the culture is telling her she should be*. I will talk a lot about this sense of self throughout the book, as it is central to a girl's ability to be resilient to cultural expectations. If she does not have an authentic identity whereby she knows what she believes and values, she will bend and sway in the face of pressure. If she does not know who she is, she will be pulled toward making decisions based on what other people want from her or what is just easiest in the moment. Instead, with your help, she can learn who she is apart from cultural values and start to thrive in spite of the toxic culture surrounding her. She can survive while going with the flow, but to thrive she will have to learn to swim upstream.

OVERVIEW OF THE BOOK

In Part One you will take a tour of current girl world. I will provide a foundational background of girls' culture, their development, and their mental health. In Chapter One, "**Appearance, Attention, Accomplishments: Toxic Cultural Expectations for Girls**," I paint a portrait of popular culture to help you understand the standards that are held out for girls today. When girls internalize these expectations as requirements for themselves, they are not able to recognize that these are not the only avenues available for building a meaningful life. These messages about how she should measure her worth are classified into three themes:

- **Your worth is based on your appearance**. Even from an early age, today's girls learn that their worth is based on looking as "hot and sexy" as possible. I provide examples of clothing, products, music, advertisements, movies, books, and television programs to demonstrate current socialization processes for girls that emphasize sexiness and looking older than they are as the key to success and value.
- **Your worth is based on getting attention and approval from others**. I first discuss expectations for a girl to be a Princess/Diva. When a girl

grows up with the label "Princess" or "Diva," she learns to demand what she wants, believing that she deserves to be pampered and to own the "right" merchandise. She may also learn to behave in edgy, outrageous, often sexually provocative ways in order to seek and keep the attention of others. I also discuss the current culture of meanness among girls, which can fuel competition, the cultivation of frenemies, cyberbullying, and relational aggression. Next I explore the pressure girls experience to maintain a carefully crafted online image—one that emphasizes the *appearance* of popularity rather than actual relationships. The pressure to cultivate and present the right online image ultimately impedes the development of an authentic sense of self.

- **Your worth is based on your accomplishments**. Many girls feel pressure to compete and achieve in all arenas—academics, athletics, extracurricular activities—while still maintaining their relationships and doing what it takes to look as attractive as possible. I describe how the pressure for perfection and for meeting unrealistic and often contradictory goals sets girls up to feel that they can never measure up.

To end the chapter, I also discuss research showing that the more immersed in media and current culture a girl is, the more likely she will be to adopt these cultural standards for herself. I then provide important strategies for limiting and monitoring her use of media.

In Chapter Two, "**Girls in Transition: Who Am I?**" I explore the developmental changes that a girl will be experiencing in terms of her body (puberty), her cognition (based on her changing brain), and her overall identity. I first discuss physical changes and highlight issues related to early puberty and the problems that arise when a girl matures early. Next I turn to the brain changes that will be occurring as she reaches adolescence, with a focus on why she seems to be more emotional and drawn toward her peers. She may also start to engage in thrill-seeking behaviors without giving much thought to the consequences of her actions. With this in mind, I also provide strategies for helping you give your daughter ample guidance and structure while balancing this protection with opportunities for her to strengthen her decision-making skills in safe situations. Finally, I explore how a girl begins to weave the strands of her identity together into a coherent whole, noting the ways in which she is simultaneously working to stand out, fit in, measure up, and take hold of her own beliefs and values.

Next, in Chapter Three, "**Vulnerable Girls: Common Mental Health Problems in Girls**," I uncover what can happen when developmental stressors and cultural pressures become too much for a girl to handle on her own and how mental health problems can result. I first review the research-based consequences that occur when girls learn to self-objectify, to define themselves in terms of how they appear to others, and to present themselves in an inauthentic manner, resulting in a lack of a stable identity as well as feelings of emptiness, frustration, and unexpressed anger. I then show how these problems increase girls' vulnerability to the development of mental health problems such as depression, anxiety, substance abuse, eating disorders and weight-related problems, self-injury, sexual victimization and dating violence, and suicide risk. For each mental health issue, I describe what the problem looks like, who is most at risk for the development of this problem, and what parents can do to prevent its onset or to seek help once it has developed.

In Part Two of the book, I provide a guide designed to equip you with skills for helping your daughter build resilience as she attempts to swim upstream against the toxic cultural pressures and stressors that she may experience during these years. In Chapters Four through Eight, I cover five resilience dimensions. I start the section with a chapter dedicated to helping you develop your own resilience to cultural pressures around parenting. In Chapter Four, "**Resilience Dimension One: Parenting From Your Inner Core,**" I discuss the importance of being consciously aware of your choices as a parent. I then provide foundational parenting strategies designed to promote girls' overall resilience and well-being. These include familiar tenets such as the importance of love, warmth and connection balanced with limits, structure, and consequences. Next, I describe some current parenting trends and how they often fail to support the development of adolescent girls. Parenting practices such as micromanaging, overscheduling, "friending," and disconnecting are discussed extensively. I provide opportunities for you to reflect on these trends and to decide whether or not they fit with your own values as a parent.

Chapters Five through Eight are dedicated to building resilience in girls and to help your daughter move past an excessive focus on *appearance* (Chapter Five), *attention* (Chapter Six), and *accomplishments* (Chapter Seven) in determining her worth. In Chapter Five, "**Resilience Dimension Two: Developing a Positive Body Image,**" I discuss the thin-beautiful-hot-sexy ideal that many girls feel pressured to emulate and how your daughter can learn to reduce the emphasis on attractiveness in how she evaluates herself. I talk about the resilience factors that lead to a more positive body image, including modeling by mothers and fathers, and the importance of a family emphasis on all life areas—not just appearance—as the basis of self-acceptance, success, and worth. This chapter also includes a description of ways in which parents can help their daughters develop a healthy nutrition and exercise regimen that promotes a positive lifestyle (e.g., taking a nondieting approach to eating and exercising for fitness and health rather than for burning calories).

In Chapter Six: **"Resilience Dimension Three: Cultivating Healthy Relationships,"** I highlight the difficulty many girls experience in developing an authentic sense of self while also holding onto relationships—first with friends and later with romantic partners. Often these two goals come into conflict as girls sacrifice their own wants and needs in order to please others. To be resilient, girls must have comfort with their own identity while understanding what it means to set boundaries in healthy relationships. In this chapter, I specifically describe the importance of friendships for girls' well-being and present problems related to friendships and relational aggression (including the idea of frenemies and the common occurrence of cyberbullying). I also talk about romantic relationships, including problematic current social trends that teach girls to view other girls as competitors for male attention and to prioritize romantic relationships over friendships and other life areas. I also describe qualities needed for successful romantic relationships and warning signs for unhealthy romantic attachments, which is particularly important given the frequency of sexual harassment, sexual assault, and dating violence during the adolescent years.

In Chapter Seven: **"Resilience Dimension Four: Keeping Success in Perspective,"** I review pressures that girls experience around achievement and accomplishments. Girls are often socialized to achieve at exceptional levels in school in order to be "successful" in the eyes of parents and other significant adults in their lives. To be resilient, girls need an internally derived sense of worth and value that is not based solely on their achievements. If girls learn that they are acceptable or successful only if they make top grades or perform at extraordinary levels, they feel highly pressured to do what it takes to achieve success as others define it. I also explore the problems girls experience when such pressures become too much for them to manage. Some girls choose to drop out of the accomplishment race and focus on finding their worth in other areas (like popularity and male attention). Finally, I provide research-based strategies to help you reevaluate your definition of your daughter's success so that you can help her to follow her authentic identity, unique values, and interests. I discuss how the period from childhood through adolescence does not have to be hurried and stressful or steeped in peer pressure and conformity. I encourage you to help your daughter create an alternative vision for girlhood as an exciting time for discovering herself and her passions, and for seeing school as a place for learning new things about the world while also mastering new challenges.

In Chapter Eight, "**Resilience Dimension Five: Charting My Life Course,**" I discuss the importance of self-regulation: the ability to catch yourself in a moment, reflect on what you are thinking and feeling, consider your options, and make decisions based on your values or on what is best for you as well as for others in any given situation. The ability to self-regulate means the difference between your daughter impulsively diving into situations versus remaining aware of her options and in control of her responses. These skills are important for resilience because they enable her to be an active agent in her life rather than a passive victim of her circumstances. To help your daughter learn self-regulation, I present two skill sets: problem solving (when you need to take action in a situation) and active coping strategies (when you can't really do anything to make the situation go away but you can learn to do things to improve your reaction to the situation). Active coping involves skills like cognitive restructuring, mindfulness, the regulation of emotion, and being able to tolerate distress and frustration. I also discuss spirituality, gratitude, and compassion as important aspects of coping that can significantly change your daughter's perspective on her perceived problems.

I am excited to share these ideas and resilience dimensions with you in the forthcoming chapters. Before we get started, there are two additional points I would like to make. The first is related to *compassion* and *empathy*. Writing about parenting is a daunting task at any point, but living it while writing about it is an extra challenge to say the least! So here is a disclaimer: I am not a perfect parent of my own two children, a son who is almost twelve and a daughter who is approaching ten. Please know that I am not writing this book from an ivory tower or from a position of judgment. I have already stated that I know from daily experience that parenting is hard, and it is even harder to go against the cultural tide. It takes extra energy to swim upstream. Sometimes I have the energy to fight, and other times I don't. Some days while writing this book I have buried myself in research articles and books by parenting experts, and have written about these issues all day. I am bolstered by all of this sound parenting expertise and am pleased with my writing; all is right with the world. Then I pick up my kids from school and within 30 minutes of interacting with them, everything seems to fall apart, and I realize I am not even close to following my own advice! I hope it is reassuring to you to hear that even when we know the right thing to do, it doesn't happen perfectly every time. Please know that while I am providing you with information based on research and theory, I am also writing from a place of compassion and empathy as a fellow parent along this journey.

The final point is related to *urgency*. With all of these new cultural changes affecting girls at such early ages, we don't fully know how this will affect the mental health and development of our next generation of girls. Never before have girls been faced with so many pressures to live up to confusing and often contradictory expectations. With so much uncertainty, the stakes for our girls are high. I am writing this book because I want to speak up for girls who are living in a toxic culture that holds an unknown future for them. I want to empower you to speak up as well. Our girls do not yet have a voice, but we do. They don't know any better than to follow current trends, but we do. We have what it takes to help them stand strong and remain resilient. I am writing this book as a challenge for us to change course and help our daughters do the same. It is time for us to change our direction and to start swimming upstream.

PART ONE

Taking a Tour of Girl World

CHAPTER ONE

Appearance, Attention, Accomplishments

Toxic Cultural Expectations for Today's Girls

Imagine that you have just dropped in on Planet Earth for the first time. You know nothing about this planet and your assignment is to study what is known as *girlhood*. Exactly what is expected of girls in this culture? What are girls all about? After you had conducted your investigation, I wonder whether your final report might read something like this:

> After collecting evidence from this planet, I have determined that this culture expects girls to *look* a certain way:
>
> *"Girls must be sexy no matter what their age."* I saw Playboy lunchboxes for elementary school girls. Padded plunge bras for girls' sizes 7 to 14. Their toys look like plastic versions of mature women: Bratz dolls in heavy makeup, fishnet stockings, and feather boas. And the clothes sold for 8-year-olds are not all that different from those for 18-year-olds.
>
> *"Girls must be sexy but also thin and beautiful."* Many young girls were on diets and said that they needed to lose weight. Each day I observed thousands of girls visiting "Thinspiration" websites promoting extreme thinness. Thousands more posted pictures online with the question "Am I pretty or ugly?" and asked for anonymous comments to tell them how good (or not) they looked.

This culture also expects girls to *act* a certain way.

"You must be mean to other girls." This one is confusing because I also heard the phrase "Be nice and don't cause problems." On the other hand, I saw that it is common to have frenemies— friends who are actually enemies. There is cyberbullying and relational aggression. There are reports of frequent girl-fighting. Girls here seem to have close friends but don't really trust them. I don't understand how they are supposed to be nice and mean at the same time.

"Girls must seek male attention." Girls in this culture get frequent requests to engage in sexting — sending sexually explicit messages or images by cell phone — by the time they are in middle school. They are pressured to perform oral sex for boys they call "friends with benefits." I noticed that this culture somehow teaches girls to be independent but then also teaches them to worry about doing whatever it takes to make boys happy and keep them interested.

"You must be a diva." Girls on this planet hear things like "Demand what you want with an attitude!" "Be a princess!" "You deserve the best!" They are encouraged to shop a lot and to want the best things for themselves. They learn that it is important to seek fame and lots of attention both in real life and online.

"You must plaster yourself online." Girls here, on average, have cell phones by age 11. They commonly send and receive over 100 texts per day. They may check social media hundreds of times a day out of "fear of missing out" (FOMO). They may spend hours poring over photos to post on Facebook. They are "living for likes" on social media.

And on top of all of these messages, I also heard:

"You must be perfect!" Girls seem to be expected to "do it all." I observed that they are really busy and have high expectations for themselves. Girls here admit that they are stressed out and anxious about meeting others' expectations. Some try very hard to meet these standards and others simply give up.

Final conclusion: It is a difficult time to be a girl on this planet!

As the parent of a girl living in today's culture, you were probably not shocked by some of the examples included in this report. Yet seeing these cultural expectations packaged in this way may have led you to stop and think about the impact of the multiple pressures being placed *all at once* on your daughter. Over and over again she will get the message that *a girl must live up to these standards or she will not be acceptable.* The problem with this is that many girls listen to these cultural messages and then accept them as *requirements for themselves.* The external expectations become internalized, so that girls no longer question whether the standards are even valid or reasonable. They accept them as truth. This is understandable because they are young and do not have the life experience to know that these are not the only avenues for building a meaningful life.

Fortunately your daughter has you. You are the buffer between her and the messages that tell her she is not good enough as she is. You have the wisdom and life experience to know that there are choices and options. You have the ability to step back and evaluate whether these standards are the ones you want your daughter to accept and live by. You have a powerful role to play in how frequently she is exposed to these messages and how she will interpret them. You are in a position to make choices as to whether or not your family will follow cultural trends. This responsibility requires that you be informed about cultural expectations for girls so that you can make the best choices for your daughter. I will now take some time to explore these current expectations.

TAKING A TOUR OF POPULAR CULTURE

Girls spend much of their time immersed in media. When I discuss media, I am using the term in the broadest sense—television, movies, magazines, advertisements, books, music, videos, Internet, cell phones, video devices and games, as well as clothes, toys, and other merchandise. Consider the following statistics on media use:

- *Regarding TV*: Children aged 2 to 5 watch about 32 hours of television per week and those aged 6 to 11 watch an average of 22 hours per week.
- *Regarding combined media*: According to a Kaiser Family study, the average 8- to 10-year-old spends nearly 8 hours a day using media (television, movies, computers, gaming devices) and 11- to 17-year-olds spend more than 11 hours per day on media. When asked specifically about how much they use media for "fun," children between the ages of 8 and 18 report that they spend 7 hours and 38 minutes per day just on fun (not school) screen-related activities.
  (Note: It should be clear by these numbers that school-age children spend more time with media than they do at school, and studies bear this out. Media use is the leading activity for children and teens, second only to sleeping.)

- *Regarding media limits*: When children are asked about whether their parents monitor the time they spend using media, two-thirds of 8- to 18-year-olds say they have no rules about how much time they spend watching TV, playing video games, or using a computer.
- *Regarding social media use*: Eighty-one percent of 13- to 17-year-olds use social media sites, with Facebook being the most popular by far (77 percent), followed by Twitter (24 percent) and Instagram (11 percent).
- *Regarding cell phones*: Eighty-two percent of adolescents have a cell phone of their own. When broken down by age group, 74 percent of 13- to 14-year-olds and 87 percent of 15- to 17-year-olds own a cell phone.
- *Regarding texting*: Sixty-four percent of adolescents send text messages on a daily basis; not surprisingly, this is higher than the percentage of teens who report talking with friends face to face on a daily basis. Girls do the most texting: they send/receive as many as 4,000 texts per month (this averages out to 135 per day!).[1]

Because girls are such heavy consumers of media, they are highly attuned to media messages. Remember, your daughter doesn't hear a cultural message spoken directly from any one advertisement or movie; she is bombarded with consistent messages from multiple sources. When everywhere you look you start to hear and see the same themes, they become hard for anyone to ignore. And we know that the more immersed a girl becomes in popular culture through her media use, the more likely she is to adopt the media's cultural standards for herself.

In this section of the chapter we will take a tour of current culture and unpack cultural expectations for today's girls that tend to undermine their sense of worth and value. As a reminder, as a parent it is important for you to be aware of the messages she receives on a daily basis so that you can stop and ask yourself whether you believe that this is an appropriate expectation for her to place on herself. If you don't help her question these expectations, she will accept them at face value. I have categorized these messages in three primary categories: expectations that cause girls to believe their worth is primarily determined by (1) their *appearance*, (2) their ability to gain *attention*, and (3) their *accomplishments*.

PRESSURE ONE: "YOUR WORTH IS BASED ON YOUR APPEARANCE"

The popular media have long proclaimed the message that girls and women should focus their efforts on achieving a thin, beautiful ideal. From an early age, girls learn that appearance is what matters most in how a woman is evaluated. This message is still in place, but a new layer has been added: girls now learn that it is important for them to be not only thin and attractive but also to look as "hot and sexy" as possible. They learn that a thin + beautiful + hot + sexy appearance is the formula for getting attention or achieving the status to which they aspire. This is concerning to parents of all girls because it sets our daughters up for a never-ending cycle of feeling bad about themselves. When this ideal standard of weight, shape, and appearance is unattainable for all but a highly select few, how can a typical girl ever feel that she measures up to such limiting standards? If she bases her value on whether she looks like the images she sees in magazines or how she compares with other girls, she will be vulnerable to the development of serious mental health challenges such as depression and eating disorders (discussed in Chapter Three). Again, the message is that she will never be good enough as she is.

An additional concern is that this message for girls to look not only thin and beautiful but also "hot and sexy" has now trickled down to girls at younger and younger ages.[2] Starting in the preschool years, media messages tell girls that a hot and sexy appearance is the required standard for success. This is what is meant by the phrase *the sexualization of girlhood*.

The American Psychological Association brought widespread attention to this issue with its *Task Force Report on the Sexualization of Girlhood*. According to the report, the sexualization of a person is defined in the following ways: (1) when a person's value comes only from his or her sexual appeal or behavior to the exclusion of other characteristics, (2) when a person is held to a narrowly defined standard that equates physical attractiveness with being sexual; (3) when a person is sexually objectified, made into a thing for others' sexual use, rather than being seen as a person with the capacity for independent action and decision making; and/or (4) when sexuality is inappropriately imposed on a person.[3]

When you consider this definition and apply it to popular culture today, you can start to see how the sexualization of girlhood has crept in and is increasingly becoming normalized. I have been closely observing this trend for over ten years and what is most concerning to me is how things that were considered shocking a decade ago are currently considered normal for young girls' clothes, toys, shows, and overall media. When trends become so pervasive, we all tend to become desensitized to them; we fail to stop and ask "Is this healthy for little girls?" When we stop paying attention, when we accept that "*this is just this just the way things are*," we lose sight of the fact that *this isn't the way things have to be*. So keeping these definitions of sexualization in mind, let's take a step back and view the landscape through a critical lens, asking the question "Is chasing a hot-and-sexy standard" best for my daughter?

Hot and Sexy Clothes

Let's start with clothes. A recent study showed that 30 percent of clothing items available for preteen girls had sexualized characteristics—meaning that they emphasized or revealed a sexualized body part or had characteristics associated with sexiness. The researchers culled the websites of fifteen national stores—department stores (e.g., Macy's, Kohl's), discount stores (Target, Walmart), specialty stores (Justice)—and rated each piece of clothing. Not to pick on any one store, but Abercrombie Kids had the highest ranking, with 72 percent of their clothes containing at least one sexualized characteristic.[4]

If you have recently been to a mall or visited a large retailer, you know the clothing offerings in the girls' departments and you are well aware that the 30 percent rating is probably a gross underestimate. Have you been to specialty stores where they sell tank tops with words such as "Hottie" and "Future Porn Star" in little girls' sizes? Or retail stores selling T-shirts that promote the value of being "hot" by selling pajamas printed with "Cuties vs. Hotties" and "Hello my name is Hottie"? Lingerie for young girls is now the norm, with thong underwear decorated with slogans such as "wink, wink," "eye candy," or "feeling lucky?" Even the question "Who needs credit cards?" is written on the crotch of some recently popular girls' underwear. (On a positive note, when I last checked, Abercrombie and Fitch Kids was no longer selling these "wink wink" thongs, and Walmart pulled the "credit card" underwear after pressure from consumers.)

Mainstream stores sell padded bras in young girls' departments, starting at size 30AA, and bralettes are regularly sold for girls as young as age 5. Then there are the push-up string bikinis for young girls (many in exotic animal prints, many more with fringe and often with the new "cheeky bottom" cut). There is no doubt that the string bikini has taken over the world of girls' swimwear. As a parent, I know that it is hard to find a one-piece swimsuit anywhere! I went to a local water park with my children at least a half dozen times last summer, and each time I was amazed at how many elementary-age girls were walking around with heavily padded push-up string bikini tops and cheeky string bottoms. They appeared to be trying too hard to look much older than they were yet they also seemed so very young and vulnerable.

In addition to the pushup string bikini trend, there is also the trend toward highly sexualized Halloween costumes for young girls. We were coming up on Halloween season when I wrote this chapter, so my mailbox was flooded with Halloween catalogs; the offerings were ripe for sexy witches, pirates, waitresses, even sexy superhero girls like Batgirl, Supergirl, and Wonder Woman. It's hard for parents and girls to know what's appropriate when costumes designed for women are marketed in small sizes to young girls. (This year I too struggled to find a cute and colorful costume for my daughter that was not sexy or suggestive; fortunately a rainbow unicorn outfit met both requirements!) Add to these examples the current popularity of "Juicy" girls' fashions, featuring T-shirts with slogans like "Young, Wild, and Juicy." Several years ago the terms "prostitot" and "pimpfant" were coined by commentators as a response to current girls' fashion, implying that this was the "hip" way to dress our children.[5]

As a parent you might be reading this section with a jaded eye. "But you don't know my daughter" you say, "She begs me to let her dress in these clothes!" Of course she does. She looks around and sees that there are certain benefits to dressing in a sexy manner, such as appearing older, becoming more popular, and receiving more attention. She can see only the rewards of dressing this way and is not yet able to foresee any negative consequences.[6] She doesn't yet have the developmental capability or life experience to understand that the hot-and-sexy trend can cause her to overly focus on and worry about her appearance and to become self-conscious about her body. She also has no idea how her appearance could be perceived by others, particularly older males. Or if she does have ideas about this, the ideas will likely be about attention and romance; she is not yet able to have a clear understanding of the dangers that might be associated with unwanted sexual attention.

I found one study on this issue very eye-opening. The researchers recruited a group of college students and showed them images of a fifth-grade girl who was presented in either child-appropriate clothes, somewhat sexualized clothes, or highly sexualized clothes. She was described as being either a below average or above average achiever for her age. The students rated this hypothetical girl on ten different traits. The girl in sexy clothes was seen as the least intelligent, least competent, least determined, and least capable. This girl was also rated as relatively low in self-respect and morality. Somehow the students were equating her clothing choice with her moral character![7] This is only one study and the ratings were performed by college students, but it offers us some initial evidence showing that even elementary-age girls can be viewed as less competent when they dress in a hot-and-sexy manner. And if they are treated that way by others, they may start to adopt this same view of themselves.

But what do girls themselves actually think when they see other girls dressed in a sexy manner? How do they view other girls who sport the hot-and-sexy look? When researchers showed 6-year-old girls a pair of paper dolls (one dressed in a sexy manner and the other in "regular" play clothing; see Box 1.1), most girls chose the sexy doll as the one they would prefer as their "ideal" self and as the one that they believed would be most popular. Interestingly, more girls chose the regular doll as the one that they actually look like and as the one they would want to play with.[8] Even at the young age of 6, girls have already learned that looking "hot and sexy" means you will get more attention, and that being popular is something to aspire for. They also know, and wisely so, that the girl dressed in

Box 1.1: AN ACTIVITY TO TRY WITH YOUR DAUGHTER

In a recent study, 6-year-old girls were shown these two images and asked which they would like to be like, which would be most popular, which they actually looked like, and which they would prefer to play with. Ask your daughter these questions and ask her why she thinks this way. How do these answers compare with the findings reported in the study?[9]

Source: Dollz Mania's ChaZie Dollmaker, http://dollzmania.net/ChaZieMaker.htm

the sexy outfit would not necessarily be that much fun to play with! She would probably not be very comfortable or able to run very far!

Resilience Strategy: What Can I Do When My Daughter Wants to Wear the Latest Hot and Sexy Fashions?

First, reassure yourself that it is okay to follow your instincts and say no to your daughter when you don't want to buy into the latest clothing trend. While the clothing is everywhere and every other parent in your daughter's social circle may be willing to buy it, it is still your job as a parent to do what you believe is necessary to protect your daughter and shield her from inappropriate attention from others. While it takes extra effort to find them, there are other clothing options available. Take the time to search them out. Here are some ideas to help you make your decisions:

- **Your decision is based on your daughter's safety.** Focus your comments on her *safety* and try to explain in simple terms that you are concerned about the ways in which older people might view her if she wore a particular outfit. I suggest the following type of response, which I have adapted from Greenspan and Deardorff in their highly recommended book *The New Puberty: How to Navigate Early Development in Today's Girls*:

   Julia, I am not going to buy that outfit for you. We have rules in this family, and saying no to outfits that look like they are made for much older girls is one of them. Every family has different rules, so your friends' parents might see things differently. That's how life works. I'm sorry if it upsets you, but this is the way we do things in our family. The rules we have in place are to keep you safe. Remember, we love you and want you to stay safe.

- **Your decision is based on her comfort.** When she is wearing sexy clothing, she will be thinking about managing the clothes (tugging to keep them in place) rather than being comfortable and having the freedom to run and play. As an example, Anea Bogue writes about how there is nothing wrong with the current trend of mommy/daughter mani/pedis (manicures/pedicures) that are so popular at today's salons. But, she argues, "How can we expect a girl with a manicure to run freely, play sports, get dirty, or climb a tree? We are teaching girls to be dainty and decorative at an alarmingly young age."[10] Several years ago I taught a class of kindergartners and took the children outside to play. I recall seeing a group of the girls sitting on a bench because they didn't want to mess up their shoes. One had semi-high heels and said she couldn't really walk well in them so she didn't want to play. So these 5-year-old girls sat and stared at their feet while the rest of the class had a wonderful time laughing and running around the playground. The lesson is this: try to keep her clothing simple and comfortable so that she feels free to run and play!

- **Your decision is based on keeping her free from appearance concerns.** When you want to tell your daughter "no" but feel unsure about your decision, another thing you can remember is that you want her to focus on being strong and free from concern about how others might be judging her appearance. When you are wearing hot-and-sexy clothes, you are more likely to think about yourself and how you look; it's harder to turn this part of your brain off and focus on other things (this is called self-objectification, and I will talk more about it in Chapter Three). One of my favorite things about watching my daughter play on a recreational soccer team for 9- and 10-year-old girls is that the girls get dirty and sweaty. They fall down, get dirt on their clothes, and keep running. I love that the female coach makes them run sprints and endurance drills at the end of practice in the 100-degree Louisiana heat and humidity. (Last week, in mid-September, I was soaked with sweat just standing there watching them run!) This sort of activity not only builds character and endurance but also, for a few hours per week, the girls on the team are not thinking about their appearance. They are not at all self-conscious; they are not worried about what other people will think of their looks, their bodies, or their hair. They are just running, sweating, kicking, and actually having fun. They are acting like 9-year-olds! So for as long as possible, do what you can to keep your daughter's focus on dressing for comfort and strength, not for her appeal to others.

Hot and Sexy Toys

No discussion of the hot and sexy trend would be complete without a discussion of girls' dolls. We can start with Barbie, because 90 percent of girls own a Barbie, she has been around the longest, and, in fact, she just celebrated her fifty-year anniversary! It is interesting that Barbie was first marketed to 9- to 12-year-old girls but is now primarily marketed and advertised to 3- to 5-year-olds. Barbie has definitely had an impact—first on preteen girls and now, fifty years later, the preschool set. Consider this fact as you realize that just this year Barbie was included as a model in the fiftieth anniversary *Sports Illustrated* Swimsuit edition. For its special issue, *Sports Illustrated* gathered twenty-two former SI Swimsuit cover models to reunite in a photo shoot and editorial production called "Salute to the Legends of Swimsuit" (including supermodels Tyra Banks, Christie Brinkley, Heidi Klum, and Kathy Ireland, among others, as well as Barbie). I wrote a blog about that issue and I will excerpt some of it here:

Barbie's presence in a magazine intended for adults is only part of an overall campaign that Mattel has titled, "Unapologetic"—it will also involve a billboard in Times Square and the release of a new SI Barbie doll. According to a Mattel spokesperson as cited in *Adweek*: "Unapologetic is a rally cry to embrace who you are and to never have to apologize for it." Evidently this campaign is a new way to try to fight back against the criticisms Barbie receives for her incredibly unrealistic image of "perfection"—a perfection so far reaching that her long, lean proportions would prevent her from being able to walk if she were human. In my view, it is hard to see how Barbie as an "Unapologetic" role model helps girls and women to "embrace who they are" if they believe they should look like Barbie.

There was lots of media buzz around the decision to include Barbie, a toy for young girls, in a Swimsuit edition intended for adults. In its defense, *Sports Illustrated* argues that the Swimsuit issue actually *celebrates* women and that Barbie fits in with this image: "From its earliest days, Swimsuit has delivered a message of empowerment, strength and beauty, and we are delighted that Barbie is celebrating those core values in such a unique manner," said Swimsuit editor M. J. Day. This quote poses a question for me: In what ways are pictures of models posing in (and out of) swimsuits included in a magazine designed for sports enthusiasts empowering to women?

On the other side of the Barbie SI Swimsuit controversy, some people are simply dismissive: "What is the big deal?" After all, she *is* just a doll. But if that is the case, I wonder why Mattel and Sports Illustrated believe that a doll is appropriate to include alongside human models, as if it didn't matter that she is not a real person and as if Heidi Klum and Barbie were interchangeable. According to a spokeswoman at Mattel, Barbie is definitely not just a doll: "Barbie is a legend in her own right, with more than 150 careers and a brand valued at $3 billion. She is in great company with the other legends such as Heidi Klum and Christie Brinkley, to name a few." With quotes such as these, her inclusion in Swimsuit does become a big deal. Calling her a "legend" takes her out of toyland and into the realm of influence and power. She becomes larger than a toy and takes on even more importance as a potential ideal for girls to emulate. Little girls do soak in the cultural messages around them: look like this, act like this, and you will be happy, popular, successful—in other words, follow the formula and you can have it all. Even if you have a career, even if you break the glass ceiling and become fabulously successful, you should still look perfect; you should still look like Barbie.[11]

Barbie has her critics (I admit that I am one of them; I'll talk more about why in Chapter Five), and she definitely has her fans, but there is no doubt that girls are affected by her image. Several research studies have called into question Mattel's claim that Barbie is a positive role model for girls, and I will describe two of them here. In one study, young girls aged 5 to 8 were shown either images of Barbie, an Emme doll (a plus-size model), or no doll at all. They were then asked questions about their own body image. Compared with the other groups, the girls who had just seen pictures of Barbie had less body satisfaction and reported a greater desire for a thinner body shape. This effect was present for girls starting at 5½ years but was most pronounced among the 6½- to 7-year-olds.[12]

Another study also questions Mattel's claim that Barbie is a strong role model for girls because Barbie has had over 150 careers. Girls aged 4 to 7 were randomly divided into three groups: one group played with Dr. Barbie (Barbie dressed as a doctor), another with Fashion Barbie, and a third with a Mrs. Potato Head. Afterward they were given a list of careers and were asked select careers that they saw as possibilities for themselves as girls and then to select those careers that they thought were possible for boys. Compared with girls who played with Mrs. Potato Head, girls who played with the Barbie dolls reported significantly fewer careers as future possibilities for themselves than they reported were possible for boys. Playing with Barbie, as opposed to a Mrs. Potato Head, actually affected girls' notions of future careers! Note that this was true whether they played with Dr. Barbie in a lab coat or Barbie as a fashion model. The study authors conclude that Barbie is a sexualized toy even when wearing the physician costume and actually restricts a girl's sense of what is possible for herself.[13]

However, Barbie has been around awhile and she almost appears old fashioned compared with her new competitors. Her first major rivals were the Bratz Dolls, who quickly became the most popular dolls for young girls, even outselling Barbie. Bratz dolls—known for their long hair, heavy makeup, short skirts, fishnet stockings, stiletto heels, and feather boas—are highly sexualized representations of older adolescent girls, but they are targeted to very young girls (including even a "Bratz Babyz" line). Their advertising campaign teaches girls to "hit the town and dance the night away" and to "know how important it is to be seen!" To attract additional girls, Bratz has released a "Bratzillaz" line ("Where glam gets wicked!" "Witchy princesses!") to compete with the newer Monster High dolls.

As a parent of a daughter, you are probably well aware of Monster High dolls—dolls that feature heavy makeup and sexualized fashions but who are also monsters (e.g., modeled after werewolves, vampires, Frankenstein). Some researchers examined today's dolls and rated them according to their sexualized characteristics (low-cut tops, very short skirts, etc.). The "winner"? Monster High dolls followed by Bratz dolls. Barbie came in third.[14]

These toys also represent a marketing trend geared to young girls: pressuring them not only to look hot-and-sexy but also older than they are. The terms "age compression" (marketing products intended for older girls to younger girls), "age aspiration" (marketing products that tap into girls' desires to emulate older girls' lifestyles), and the idea of KGOY ("Kids Growing Older Younger"—capturing girls' brand loyalty in their youngest years) are definitely driving marketers' product campaigns. Lamb and Brown cite a management executive who claims "If you don't target the consumer in her formative years, you're not going to be relevant through the rest of her life."[15] Just a few examples of KGOY include Juicy Couture dolls and girls' clothing line; Victoria's Secret Pink line of stuffed animals, and the Forever 21 clothing line for young girls.

As a media example, the popular Dora the Explorer—the beloved young girl cartoon character with T-shirt, shorts, and tennis shoes—has now been remodeled as a tall, thin adolescent girl wearing a dress, leggings, ballet flats, and a "map app" for her phone. In this way, marketers hope that girls will embrace the new, older Dora and will remain interested in her as they enter the middle childhood years. It is hoped that they won't outgrow her as quickly. However, representatives indicate that the new Dora show is still being marketed to preschoolers, not to the older set:

> Despite her preteen look, the older Dora is not necessarily intended for older kids. The show's target audience, much like "Dora the Explorer," is the preschool set of 2- to 5-year-olds. Older Dora is meant as a companion piece—an aspirational figure to little ones—according to creators Chris Gifford and Valerie Walsh Valdes, who also were behind the original show.[16]

In addition to Dora, there are ample childhood images that have been updated for a more mature, sexualized look; consider, for example, the new cover of the Candyland game, Strawberry Shortcake dolls and merchandise, and the Trolls dolls. For more, see the Sociological Images pages at http://thesocietypages.org/socimages/?s=sexy+toy+makeovers.

Summary Box for Pressure One: There is currently a strong expectation for your daughter to look thin, beautiful, hot, and sexy and to draw her self-worth from her appearance. While this is a relatively new trend, we are already starting to see how today's clothes, toys, and merchandise can have a negative effect on the way your daughter sees herself and the importance she will place on her appearance. As a parent, you can make more informed decisions about your purchases for your daughter when you are armed with this information. In addition, you can learn specific resilience strategies for helping her stand strong against pressures regarding her appearance. This will be the focus of Chapter Five.

PRESSURE TWO: "YOUR WORTH IS BASED ON GAINING ATTENTION"

This expectation describes the pressure girls experience to gain attention, often wherever and however they can. In this section I will first explore how girls learn to gain attention: by acting like a princess/diva and seeking out fame, male attention, and competing with other girls. Then I will turn to a discussion of the powerful ways through which she is socialized to seek online attention.

The diva/princess value is taught to girls even when they are very young, with common labels for little girls like "Diva," "Drama Queen," and "Princess." We often think of this as cute when we see little pink T-shirts imprinted with "Diva," "Professional Drama Queen," "Spoiled Princess Soccer Club," or "My Selfie Is a Winner." I saw a T-shirt today that had all three labels: "Princess Diva Queen."

Part of this princess/diva trend stems from the popularity of "girl power," a marketing phrase that is geared to younger girls and implies that to be powerful as a girl, you have to be powerful as a *consumer*. "Girl power" in a marketing sense attempts to suggest that the achievement of a successful identity as a girl is based on looking just right and owning the right things—that is, to have a "passion for fashion" and to "shop 'til you drop." Girls pick up on the message that the more you have, the better you are; your belongings somehow signify your overall worth as a person.[17] *So part of becoming a princess/diva means having the "right" things.*

As a result, girls also observe a cultural norm wherein it seems okay not just to *want* the right things but also to *demand* everything they desire. What is interesting is that while the *princess* trend for girls has been around for generations, part of what is new is the *diva* part of the equation: although a princess has everything she wants, a diva wants what she wants when she wants it, and she wants it *now*. This cultural value is teaching girls that being both entitled and demanding is an expected part of what it means to be a girl today. It also means that girls learn it is important to be the center of attention and to do whatever it takes to make this happen. Clearly this can lead to a sense of self-importance and a belief that their needs are more important than those of others, as I will discuss in later chapters.[18]

Become Famous

The princess/diva expectation is also tied to the pressure girls feel to be as popular and famous as possible. More girls say they want to be famous today than they did in the past; this is fueled in part by the popularity of reality television and Internet sites such as YouTube or Facebook, wherein a girl who posts a video clip or image that goes viral can become an instant celebrity. To do so she doesn't have to have a particular talent or skill set; she can now become famous just for her ability to gain attention! The value of fame has also increased in our culture through the massive rise of YouTube accessibility, where the prospect of being discovered is an ever-present reality (recall that Justin Bieber was discovered on YouTube when he was only 13). Television programs designed for preteens also push the importance of fame. In one interesting study, researchers looked at the values represented in preteen TV programs during the past decade and found that fame was the number-one value portrayed in preadolescent television programs in 2007 while it had been the fifteenth most common value just ten years earlier, in 1997. As cited in an interview in *USA Today*, the lead author of the analysis noted that

> Preteens are at the age when they want to be popular and liked just like the famous teenagers they see on TV and the Internet. With Internet celebrities and reality TV stars everywhere, the pathway for nearly anyone to become famous, without a connection to hard work and skill, may seem easier than ever.[19]

In another study of children aged 10 to 12, researchers asked children about their values for the future. The children rated "being famous" as by far their most important future value. The bottom line is this: if you are a girl growing up today, compared with girls in the past, you are learning that it is important to aspire to be famous.

Bad Is the New Good

Part of the message girls also receive is that they can become famous by gaining negative attention. From what they see in popular media, girls learn that they can achieve fame and notoriety by acting out in edgy, sexually provocative ways and fighting with one another. Who gets the most attention? Often it is the girls who display dramatic, impulsive, high-risk behaviors.[20] Think of Miley Cyrus and her transformation from Disney's Hannah Montana to a pop star who is known for "twerking" and singing songs that glamorize partying, sex, and drug use (the lyrics to her current song "We Can't Stop" serve as an example). Girls imitate the "Bad is the new good" behaviors displayed by media stars and try them out by acting out online in a sexual manner (or by sexting, explored in Chapter 6) and also by public acts of meanness and aggression. As I discuss later in the book, today's girls learn that being mean to other girls and getting in physical fights with them is an expectation and will gain them much attention. All they have to do is watch music videos, reality television, or YouTube videos to be bombarded with this message.

Another aspect of this value is that other girls are viewed as competitors. They may find that friends are not what they seem: "they are your competitors, not just your friends."[21] For example, the most popular show among older children and teens was most recently *Pretty Little Liars* (it was voted the Top Choice for TV-Drama in the Teen Choice Awards in 2012, 2013, and 2014[22]). Popular reality shows like *The Bad Girls' Club, The Real Housewives*, and *Real World* also pit young women against each other as competitive rivals, and they are frequently featured fighting, gossiping, and criticizing one another regarding their appearance, relationships, and financial status. In fact, it is difficult to list popular shows or movies that feature positive female friendships. To explore this theme further, try the following activity with your daughter and family (see Box 1.2).

Several surveys conducted by the Girl Scout Research Institute indicate that girls are paying attention to these messages about other girls: One such survey found that girls who watch reality TV (compared with those do not watch these programs) are more likely to agree that:

- "By nature girls are catty and competitive."
- "You have to lie to get what you want."

- "Gossip is a normal part of relationships between girls."
- "Being mean earns you more respect than being nice."
- "Girls often have to compete for guys' attention."
- "It's hard for me to trust other girls." [23]

I will fully explore the importance of girls' friendships and their need for strong social support in Chapter Six. For now, be thinking about these messages regarding "bad is the new good" and the pressures to view other girls as competitors. How might these ideas be affecting your daughter's views of herself and of other girls?

Rescue Me

The cultural value of gaining attention also includes the importance of specifically gaining and prioritizing *male* attention. Just this week I read a *Huffington Post* parents' blog about the release of a new, popular girls' T-shirt printed with the slogan *Training to Be Batman's Wife* (sold at Walmart and sold out on Amazon at the time of this writing). Creating a stir among parents and comic fans alike, the T-shirt slogan raises questions about why parents (usually those who purchase the shirts for their daughters) would want girls to aspire to *marry* a superhero instead of seeing *themselves* as the superheroes.[24] According to this cultural value, a girl does not need to worry about taking care of herself because she should wait to be saved by someone else. Traditional Disney movies like *Cinderella* *(also remade and re-released in 2015), Snow White, Sleeping Beauty,* or *The Little Mermaid* are well known for their perpetuation of these themes: *Be beautiful and clever, attract a prince, and wait to be rescued.*

In a time when most parents hope that their daughters will grow up to be active, not passive problem solvers, slogans such as these reflect a confusing message to girls, who may then ask themselves "Should I be a 'Supergirl?'" or "Should I play the part of a damsel in distress, waiting for Prince Charming to swoop in and rescue me?" Which cultural imperative does she accept? Fortunately there are some recent princess movies that have provided a more positive message in this regard. Starting with the movie *Brave*, I have seen two other recent blockbuster Disney films that have somewhat defied these stereotypes. (Spoiler alert: If you haven't seen these movies, I am about to ruin the surprise endings for you. Note also that I am not necessarily recommending these movies for your daughter; they are just the most recent examples of the "rescue me" trend reversal.) In the very popular *Frozen* movie, the viewer is led to believe that it is going to be Prince Hans or the strong Kristoff who will save Princess Elsa from her impending death, but it is actually her sister who rescues her (well, actually they save each other). Another 2014 movie, *Maleficent*, a retelling of the story of Sleeping Beauty, surprises audiences when the kiss of a handsome prince does nothing to awaken Sleeping Beauty while true love's kiss comes from Maleficent herself, the mother figure in the movie.

Even with these surprising twists emerging in several princess movies, it is hard to understand the contradictions presented to girls in popular culture today. A girl is told to become a powerful princess/diva, yet she is simultaneously encouraged to be a passive damsel in distress, waiting for a boyfriend. Cultural expectations pressure her to become a girl who has to work hard to please males and to keep their attention, yet still she hears the message of "Girl Power." How *is* she supposed to act? And for girls who are not interested attracting a boyfriend or being a princess or being perfect, what are the options? These are the kinds of ideas I will explore throughout this book. For now, just remember that these questions are also swirling around in your daughter's head as she is trying to grow up and figure out who she is and what is expected of her.

Not only are girls expected to seek and get attention IRL (in real life), this pressure is amplified exponentially through texting and social media. Earlier in the chapter, I highlighted the pervasive use of social media and technology in girls' lives, with staggering numbers like 81 percent of 13- to 17-year-olds using social media sites, 78 percent having their own cell phones, 64 percent sending text messages on a daily basis, and girls in particular sending/receiving as many as 4,000 texts per month (over 100 per day).[25] Needless to say, social media and texting have become not only an important part of girls' social lives in terms of the way they communicate with one another but also comprise a critical aspect of girls' overall identities—their online activities greatly affect how they see *themselves*. It is hard to imagine how large the impact this will have on your daughter's life. Consider that at the very time a girl is figuring out who she is and how she wants to present herself to the real world, she is also required to craft an online identity.

To put this in perspective, take a moment to imagine the pressure that your daughter does (or will) experience as she carefully works to manage her online image. She has to worry not only about how she looks, what she says, and what she does IRL but also has to agonize about how her appearance and actions will come across online or in a texted soundbite! Every social event becomes a big deal as she becomes a microcelebrity, with pictures of her every move potentially posted within seconds.[26] Steiner-Adair writes about how girls she interviewed described their actions during and after any social event. They told her that it is not unusual for them to take hundreds pictures at one party and to stare at these photos for hours, only to select two or three to actually post on their social media sites. According to these girls, this selection process involves a lot of pressure because any perceived miscalculation about the way the pictures come across to others will be an online mistake posted forever for the world to see.[27] Many girls also say that they spend hours poring over others' online photos, worrying about whether they have been left out of events (up to 43 percent say that they have felt left out or excluded from events after viewing social media photos), what kinds of comments have been made about their pictures, and whether others have posted unattractive photos of them (up to 35 percent say that this is a concern).[28] Girls also visit social media sites asking directly for comments about their pictures" (e.g., Reddit.Com; YouTube videos such as "Am I Ugly? "Am I pretty? Please be honest").

As is evident from even a cursory glance at popular social media sites, girls are spending a lot of their time and energy creating their social media pages/images, monitoring them, and viewing others' pages to see how they might be missing out. Girls can then actually try to measure how they are doing in terms of getting attention. As opposed to the past when we had to guess about whether or not people "liked" us, now girls can look to their actual numbers of friends, followers, likes, and views to provide evidence of their popularity. A recent *Good Morning America* segment brought this issue to light by reporting on teens' current obsession with "likes" on social media, primarily on Facebook and Instagram. To be in the "100 Club," a girl has to accumulate at least 100 "likes" for her pictures or they are considered an embarrassment. According to a teen girl interviewed for the segment, "If I get less than 100 likes ... I will delete the picture because it wasn't good enough." Her friend chimes in, "Everyone at school gets 100 or more; it's not good to be the only one who doesn't have it." To be measured by whether your pictures get 100 likes puts a great deal of pressure on girls; if they can't reach the 100 mark, they believe they don't have approval of their peers.

While most adults can reason that this is not a valid way to measure whether or not you are likeable, popular, or attractive, it is important to remember that a girl can easily get caught up in using these numbers as a measure of her worth. It is a tangible way for her to assess whether or not she is acceptable, and she learns that she is not okay unless others are providing validation of her worth by paying attention to her online. It is easy for "living for likes" to become her new reality.[29]

As a parent you are probably thinking that this sounds like an exhausting way to live. How can you relax when everything you say and do is analyzed, photographed, posted for an audience, and evaluated? It's stressful to feel that you have to be "on" at all times and always available—that if you go for too long without checking your phone or computer, life might leave you behind (this is termed "fear of missing out," or FOMO). It is estimated that people check their phones over 100 times a day for that reason; *what if I am missing out on something?*[30] As a result, it is interesting that teens aged 13 to 17 do report some weariness over always being "on." Up to 43 percent of teens say they sometimes wish they could just unplug for awhile (which implies that they feel that they want to but don't feel they are able to do so), and up to one third say they sometimes wish they could go back to a time before Facebook existed (Common Sense Media aptly terms this trend "Facebook Fatigue").[31]

This results in a new cultural expectation for girls that simply did not exist even a decade ago. What are the results of what Ana Homoyoun calls *hypersocialization* in today's girls? Since this trend is so new, we don't really know the range of its far-reaching effects. For now, here is a sample of current research findings.

- *It can impede authentic identity development*. When you are always "on," you don't have time to have a complete thought, much less a moment to figure out who you are and what you want for your life. Developing an authentic identity requires downtime and reflection, and a hypersocialized life does not allow for this development.[32]
- *It can impede healthy self-esteem development*. **When she bases her sense of who she is on how many** "likes" she can get, you daughter will never feel good enough as she is; she will always be looking for external validation of her worth. Even when this validation is superficial, she will continue to seek it out. According to Robyn Silverman, your daughter's "quality of life is not about her quantity of likes."[33]
- *It can impede the development of social skills*. In an ironic twist, online hypersocialization can actually get in the way of the development of social skills. According to the American Academy of Pediatrics Council on Communication and Media, a major part of this generation's social and emotional development is occurring while they are on the Internet and on cellphones. Steiner-Adair agrees when she writes that the more energy your daughter spends on socializing through texts and social media, the more likely she is to miss out on the kinds of conversations and experiences that contribute to the development of the relational skills needed for healthy friendships and emotional intimacy. All of the skills that are required for actual face-to-face conversations—skills like getting up the nerve to express yourself in full sentences, stating your feelings openly, making eye contact, reading the other person's social cues and body language, and figuring out what to say next—are all bypassed when your daughter communicates primarily through texting or social media. These are skills historically learned in adolescence, but many of today's preadolescents and adolescents are missing out on this necessary practice and skill development. As a result, Steiner-Adair claims:

> The less practice they have with face-to-face interaction, communicating their ideas and feelings in person, the less ready they are for relationships of greater emotional complexity. . . . Texting is the worst possible training ground for anyone aspiring to have a mature, loving, sensitive relationship.[34]

- *It impedes the development of empathy*. Another problem that results from social development that occurs in large part online is an increase in cruelty and lack of regard for others' feelings. In the absence of face-to-face conversations in which girls learn to interpret social cues, they are less likely to develop empathy and awareness of the impact that their communication can have on other people. In this type of environment, trends like cyberbullying, sexting, and harassment will continue to flourish (I will talk more about these trends and what to do about them in Chapter 6).

In case you are getting discouraged, one positive note in this area is the finding that even when children are missing out on learning appropriate social cues, they can improve quickly with practice and with time away from technology. In a notable study, researchers examined two groups of preteens who were preparing for a five-day technology-free outdoor education camp. All of the children were tested on their ability to read emotional cues in people's facial expressions. Then half of them went to the five-day camp where no electronics were allowed. The other group stayed at home, still using their electronics, while they waited to go to the camp. After only five days away from their tech screens and engaging in outdoor camp activities that required face-to-face interactions, the campers became significantly better at reading facial emotional cues (the group who remained at home showed no changes). These findings highlight the importance of making the extra effort needed to increase opportunities for your daughter to engage in face-to-face conversations and to leave her technology devices behind for a few hours. When she interacts with others without escaping into games or worrying about the texts or updates she is missing, she learns to be present and to develop the social skills she will need for the future.[35]

Summary Box for Pressure Two: It can be complex and confusing to live in a princess/diva culture where your daughter is taught to be both entitled and demanding but also nice and pleasing to others. If she listens to current cultural messages, she will be taught not to trust other girls, to view them as competitors, and to prioritize male attention over friendships with her peers. She will hear that being famous is important, whether she achieves fame by acting out or doing whatever it takes to be popular. In addition to seeking attention IRL, she will experience 24/7 pressure to gain attention online—to get as many "likes" as possible, to never miss a text, to be constantly "on." Instead of looking only for validation from others, your daughter needs your help to develop an authentic sense of self that is not based solely on others' approval. Resilience strategies for healthy relationships and promoting these qualities in your daughter are the focus of Chapter Six.

PRESSURE THREE: "YOUR WORTH IS BASED ON YOUR ACCOMPLISHMENTS"

As already reviewed in this chapter, girls learn that they are expected to look not only thin and beautiful but also hot and sexy, all the while gaining attention from the world around them in order to feel okay about themselves. These goals in and of themselves are nearly impossible for anyone to meet. On top of this, girls learn that they must also excel by accruing a long list of *accomplishments*—they must be perfect in all areas including academics, sports, and other extracurricular activities. In his book *The Triple Bind*, Stephen Hinshaw identifies this bind for today's girls: they must excel at traditional "girl" skills (caretaking, nurturing, relationship building, keeping a boyfriend) while also excelling at traditional "boy" skills (competitive at sports and in school, being aggressive, staying focused on winning, and being the best). And they must do this all flawlessly, perfectly, with little or no perceived effort. In other words, a girl must achieve at high levels in all areas—school, sports, extracurriculars, her appearance, her clothes, even her online presence—but never show that she is trying too hard.[36] According to Peggy Orenstein, she must be both Cinderella and Supergirl, achieving effortless perfection in every area of her life.[37]

Part of this pressure is positive in that girls now have opportunities that were closed to them in the past. Look at the millions of girls who are now able to play sports and go on to achieve advanced degrees in law and medicine, pursuing careers that were not available to women of past generations. But now that more and more doors are open to them, girls are starting to feel that these same opportunities have become obligations to take advantage of every opportunity that comes their way. Girls learn "You can do *anything!*" but they interpret this to mean "You have to be *everything.*" They feel pressure: "If I *can* do it, I *should* do it." They feel that they should be everything to everyone yet end up believing that they will never be good enough.[38] They are spinning multiple plates in the air but still don't feel that they are living up to what is expected of them.

As Cohen-Sandler writes in *Stressed Out Girls*, as a result of these pressures, many of today's girls are "totally stressed out," overwhelmed, and completely exhausted. They believe that they have to be perfect—that if they just work harder, they will finally become acceptable. Up to three out of four girls agree that today's girls feel intense pressure to be everything to everyone all the time, that they must please everyone.[39] Understandably the accumulation of pressures and expectations can become too much for some girls. Some push themselves too hard to achieve and meet these expectations while others give up and stop trying altogether.

Summary Box for Pressure Three: There is an expectation for girls to achieve in all areas, and when they accept this as their goal, they will start to base their worth and value on the accumulation of a long list of accomplishments. This causes many girls to experience anxiety and emptiness as they run frantically toward achievement after achievement in order to feel acceptable. Resilience strategies for helping your daughter to let go of some of this pressure and develop more realistic yet meaningful goals for herself will be the focus of Chapter Seven.

To Conclude Our Tour: A Media Wakeup Call

The purpose of this section was to take a tour of popular culture and to highlight the strong cultural expectations placed on girls today regarding their need for a thin-beautiful-hot-sexy appearance, the need to gain attention, and the need for accomplishments in order to have a sense of worth and value. These expectations are strongly conveyed through a variety of popular media and can be confusing and toxic to your daughter's development. In addition, the more your daughter is immersed in today's media, the more likely she will be to absorb these cultural expectations and to hold them as standards for herself.

While the purpose of Part Two of this book is to help you teach your daughter ways to stand strong against these cultural pressures, sometimes the best place for you to start is with *protection and prevention*. Put simply, she needs to be protected from the powerful impact of the media, and the best way to do this is by placing limits on its use and by monitoring what she views. This is a countercultural idea in a world with televisions, computers, and Internet-enabled smartphones and devices within constant arm's reach of almost every girl. But if you want your daughter to thrive, you need to start with sensible limits on media and with monitoring its use.

Here are several suggestions to help you start to think about how you will limit and monitor media in your home. If any of this seems overwhelming, start with a small change and then work from there.

- **Keep TV out of your daughter's room**: This might seem like an outlandish statement because so many families have televisions in their children's bedrooms. However, every expert parenting organization, including the American Academy of Pediatrics (AAP), recommends that children's rooms be kept TV-free. There is ample research to indicate that children who have TVs in their bedrooms perform worse in school, have more trouble falling asleep, and are at greater risk of being overweight than are children without TVs in their rooms. In addition, children who have TV's in their bedrooms watch the most TV, and those who watch the most TV are the most likely to have emotional and behavioral problems that stem from cultural messages commonly found in popular media. (This does not mean that all children who have TVs in their bedrooms have these problems; it just means that statistically speaking, they are more likely to have problems than are children without TVs in their bedrooms.)[40]

Here is some research to help you put this recommendation in perspective:

- **TV viewing can make her feel worse about herself**. When your daughter frequently watches TV, commercials, music videos, movies, video games, and social media sites, she is likely to feel worse about herself. One 2012 study showed that after viewing TV for a short period of time, White boys immediately felt better about themselves, but White girls, Black girls, and Black boys felt worse. There are likely many reasons for this result, but part of it stems from girls' comparisons with the women they see on television; they see women who are in limited roles and who are primarily valued because of the way they look.[41] This, in turn, can cause a girl to feel that she doesn't have what it takes to measure up.
- **She starts to believe the sexualized values endorsed by the shows she watches**. The more frequently your daughter watches television and other media, the more likely she is to run across highly sexual content and to be influenced by it.[42] In addition, she will be exposed to sexualized, gender-stereotypical images and messages regarding how she is supposed to look and act as a girl in today's culture.[43] As a striking example of the impact of sexualized media, when your daughter watches music videos, she is highly likely to see sexually objectified women in the videos and hear lyrics that degrade and objectify them. That of course, is no surprise and is nothing new. But what you might not know is this: frequent viewing has an impact on your daughter's

actual attitudes and beliefs about *herself*. One striking study of girls between the ages of 12 and 14 found that the more a girl views music videos, the more likely she is to actually believe that it is acceptable for women to be treated as sexual objects and to be sexually harassed. In other words, girls who watch the most music videos are more likely to accept the treatment of women according to the way that women are treated in these videos. In the study, these same girls were also more likely to believe that attractiveness was a high priority for them and were more likely to have negative body image, excessive dieting behavior, depression, anxiety, and even lower math confidence than girls who did not watch as many videos.[44]

- **She is more likely to engage in the same sexualized behaviors as the characters she sees on TV.** While the previous study I discussed examined media use and girls' attitudes, there is evidence that watching sexualized images on television is related to actual sexual *behaviors*. Researchers conducted a longitudinal study of the movie-watching patterns of 12- to 14-year-olds and then followed up with them six years later. The preteens who watched movies with more sexual content at a younger age were more likely to say that they had been influenced by what they watched, were involved in sexual activity earlier than other children who had watched less sexualized content, and were more likely to report that they had imitated the sexual behaviors they had seen in the shows they had watched.[45]

Note that although these studies were done just a few years ago, they measured only the effects of television viewing. Television is, of course, only one part of the problem with media. You are probably thinking *if TV was the only thing I had to worry about, life would be much easier!* Therefore stay tuned for the next recommendation:

- ***Keep computers and Internet-equipped devices out of your child's bedroom***. This is also a recommendation of AAP. In the past, the guidelines could be more basic: keep the family computer out of the child's bedroom and locate it in a public place in your home. This single step would take care of the problem of unmonitored Internet use. Today it is just not that simple if your child is older or if you have a child who owns a smartphone, tablet, laptop, or game device. It is quite a challenge (although not impossible) for families to require that all Internet use be done in public areas of the home, particularly when the use of devices is a requirement for homework. So consider a requirement that your daughter will turn over all Internet-equipped electronics to you at a certain time and that you will keep them out of her room at night. This includes her phone and laptop. She needs sleep and she needs your protection from the influences she might encounter online and through texting.

- **Limit overall screen time.** The AAP recommendation is to limit your child to no more than one or two hours of combined screen time per day. Children under 18 who spend more than this recommended time period are more likely than others to have emotional, social, and attention problems.[46] Your daughter really needs your help on this. She does not have the developmental ability to limit herself; think about the lure of games, social media, videos . . . it is all so enticing and reinforcing that it is very difficult for anyone to put the brakes on media use, let alone a child. So be the brakes for her.
  - Eye-opening activity: Try to estimate how much time your daughter spends with media on a daily basis. Then keep a media-use log for one week. Record her time spent playing on gaming devices, watching TV or movies, texting, using social media sites, surfing the Internet, playing game apps on her phone (or yours), and so on. Compute the daily totals and compare the results with your estimated total. Does the number surprise you? Based on these results and after reading this chapter, what changes would you like to make?[47]
- **Designate required breaks from technology.** For her optimal development, your daughter needs unplugged time each day. She can't learn who she is if she is always "on" for an online audience and is never present for the actual life she is living. Plan on designated times during the day when she takes a break from her screens. One example might be a family decision that no one will use any form of technology at mealtime (e.g., no texting under the table). Another idea might be to make plans for a family outing where no one brings along technology devices, thus forcing your family to have face-to-face conversations and be present with one another.
- **Monitor what she is viewing.** The purpose of monitoring is twofold. First, it is important to monitor what she is doing so that you can determine whether it is appropriate according to your family's values. It is okay to be selective and to place limits on what she can watch, visit, and view. In fact, research indicates that parental monitoring of media has a protective effect on a variety of positive outcomes—including improved school performance, quality of sleep, decreased aggression, and positive social behaviors.[48] Second, it is also important for you to view media *with* her, so that you can help her decipher the contradictory and confusing messages I have discussed in this chapter. Co-viewing media also helps you better understand her world and what is important to her (e.g., What are her favorite websites and why? What does she like about

a certain song?). Ask questions to help her uncover the values conveyed by a particular show, advertisement, or website. What is the underlying message about how girls should look and act? (To provide more information on this essential topic, I will discuss how to teach your daughter media literacy skills in Chapter Five.)

- **Be mindful of your own media use.** I will cover this strategy extensively in Chapter Four. If you are asking your daughter to limit her media use and to be more tuned in to real life, you need to be willing to do the same. When you ask your daughter to put her cell phone down during dinner, take the extra step of putting yours out of reach as well. Take steps toward making more face-to-face connections with your daughter and with your family.[49]

I would like to end this section with a note of encouragement. Placing limits on your daughter's media usage isn't an easy task and it certainly will not make you popular with anyone in your family. You probably won't see many other parents modeling these behaviors. But press on. When in doubt, reflect on the toxic messages that your daughter is receiving from popular culture and remember that the more media she uses, the more likely it is that she will believe in and act on these messages. Ponder this powerful quotation from Anea Bogue:

> What we must take the time to do, if we hope to protect our daughters from one of the most pervasive sources of disempowering messages to our girls, is to filter and monitor what she is allowed to read and view when she is young, and ensure that her media literacy skills and her own media filter become really strong as she grows older. Her overall health and well-being, not to mention her ability to reach her highest potential, may depend on it.[50]

In this chapter, you went on a tour of popular culture in order to better understand what is being held out as the standard for girls today and had a chance to consider how these expectations can become toxic for girls. This is the external chaos she is facing as she grows up in our current culture. But this is not all. At the same time she is dealing with *external* pressures, we have to remember that she is also undergoing an *internal* transformation that will change every aspect of her life. She is undergoing major physical changes, brain changes that dramatically influence the way she thinks and feels, and is developing her overall sense of who she is and who she wants to become. It is a tremendous amount of pressure and change. It is this internal process of development that I will explore in Chapter Two.

NOTES

1. Lenhart, A. (2012, March 19). What teens do with their phones. *Pew Research Center's Internet and American Life Project*. Retrieved from: http://www.pewinternet.org/2012/03/19/what-teens-do-with-their-phones/Common Sense Media Report (2012). *Social media, social life: How teens view their digital lives*. Retrieved from file:///C:/Users/hgarre3/Downloads/socialmediasociallife-final-061812.pdf.

2. Lamb, S., & Brown, L. M. (2006). *Packaging girlhood: Rescuing our daughters from marketers' schemes*. New York: St. Martin's Griffin; Oppliger, P. A. (2008). *Girls gone shank: The sexualization of girls in American culture*. Jefferson, NC: McFarlan; Choate, L. H., & Curry, J. R. (2009). Addressing the sexualization of girls through comprehensive programs, advocacy and systemic change: Implications for professional school counselors. *Professional School Counseling, 12*(3), 213–221. doi: 10.5330/PSC.n.2010-12.213; Levin, D. E., & Kilbourne, J. (2008). *So sexy so soon: The new sexualized childhood and what parents can do to protect their kids*. New York: Ballantine; Choate, L. H. (2014). Adolescent girls in distress: A guide to mental health treatment and prevention. New York: Springer.

3. American Psychological Association (2007). *Report of the APA task force on the sexualization of girls*. Washington, DC: Author.

4. Goodin, S. M, Van Denburg, A., Murnen, S. K., & Smolak, L. (2011). "Putting on" sexiness: A content analysis of the presence of sexualizing characteristics in girls' clothing. *Sex Roles 65*, 1–12. doi: 10.1007/s11199-011-9966-8

5. Oppliger, P. A. (2008). *Girls gone shank: The sexualization of girls in American culture*. Jefferson, NC: McFarlan.

6. Graff, K., Murnen, S. K., & Smolak, L. (2012). Too sexualized to be taken seriously? Perceptions of a girl in childlike vs. sexual clothing. *Sex Roles, 66*, 764–775. doi: 10.1007/s11199-012-0145-3

7. Ibid.

8. Starr, C. R., & Ferguson, G. M. (2012). Sexy dolls, sexy grade schoolers? Media and maternal influences on young girls' self-sexualization. *Sex Roles, 67*(7/8), 463–476. doi: 10.1007/s1119-012-0183-x

9. Choate, L. H. (2014a). *Adolescent Girls in Distress*. New York: Springer.

10. Bogue, A. (2014). *9 ways we're screwing up our girls and how we can stop. A guide to helping girls reach their highest potential*. Dunham Books.

11. Choate, L. H. (2014b). *Barbie on Sports Illustrated Swimsuit Issue 2014: "Unappologetic" to girls and women?* Retrieved from http://www.springerpub.com/w/psychology/barbie-on-sports-illustrated-swimsuit-issue-2014-unapologetic-to-girls-and-women/

12. Dittmar, H., Halliwell, E., & Ive, S. (2006) Does Barbie make girls want to be thin? The effect of experimental exposure to images of dolls on the body image of 5- to 8-year-old girls. *Developmental Psychology, 42*(2), 283–292. doi: 10.1037/0012-1649.42.2.283

13. Sherman, A.M., & Zurbriggen, E.L. (2014). "Boys can be anything": Effect of Barbie play on girls' career cognitions. *Sex Roles, 70*, 195–208. doi: 10.1007/s11199-014-0347-y

14. Boyd, H., & Murnen, S. K. (2011) *How sexy are girls' dolls? A content analysis of the sexualized characteristics of age 3–11 girls' dolls*. Paper presented at the Ohio Undergraduate Psychology Conference. Gambier: Kenyon College.

15. Lamb, S., & Brown, L. M. (2006). *Packaging girlhood: Rescuing our daughters from marketers' schemes*. New York: St. Martin's Griffin.

16. Villarreal, Y. (2014, August 18). Dora the Explorer is growing up and getting a spinoff series. *New York Times*. Retrieved from: http://www.latimes.com/entertainment/tv/la-et-st-aging-dora-20140818-story.html

17. Harris, A. (2004). *All about the girl: Culture, power, and identity*. New York: Routledge; Hartstein, J. L. (2012). Princess recovery. *A How-to guide to raising strong, empowered girls*. Avon, MA: Adams Media.

18. Hartstein, J. L. (2012). Princess recovery. *A How-to guide to raising strong, empowered girls*. Avon, MA: Adams Media.

19. USA Today. Retrieved from http://www.cdmc.ucla.edu/Published_Research_files/CDMCpressreleaseUhls%26Greenfieldfinal4.pdf

20. Sax, L. (2010). *Girls on the edge: The four factors driving the new crisis for girls*. New York: Basic Books

21. Lamb, S., & Brown, L. M. (2006). *Packaging girlhood: Rescuing our daughters from marketers' schemes*. New York: St. Martin's Griffin.

22. Teen Choice Awards Vote (2014). Retrieved from http://www.teenchoiceawards.com/votetv.aspx

23. Girl Scout Research Institute. (2011b). *Tips for parents: Real to me: Girls and reality tv*. Retrieved from http://www.girlscouts.org/research/pdf/real_to_me_tip_sheet_for_parents.pdf

24. Samakow, J. (2014, August 30). "Training to be Batman's wife": Shirt for teen girls sends all the wrong messages. Retrieved from http://www.huffingtonpost.com/2014/09/30/sexist-batman-shirt_n_5907128.html

25. Lenhart, A. (2012, March 19). What teens do with their phones. *Pew Research Center's Internet and American Life Project*. Retrieved from http://www.pewinternet.org/2012/03/19/what-teens-do-with-their-phones/Common Sense Media Report (2012). *Social media, social life: How teens view their digital lives*. Retrieved from www.commonsensemedia.org/research/social-media-social-life-how-teens-view-their—digital-lives

26. Sax, L. (2010). *Girls on the edge: The four factors driving the new crisis for girls*. New York: Basic Books.

27. Steiner-Adair, C. (2013). *The big disconnect*. New York: Harper Collins.

28. Common Sense Media Report (2012). *Social media, social life: How teens view their digital lives*. Retrieved from www.commonsensemedia.org/research/social-media-social-life-how-teens-view-their—digital-lives

29. Silverman, R. (2014). Am I Like-able? Teens, self esteem and the number of likes they get on social media. Retrieved from drrobynsilverman.com

30. "Fear of missing something" drives home screen alert usage (2014, January 22). Retrieved from http://www.emarketer.com/Article/Fear-of-Missing-Something-Drives-Home-Screen-Alert-Usage/1010546

31. Common Sense Media Report (2012). *Social media, social life: How teens view their digital lives*. Retrieved from www.commonsensemedia.org/research/social-media-social-life-how-teens-view-their—digital-lives

32. Homayoun, A. (2012). *Myth of the perfect girl: Helping our daughters find authentic success and happiness in school and life*. New York: Perigree.

33. Silverman, R. (2014). Am i like-able? Teens, self esteem and the number of likes they get on social media. Retrieved from drrobynsilverman.com

34. Steiner-Adair, C. (2013). *The big disconnect*: Protecting childhood and family relationships in the digital age. New York: Harper Collins.

35. Uhls, Y., Michikya, Morris, J., Garcia, D. Small, G. W., Zgourou, E., & Greenfield, P. M. (2014). Five days at outdoor education camp without screens improves

preteen skills with nonverbal emotion cues. *Computers in Human Behavior.* doi: 10.1016/j.chb.2014.05.036

36. Hinshaw, S. (2009). *The triple bind: Saving our teenage girls from today's pressures.* New York: Ballantine.

37. Orenstein, P. (2011) *Cinderella ate my daughter: Dispatches from the front lines of the new girlie-girl culture.* New York: Harper.

38. Bogue, A. (2014). *9 ways we're screwing up our girls and how we can stop. A guide to helping girls reach their highest potential.* Dunham; Cohen-Sandler, R. (2006). *Stressed-out girls: Helping them thrive in the age of pressure.* New York: Penguin; Martin, C. E. (2007). *Perfect girls, starving daughters: The frightening new normalcy of hating your body.* New York: Free Press; Homayoun, A. (2012). Myth of the perfect girl: Helping our daughters find authentic success and happiness in school and life. New York: Perigree.

39. Girls Incorporated (2006). *The supergirl dilemma: Girls grapple with the mounting pressure of expectations. summary findings.* Retrieved from http://www.girlsinc-monroe.org/styles/girlsinc/defiles/The%20Supergirl%20Dilemma—Summary%20Findings--low%20res.pdf

40. American Academy of Pediatrics (2014). *Managing media: We need a plan.* Retrieved from http://www.aap.org/en-us/about-the-aap/aap-press-room/Pages/Managing-Media-We-Need-a-Plan.aspx

41. Martins, N., & Harrison, K. (2012) Racial and gender differences in the relationship between children's television use and self-esteem: A longitudinal panel study. *Communication Research, 39,* 338. doi: 10.1177/0093650211401376

42. Grabe, S., & Hyde, J. S. (2009). Body objectification, MTV, and psychological outcomes among female adolescents. *Journal of Applied Social Psychology, 39*(12), 2840–2858. doi: 10.1111/j.1559-1816.2009.00552.x; Starr, C. R., & Ferguson, G. M. (2012). Sexy dolls, sexy grade schoolers? Media and maternal influences on young girls' self-sexualization. *Sex Roles, 67,* 463–476. doi: 10.1007/s1119-012-0183-x

43. Martino, S. C., Collins, R. L., Elliot, M. N., Strachman, A., Kanouse, D. E., & Barry, S. H. (2006). Exposure to degrading versus nondegrading music lyrics and sexual behavior among youth. *Pediatrics, 118,* E430–E441. doi: 10.1542/peds.2006-0131; Ward, L. M., & Friedman, K. (2006). Using TV as a guide: Associations between television viewing and adolescents' sexual attitudes and behavior. *Journal of Research on Adolescence, 16,* 133–156. doi: 10.111 1/j.1532-7795.2006.00125.x

44. Grabe, S., & Hyde, J. S. (2009). Body objectification, MTV, and psychological outcomes among female adolescents. *Journal of Applied Social Psychology, 39*(12), 2840–2858. doi: 10.1111/j.1559-1816.2009.00552.x

45. Ohara, R., Gibbons, F., Gerrard, M., Li, A., & Sargent, J. D. (2012). Greater exposure to sexual content in popular movie predicts earlier sexual debut. *Psychological Science, 23*(9), 984–993. doi: 10.1177/0956797611435529

46. American Academy of Pediatrics (2013). Policy statement on children, adolescents, and the media. Available at www.pediatrics.aappublications.org/content/132/5/958.full?sid=f31bfb76-437f40c0-8101-267c2d1cc581; Ginsberg, K. (2011). *Building Resilience in Children and Teens* (2nd ed.). Elk Grove Village, IL: American Academy of Pediatrics.

47. Donaldson-Pressman, S., Jackson, R., & Pressman, R. (2014). *The Learning Habit: A Groundbreaking Approach to Homework and Parenting that Helps Our Children Succeed in School and Life.* New York, NY: Penguin Group.

48. Gentile, D. A., Reimer, R. A., Nathanson, A., Walsh, D. A., & Eisenmann, J. C. (2014). Protective effects of parental monitoring of children's media use: A prospective study. *JAMA Pediatrics, 168*, 479–484.
49. Steiner-Adair, C. (2013). *The Big Disconnect*. New York: Harper Collins.
50. Bogue, A. (2014). *9 ways we're screwing up our girls and how we can stop. A guide to helping girls reach their highest potential*. Dunham Books.

CHAPTER TWO

Girls in Transition

Who Am I?

As I mentioned in Chapter One, just when your daughter is grappling with the impact of confusing and often incompatible cultural expectations, she will also be going through dramatic upheavals in her physical, cognitive, social, and overall identity development. An important task for you as a parent, then, is to understand adolescent development and to begin to view her current attitudes and behaviors through this developmental lens. Even when life with her feels chaotic, knowing what is normal and to be expected will help you to make more sense of her behavior. With your support, it can become possible for her to manage all of these transitions well, particularly if you are equipped with knowledge, lots of patience, and the resilience strategies described in Part Two of this book.

To help you with your understanding of girls' development, in this chapter I will first discuss some of the physical changes of puberty and then describe girls' rapidly changing brains and the impact of this on their thinking and emotions. Finally, I will highlight the changes that are occurring as she struggles to answer the question "Who Am I?" As you know, the answer to this seems to change daily, but as she progresses through adolescence, one of her goals will be to develop a somewhat stable identity, one that is based on an authentic core of who she is and what she values.

For some of you with younger daughters, this chapter might be a look ahead: you have time to prepare and to know what to expect in the years to come. Others of you with daughters who have already undergone the initial phase of puberty might already be helping them to cope with their developing bodies, minds, and identities. It is my hope that this chapter will give you a solid grounding in understanding girls' development so that you can nurture and support your daughter no matter where she is located along the continuum as she transitions from girlhood to adolescence and then to adulthood.

PHYSICAL DEVELOPMENT: WHAT'S HAPPENING TO HER BODY?

It seems unfair that at the same time that girls are receiving strong cultural pressures about how they should look and act, they are also undergoing major physical developmental changes in their transition through adolescence.[1] It seems as though it were too much to ask of them, yet it all crashes down on them at once. Boys face changes and pressures too, of course, but they typically go through the physical changes of puberty much later than girls, so they have more time to learn to cope with all of the other stressors occurring in their lives before their physical maturation starts to occur.

In girls, the physical changes of puberty include dramatic hormonal changes, breast budding and growth, the development of secondary sex characteristics like pubic and armpit hair, and the eventual onset of menarche (i.e., her first period). Puberty entails the most physical changes that a girl has experienced since she was an infant; there are changes to a girl's circulatory and respiratory systems, she will grow up to 3 inches taller per year, and will experience increases in weight and body composition, mostly in the form of fat to her hips and thighs. Once puberty begins, this whole process takes about two to four years.[2]

These changes are normal; they occur for all girls, and most girls experience them with few problems. However, we know that sometimes the physical and hormonal changes that come with puberty can and do result in significant challenges for girls. There are several reasons why problems may emerge:

- **Girls experience physical changes and external stressors simultaneously.** As already discussed, it is exceedingly hard to have to deal with so much at once.
- **Girls start to worry more about their body weight, shape, and appearance.** Girls in adolescence become increasingly concerned about how they look. Many girls zero in on their body size and weight, and this heightened focus is occurring at the same time that they are undergoing significant weight gains and developing increased body fat. While they might not mind the development of breasts, many girls are not at all

happy with the weight gain that typically occurs in their buttocks, hips, and thighs. This may be a normal part of development (to prepare the body to eventually be able to bear a child), but this new body shape is often the opposite of what a girl is seeing in popular media about how she should look. As she starts to place more importance on looking like the thin-beautiful-hot-sexy ideal discussed in Chapter One, she starts to compare herself to that ideal. As her body is changing in a way that is increasingly different from the media ideal, this discrepancy often causes her to experience body dissatisfaction, lowered self-esteem, and even depression. Girls' experiences with body dissatisfaction and how it relates to the development of depression and eating disorders will be discussed in Chapter Three.

- **Girls have to deal with initial feelings related to sexual identity and sexual decision making.** As her body matures, it releases increasing amounts of oxytocin (the same hormone that is released during breast feeding, resulting in bonding between mother and child), which draws her toward romantic relationships and intimacy. If she seems increasingly pulled toward romantic relationships, know that there is indeed a biological basis for it. Because of her hormonal changes, she is also starting to experience sexual feelings for the first time and is having to come to terms with her sexual identity (and for some girls, this might mean understanding their identity as that of a person who is lesbian, bisexual, or transgender). Because she is seeking out relationships and is starting to experience sexual feelings, she will also be faced with decisions around when and how to become sexually active. I talk about sexual decision making in relationships in Chapter 6, but for now it is important for you to remember that this is a confusing time for girls, as their bodies mature at a much faster rate than does their ability to make responsible sexual decisions. Almost 40 percent of girls say that they regret their first sexual experience, and girls who engage in sexual activity at earlier ages are more likely than others to experience serious problems such as unwanted pregnancy and sexually transmitted diseases.[3]

In addition to these reasons, the biggest obstacle a girl might face in coping with the physical changes of puberty is when they occur at an early age; we know that the timing of puberty is highly linked to problems in girls' mental health,[4] and more and more girls today are experiencing puberty early. Research suggests that the age of onset of puberty has fallen dramatically for girls during the past forty years. In a study published in the *Journal of Pediatrics*, researchers found that 25 percent of African American girls, 15 percent of Hispanic girls, and 10 percent of White girls had started to develop breasts by age 7. By age 8 this number had jumped to 18 percent of White girls, 43 percent of African American girls, and 31 percent of Hispanic girls.[5] In other words, the average age for breast budding is currently 9.8 for White girls, 8.9 for African American girls, and 9.3 for Hispanic girls.[6]

An interesting thing about increases in early breast development is that although the age at which breast development begins has dropped significantly during the past forty years, the age at which a girl has her first period has fallen only slightly, from 12 years 9 months to 12 years 6 months on average. This is striking in that girls are not starting their periods much earlier than did girls in the past, but they are developing breasts up to two years earlier than before. Questions remain as to why today's girls are experiencing such a long interval between breast budding (the time at which their bodies begin to develop) and menarche (their first period, at which point they become capable of reproduction).[7] So which biological, genetic, environmental, or cultural factors are actually fueling this rise in early development for girls? Research is not yet able to provide clear answers to this question, but we know that some of the factors include the following:

- **Genetics**: There are strong links between a girl's pubertal onset and when her own mother started puberty.
- **Exposure to environmental toxins (i.e., chemicals)**: Some studies claim chemicals that are added to food and products can mimic estrogen in the body, thereby tricking the body into early puberty (e.g., the chemical BPA [bisphenol A] commonly found in hard plastics).
- **Excess body fat and weight**: One of the strongest contributors to early puberty is excess body fat and overall body weight, although the strongest link is to body fat. This link occurs because body fat causes increases in the release of leptin, a hormone that contributes to early maturation, although this connection between body fat and puberty is not completely understood.
- **Stress**: Early puberty is more likely to occur when girls live in conditions of uncertainty and stress. When the stress response is frequently triggered in a girl's body, the process of breast development and puberty is somehow stimulated for her at an earlier age than if she were living in a more stable, less stressful environment.
- **Family relationships**: Girls who experience early puberty are more likely to live in families that have high levels of conflict, lack warmth, and provide few high-quality interactions. Daughters who are insecurely attached to their parents and have parents who are harsh and

controlling are more likely to get their periods earlier. Another fascinating finding is that there is a relationship between whether or not a girl lives with her father and the timing of puberty; girls who do not have their fathers living in same the home are more likely to start puberty early. It is thought that frequent exposure to the pheromones of unrelated, sexually mature males may stimulate puberty in girls. (Pheromones are chemicals released into the air that stimulate hormonal reactions.[8]) Even though this specific explanation can't be studied directly in humans (although it has been demonstrated in animal studies), research does show that when girls' fathers don't live in the home with them, girls are likely to start puberty earlier.[9]

As you read this list, please don't see it as a prescription; just because your daughter has a stressful life, lives without her father, or has recently gained some weight does not mean that she will necessarily start puberty early. It also doesn't mean that if she did start puberty early, any of these factors were to blame. This research is based on *averages*, which means that although there is a significant relationship between each factor and early puberty, no one factor can determine what will happen to any particular girl. So keep this in mind: these studies are provided to help us understand general trends, but they can't be used to predict with certainty whether your daughter will experience early puberty or why she started puberty early. See Box 2.1 for some recommendations from developmental researchers about how to slow down the onset of puberty in girls.

Many contributors to early puberty are outside of a parent's control, but this doesn't mean that you don't have an influence on what happens to your daughter once she reaches puberty. Parents need to know that if their daughter matures early, she is at increased risk for a long list of problems (remember this means that she is at *risk*, it does not mean that these problems are *inevitable for her*). It is important to be armed with this information in order to protect her from all of the additional negative pressures she will experience. We know that some of these problems include the following:

- **Self-esteem and body image problems**: Girls who mature early are more likely than others to be uncomfortable with their bodies and weight, placing them at risk for low self-esteem, negative body image, and eating disorders.
- **Psychological problems**: Girls who mature early are more likely to experience depression, social anxiety, and substance disorders in their teen years.

If your daughter has not yet entered the preadolescent years, there are some general prevention recommendations you can consider; yet remember that many of the factors that contribute to early puberty are outside of your (or your daughter's) control. Greenspan and Deardorff offer the following guidelines, which are helpful for the health and wellness of any girl.

GUIDELINES TO PREVENT OR SLOW DOWN EARLY PUBERTY IN YOUR DAUGHTER

- Help her establish healthy habits that will keep her fit, well rested, and at an ideal weight (more about this in Chapter Eight). This includes her diet, her activities, her sleep routine, and providing a place for her to express and regulate her emotions.
- Limit her exposure to synthetic chemicals that may disrupt healthy human biology. The authors recommend the Environmental Working Group website (ewg.org) to search for the safest food and products for your family.
- Work toward maintaining a loving, supportive family environment. More about this important area in Chapter Four.[10]

- **Behavior problems**: Girls are more likely to experience increased teasing and bullying by peers, poor academic performance, disengagement from school, early smoking, sexual harassment, early and unwanted sexual activity, physical and verbal abuse in their dating relationships, social exclusion, disruptive or aggressive behaviors, and poor or little support from friends and family.
- **Physical problems**: Early-maturing girls are more likely to experience abdominal pain, sleep disturbances, headaches, and upset stomach.[11]

At this point, you might be wondering why all these problems would be linked to early puberty. Although there are many reasons for this relationship, they primarily boil down to two issues: girls might be self-conscious about being different from their peers, and they are more likely to attract attention from an older crowd. Let's look at both of these influences separately, although they go hand in glove for most girls.

First, her body is changing in ways that are very noticeable to others. She feels as though everyone is staring at her. As already discussed, during middle childhood and especially in early adolescence, girls are already comparing themselves with others to see how they measure up. Standing out or appearing "different" can cause great distress to girls who so desperately want to fit in. Every girl wants to know that she is normal, and she doesn't feel normal at all when others are teasing, harassing, or bullying her about her body. It doesn't help matters that early-maturing girls also tend to be heavier than others, so they are also likely to be teased about their weight in addition to their shape. Because girls are in a developmental stage where it is especially likely that they will compare themselves with others and base their feelings about themselves on whether or not their peers approve of them, early development can be especially distressing.

Second, girls who enter puberty early also have problems when they are prematurely forced out of childhood and into the adolescent subculture. Your daughter needs time for this transition in order to figure out who she is and what is expected of her. Early-maturing girls simply have less time just to be kids for as long as they need to be. Their teenager-like appearance will likely be attracting the attention of older friends and potential romantic interests (especially older boys), and this may become hard to resist as they are searching for a place where they can fit in and be a part of a peer group. They will learn that they can gain a lot of attention from others based on their appearance. They just want to belong, and if they don't feel that they fit in with kids their age, they will be tempted to try to blend in with an older group of friends.

Being around an older crowd, however, will inevitably expose a girl to high-risk activities, the very ones you fear the most as a parent—she will likely be encouraged to smoke, drink, try substances, date older boys, and be pressured to engage in sexual activity. Unfortunately research shows that risky behaviors tend to cluster together, so when a girl tries one behavior (like smoking) she is more likely to become involved in others (like drinking or sexual activity). This exposure and pressure starts well before she is emotionally prepared to make these types of very adult-level decisions.[12] Even though she looks more physically developed, she still lacks the emotional maturity and decision-making/coping skills needed to either remove herself from unsafe situations or to assert herself and say no to risky behaviors. While your daughter is younger, she will need you to protect her so that she doesn't end up in situations where she is forced to make serious decisions like whether or not to use illicit substances or have sex. Keep in mind that no matter how mature she may look physically, she does not yet have the skills to know how to get out of these situations easily or to assert herself effectively. She needs your help.

Resilience and Early Puberty: Parenting Strategies to Consider

- **Focus on reality versus perception**. Make a deliberate effort to treat your daughter according to the age that she actually *is*, not according to the way she looks. On the outside she may look like an older teenager, but socially and emotionally she is still a child who needs your guidance and protection.
- **Normalize**. Let her know that the changes she is going through are *normal* but just happening a little early for her. "I know you might be the only one in your class who is tall and already wearing a bra. It's okay; you've just started to change a few years earlier than the other kids." Listen to her and empathize; its so hard for her to stand out or be different at this age. Age-appropriate books about the changes of puberty might also help to normalize the process for her (see resources at end of this book).
- **Check yourself**. How you cope with what is happening can determine how well your daughter will respond. If you are embarrassed by your daughter's developing body, she will pick up on it and learn to be ashamed of her body as well. Try to cope with any negative or anxious feelings by discussing them with a counselor or trusted friend. Do what you can so that your feelings don't seep into your relationship with your daughter. She will definitely sense your disapproval at a time when what she needs most is your love, support, and acceptance.
- **Encourage resilience**. Do what you can to help her maintain a positive self-image (see Chapter Five). Maintain a loving home where she can relax and be herself. Allow her to have time to play and be a kid. Be positive about the changes in her body but try to keep most of your comments to her centered on things other than her appearance, like her character and her efforts in school and at home. Help her recognize that she is more than her body and its current changes; her physical appearance is only one aspect of who she is.
- **Protect**. Pay attention to your child's group of friends and note whether she is starting to gravitate toward an older friendship group. When she is around older friends, she will also be more likely to attract the attention of older boys and will then have to deal with pressures from them to participate in high-risk activities. Consider setting an age limit on friends and dating partners so that she will not be exposed to pressures

for drinking, smoking, and sexual activity before she is cognitively and psychologically ready to deal with these types of pressures.

COGNITIVE DEVELOPMENT: WHAT'S HAPPENING TO HER THOUGHTS AND FEELINGS?

Now that I have discussed the physical changes of puberty, let's turn to another part of your daughter's body that you can't see but that is changing just as rapidly: her brain. Her thinking and way of understanding her world is becoming distinctly different and it is helpful for you to know something about the way these changes occur.

In the not so distant past, developmental psychologists explained child and adolescent cognitive development primarily in terms of stages. The most commonly known model for understanding how a girl thinks about the world is the cognitive stage model of Jean Piaget. In Piagetian terms, most preadolescent girls are still operating at what is known as the *concrete operations* stage; they think concretely in black-and-white terms, don't plan for the future, and cannot think in abstract terms or understand multiple perspectives in approaching a problem. You might notice that your daughter tends to jump to conclusions, often based on her emotions or her own limited experiences, and she is often unable to imagine the possible consequences of her actions. You have probably seen her struggle to come up with the most practical solution to a problem and have noticed that her decisions are not based on reason and logic.

According to Piaget, once a girl enters mid-adolescence, she starts to move toward what is termed *formal operations*, meaning that she can think more abstractly about a problem, reason logically, and imagine multiple outcomes and options.[13] For example, she can begin to actually solve problems—she can consider multiple ways to plan for an upcoming event, consider the consequences of each option, and then make a decision based on a logical consideration of all the possible alternatives. This looks very different from the behavior of the emotional preteen whose ideas are jumbled and whose reasoning often seems chaotic.

Today we know more than ever about this shift from concrete to abstract thinking and from emotional to logical decision making because scientists can analyze images of the brain to actually determine how the adolescent brain works during this time. In other words, we no longer have to rely on behavioral observations to understand development; scientists can examine brain scans to see what is happening within the brain. The most recent brain imaging studies show that the adolescent brain undergoes a major remodeling and changes in drastic ways during these years, so that as she grows older, a girl's brain becomes better able to process more information and is more efficient in doing so.

An older girl's brain also becomes more geared toward reward-seeking. Her limbic system—the more primal, emotional center of her brain that is driven by her appetites and pleasure seeking—is developing especially rapidly and is highly activated during adolescence. It is no surprise to parents that brain studies show that adolescents experience their emotions more intensely, are easily excited, and are more responsive to stress and anger. Often to our surprise, their strong emotional responses can be triggered by seemingly ordinary events. In addition, they are more drawn toward thrill seeking and new, exciting experiences than are children or adults. Therefore your daughter's emotional center is especially sensitive and active during this time and has an especially strong influence on all of her actions. For several years then, much to our chagrin, the limbic system in the driver's seat.

However, brain studies also reveal that major pruning and rewiring is starting to occur in the outer layer (cortex) of your daughter's brain. It is this part that controls the brain's executive functions, including complex tasks like self-regulation, organizing and directing problem solving, self-initiation, planning for the future, goal setting, and the regulation of emotion. This CEO of the brain—the most sophisticated part—takes the most time to develop. It is not until the prefrontal cortex matures that a young woman is fully able to control the limbic system underneath or to be better able to slow down and think things through and make rational and logical decisions. This is why adolescents are not yet fully able to regulate and control their impulses or to engage in purposeful, logical, goal-oriented behavior. This is also why your daughter's erratic behavior—sometimes logical, sometimes purely emotional—is so confusing to you. Her brain is still under construction! Her prefrontal cortex is just not yet fully developed. Sometimes she uses it and at other times she doesn't.

In fact, scientists are learning that the prefrontal cortex matures much later than previously thought. They now know that it is not fully reorganized and developed until the mid- to late twenties! This is much later than what Piaget's earlier stage model of concrete to formal operations predicted. It helps us understand that although your daughter can sometimes make decisions in a rational, logical way, this does not happen consistently, and it is definitely not likely to happen when she finds herself in an emotionally charged situation. Try to think of your daughter's brain as a race car; according to Steinberg, she is like a car that has a sensitive gas pedal but has only weak brakes. The brakes are developing and are somewhat functional, but they are no match for her emotional, thrill-seeking accelerator![14] This mismatch between her thrill-seeking limbic system and the system governing self-regulation seems to be greatest between the start of puberty to around age 16.

These findings are important to keep in mind as you make parenting decisions regarding what you will allow your daughter to do or not do. It is not just about telling your daughter not to do certain things because they might be dangerous. Teens simply weigh the risks and benefits of certain behaviors differently than adults do. Research indicates that teens are well aware of the risks associated with their behaviors; they do listen to the speeches we give about why things might be dangerous. In fact, they are just as knowledgeable as adults about risks associated with reckless behaviors. Some research shows that adolescents not only understand but also even *overestimate* the risks associated with behaviors like smoking and sexual activity.

The problem is that although they do consider the *risks*, they rate the immediate *benefits* of the behavior as very high; therefore, in the adolescent mind, the benefits usually outweigh the risks. Whereas an adult might think, *if I do this, it will be exciting, but I know that getting caught might cause a lot of problems for me, so I will say no, it's not worth the risk.* An adolescent, on the other hand, will be magnetically drawn to the excitement and thrills of a new adventure or to acceptance by her peers, being lured by the benefits and greatly discounting the fact that she might get caught. The risks, while she is aware of them, play a very small role in her decision making at this point.

So especially in the period of time between the start of puberty and around age 16 when it peaks, adolescents experience pleasure intensely, and they take impulsive risks in order to experience it. Remember that the immediate benefits (driven by the limbic system which seeks thrills and novelty) will usually overpower any knowledge your daughter has of risks associated with a behavior.

This tendency to disregard longer-term consequences and seek immediate rewards is especially prevalent when girls' friends are around. According to Steinberg's research, a frightening example is that when an adolescent is driving, the presence of a group of friends in a car more than quadruples the likelihood of a crash. Contrast this with the case of an adult driver, where there presence of others in the car has no effect on the likelihood of a crash. So what is the takeaway for parents? Adolescents use poor judgment and decision-making skills when their peers are around. Even when peers don't directly pressure teens to act more recklessly, even If nothing is spoken between them, just knowing that other teens are watching causes adolescents to take more risks.[15]

Remember that when your daughter is in an emotional situation (as when she is being pressured to smoke, drink, or have sex), and especially when friends are around, her brain won't yet function like the brain of an adult. She will be in over her head; her emotions will likely win out over reason. According to Greenspan and Deardorff, "Kids might have the best intentions but succumb to their feelings when their brain rewards them for it. Welcome to the developing teenage brain."[16]

What does this mean in terms of your role as a parent? While your daughter is in this in-between period when the CEO of her brain is still under construction, you will need to provide some extra guidance and structure. She needs monitoring and oversight, especially to protect her from being alone with her peers during unstructured times; this can even mean during the hours after school. An eye-opening finding is that the primary time in which most teens initially experiment with alcohol, drugs, sex, and delinquent behavior is not on weekend nights, as you might suspect, but on weekday afternoons![17]

However, even after reading all of this, you still don't want to lock her in a room until she is 25 because her brain development is also highly influenced by her learning and experiences. She needs life experiences in order to grow and make healthy choices both now and in the future. The brain is highly plastic during these years, meaning that it is highly open to learning new skills, including self-regulation. In other words, she needs practice in order to be able to make good decisions and think through consequences. But her practice should involve safe situations. As she learns to make good decisions in low-risk situations, she is slowly being prepared for the more complex decisions she will face later on. She needs opportunities that are just slightly beyond her current level of maturity; she can progressively build her self-regulatory muscles by taking on something she is not quite able to handle now, so that she will have a good chance of success (and no serious consequences if she fails). This is what is called *scaffolding*: You provide somewhat structured experiences now so that she can practice and then succeed when the scaffolding is taken away. In this way her brain will be strengthened so that engaging self-regulation will be easier each time she is faced with a new situation.

So your guidelines can be as follows: monitor her whereabouts, keep her out of difficult situations, but also give her practice in standing up for herself and making choices in low-risk situations. She needs these skills in order to learn self-regulation, and it is self-regulation that will give her the greatest chances for success in school, in her relationships, and in life.[18] Chapter Eight of this book addresses ways in which you can help your daughter build self-regulatory skills. For now, see the resilience strategies I outlined in the following section.

Resilience Strategies for Building Self-Regulation

1. **Monitor and protect**: Now that you understand the importance of continued oversight until your daughter's executive functioning skills are more fully developed, know that she still needs adequate amounts of adult support, monitoring, and guidance until she is consistently able to engage in goal-directed, planned, less emotionally driven behavior. Even though she might look physically older and can explain her plans in a logical manner, remember that her brain is still not able to make the best decisions when she finds herself in an emotionally charged situation. Just because she can talk about it with you calmly doesn't mean that she will respond calmly in a heated moment when friends or romantic interests are pressuring her to do something she isn't ready to do. Do what you can to keep her out of situations where she is likely to be at risk for these pressures. Monitor what she is doing and provide appropriate adult supervision. When in doubt, remember the race car analogy: she can't put the brakes on consistently and effectively just yet!

2. **Let her seek safe thrills.** Because she is naturally driven to seek out new adventures, thrills, and risks, provide opportunities for her to satisfy these desires in safe ways. There are many ways in which she can seek out excitement and take risks. Think about things like adventure outings (ziplining, rock-wall climbing, laser tag). If that doesn't fit her personality, perhaps she would enjoy the risk that comes from auditioning and performing on stage (e.g., dance, acting, singing, playing an instrument). Perhaps she could take on a part-time job or volunteer for an organization that she is passionate about. Help her dream up some safe risks she can pursue![19]

3. **Teach self-awareness.** Even though her engine is racing and her brakes are weak, she can take initial steps toward implementing the skills she needs for applying those brakes effectively. This is called self-regulation: the ability to stop, think, consider the consequences, and set goals for action. The first step in this process is often the hardest: to stop and notice what she is feeling and thinking *before* she takes action. The best way for her to learn to do this is for you to practice with

her. Before she dives into something, help her to learn to visualize a stop sign that will urge her to become aware of what she is experiencing (e.g., What am I feeling right now? What are my thoughts? What is going to happen if I do this? What will happen if I choose not to do it?) It is this pause that helps her respond to a situation rather than passively reacting to it.[20] This is an essential coping skill she will need (but will not always be able to apply given her unevenly developing brain). But encourage her to practice repeatedly until it becomes automatic. I will cover this skill as it applies to parents (Chapter Four) and more extensively when I discuss self-regulatory skills (Chapter Eight).

4. **Practice appropriate scaffolding**. Your daughter will benefit most when she can practice making choices and taking small risks in gradually safe ways. For example, she may not be ready for an unsupervised boy/girl party (too much risk) but she might benefit from learning how to feel comfortable in a supervised school study group of both boys and girls that meets at the library (minimal risk, but does require her to practice social skills and assertiveness). The point is that she does need experience in standing up for herself and learning what it feels like to say, "No, I'm not interested." As with any skill, she needs practice. As she practices in safe contexts, her brain is slowly trained to follow these same steps the next time she is in a situation that requires assertiveness. With each experience, the connections in her brain are more solidified. Eventually this practice will help her know what to do when she is actually in a difficult, high-pressure situation in the future.

IDENTITY DEVELOPMENT: WHAT'S HAPPENING TO HER SENSE OF SELF?

Adolescence is the time when your daughter will find and refine her identity by struggling with answers to the question "Who Am I?" When people have a healthy sense of identity, they are able to be independent and autonomous (i.e., they are comfortable with who they are and can do things on their own) while at the same time they still have the capacity to stay connected to the important people in their lives. In other words, they are independent but also able to create and maintain positive relationships with others. This is not an easy balance to achieve, particularly for girls, who tend to get pulled toward pleasing others in relationships while neglecting the more autonomous, authentic part of themselves. A helpful way of understanding your daughter's identity development is to think about how she is trying to accomplish the following four tasks:

1. To stand out (to develop her own identity and autonomy)
2. To fit in (to gain acceptance from peers and find comfortable friendships)
3. To measure up (to develop competence and find ways to achieve)
4. To take hold (to make commitments to particular goals, activities, and beliefs)[21]

During this window of time in her life she is supposed to figure out who she is, learn to be herself, accomplish her goals, and take a stand about her own beliefs and values—all the while trying to fit in with her peers. When you take a moment to consider all that goes into developing her sense of self and add this to the cultural expectations and pressures described in Chapter One, you will start to understand the magnitude of the challenges she will be or is currently facing. That's why she needs your support, guidance, and most of all, patience.

To Stand Out

Your daughter has a drive to become her own person. She wants to be known as an individual in her own right, apart from you, and eventually apart from her friends or other relationships. She needs to take the time to figure out who she wants to be, what she likes, and what she values. I will focus on ways you can help her through this process in Chapters Five through Eight. However, as her parent, you first need to recognize that to find herself, she will take her initial steps of independence by separating from you. Remember that she will need to push you away at times in order to figure out who she is. At times she wants to stay close and connected, but at other times she needs to separate and feel more independent. So if you feel that you are being caught in a push-pull cycle, it is because you are. You have to be there for her, whichever side of the cycle she finds herself in at any given moment. She is asking, *can I be myself and still be connected to you?* If she can learn to do this with you, she can also learn to do it with others in her life. She can learn that it is possible to stand out and be her own person while also fitting in.

Often popular media portray adolescent girls in this way: a girl who spends many hours alone in her room (even while she is online with the outside world) and who spends increasingly large amounts of time away from home in order to avoid her parents and hang out with friends and romantic interests. She pushes her parents away and argues with them relentlessly. She is portrayed as someone who should just be avoided until her teenage angst has subsided. This causes many parents to think they should just give up and do their best to leave her alone. What many parents don't understand is that what she really needs is to stay close; she needs continued connection. Therefore, even when her seeming rejection of you seems painful, don't let her push you away entirely. Allow her the breathing room she needs where she can find her sense of self apart from you, but don't shut the door, because she still needs you. Many adolescents say that they wish their parents knew how much they continue to crave their parents' time and attention[22] (I will talk more about these issues in Chapter Four). During this time of push-pull, it is helpful to think of yourself as a secure home base; as your daughter explores her world and tries out new things, she still needs to be able to come back to you, her source of stability and security. She needs you to serve as the base she needs as she comes home again and again for emotional refueling. As stated in the Harvard Project on Raising Teens:

> Frustrating parents, teens want to be with them except when they don't, teens want their help except when they don't, and teens behave in excitingly more mature ways—except when they don't. Requiring moment by moment judgment calls, teens need an environment that provides opportunities for experimentation at certain times but not others; for privacy on some matters but not others; for peer influence in some areas but not others; and for negotiation and decision making on some issues but not others. Throughout, they need parents to remain available, taking the emotional high ground by providing opportunities for closeness that teens can sometimes accept and sometimes reject.[23]

As a parent, you will be called upon to live in predictable unpredictability with your daughter, sometimes letting go and other times holding on. It is truly a challenge to remain stable as she pulls away in order to learn more about who she is.

To Fit In

In addition to her drive to stand out, she is also highly drawn toward fitting in. It is a developmental task of childhood and adolescence to figure out how to relate to peers and to establish relationships. That is no surprise to any parent. But what might take you by surprise is the intensity with which she pursues this goal, often to the neglect of what she really wants and needs for herself. Recall from the previous section on brain development how puberty stimulates the regions of the brain that promote reward seeking and emotional thrills. Puberty also activates the part of the brain that focuses on relationships with others. Your daughter is experiencing heightened arousal and greater sensitivity to what others think about her, to social acceptance or rejection, and to reading social cues. In other words, her brain chemistry is actually pushing her to crave attention and close relationships right now.[24] Also recall that she is being bombarded with the strong cultural expectation for gaining attention and acceptance from others. Biologically and culturally she is being primed to pursue acceptance, often to the exclusion of the other three goals of adolescence (i.e., to stand out, to measure up, to take hold).

This relentless pursuit of peer acceptance is intensified if she feels that she does not have acceptance from her own family. If she doesn't feel accepted, liked, and validated at home, the more she will be drawn toward fitting in with whatever peer group she can find that will offer her that validation and acceptance. Remember that it is easy for this need in her life to be thrown out of balance if she does not first perceive that she fits in with you. I will talk about this powerful need for love and acceptance from you, her parent, in Chapter Four.

Another way in which your daughter's need to fit in might be thrown off balance is when her own identity becomes lost in the process of pleasing a peer group. To understand how this can occur, first take a step back and remember your daughter's middle childhood. Girls are usually blossoming at this age. More than any other time in their lives, girls like themselves, they say what is on their minds, and they do things without considering what others might think. In some of my workshops for girls, when I ask third to fourth graders what they like about themselves, they overwhelmingly raise their hands and breathlessly yell out multiple answers: "My toes!" "My sense of humor!" "My smile!" "My pretty eyes!" "How fast I run!" In group discussions, each child raises her hand, and I can't keep up with all the volunteers who want to share. For many girls, it is a time of energy and confidence.

Fast forward to middle school. I ask this same question and I hear crickets from the group. When I ask them to list ten things they appreciate about themselves, most can think of only one or two. When I ask them about their lives, feelings, and relationships, they look around at each other, worried about what the other girls will think if they speak up. In your own daughter's life, you might notice that among her friends she will say, "I don't care" if asked for her preference between movies to watch or things to do. In fact, the only time she seems willing to say no is to you! You wonder why she has stopped voicing what she really wants and you worry that soon she won't even know how to think for herself. This is a communication style girls develop in order to make others happy with them, keep the peace, and not cause any problems, and it works in the short run; it is a seemingly polite way to respond to adults and to friends. The problem with this comes later, when the choices are not about movies or menus but about peer pressure to do things that she would rather not do (and those things that you definitely don't want her to do). She might give in and say, "I don't care" when really she cares a lot. Denying her own opinions and needs, she is likely to make choices that she will later regret. I will talk more about this loss of voice in Chapter Six.

While some girls try to fit in by being nice and accommodating, others try to fit in not by being agreeable, but by being the princess/diva previously discussed in Chapter One. They might think that the best way to fit in is by gaining negative attention, demanding what they want, acting out in edgy, provocative ways, and behaving aggressively with others. Just do a YouTube search of girl-fighting and you will immediately know what I mean. (Warning: I would not recommend doing this or watching the videos around your children as they are very violent and, to me, very sad.) This attention-grabbing, defiant, aggressive persona is part of a her attempt to meet the "bad is the new good" expectation discussed in Chapter One, but it is rarely reflective of her authentic self; instead, she is trying to live up to a cultural image. So whether she is learning to take her true self underground or over the top, she is forced to choose between being *herself* or pleasing others. The empowering idea that she can be true to herself (standing out) while also having healthy, positive relationships that value her for who she really is (fitting in) is one that I will explore throughout this book.

To Measure Up

The "measuring up" part of her identity development involves her understanding of her personal strengths and capabilities. As your daughter progresses through school, she starts to learn about her particular areas of competence and develops an academic self-concept. She starts to develop a more realistic picture about possibilities for herself as she identifies academic and career goals (e.g., "I want to go to college and I think I want to study architecture," or "I love art but I will probably do it for fun and not pursue it for a college scholarship"). She is also learning about her strengths in terms of athletics and other areas of performance (e.g., music, drama, dance). This is a healthy part of her overall identity development.

As reviewed in Chapter One, this part of her identity can be thrown off balance, however, so that she learns to overemphasize her accomplishments. She may think that she has to be good at everything; there can't be *areas* of strength, they *all* have to be strengths! Or, conversely, she might believe that she is not exceptional at anything and stop trying to achieve in any area. In Chapter One I discussed the cultural expectation that a girl's worth can become based solely on her accomplishments and how harmful it can be to face so much pressure to perform at a high level at all times. The important issue here is that while "measuring up" is an important *component* of identity, it should not take over as her identity itself (e.g., "I am nothing apart from my accomplishments"). When a girl overemphasizes this area, it is no surprise that she may end up pushing too hard for perfection or even give up entirely. The cultural pressure around accomplishments is the focus of Chapter Seven.

To Take Hold

Part of your daughter's identity development will involve accepting and integrating different parts of herself into a coherent identity. She starts to take the pieces of herself and puts them together to form a whole. This process takes a considerable length of time, and for a while she will seem as if she were a different person each day. She is trying on identities for size and shedding them just as quickly. This is definitely another area that will require your patience as she seems to change preferences from day to day.

> MOM: I made our special beef lasagna tonight! I know how it has always been your favorite!
> DAUGHTER: Oh Mom, I can't eat that! You know I am a vegan!

Sound familiar? This day-to-day questioning of what she likes and doesn't like is just part of the process of developing an integrated identity. She needs a lot of practice with this before she can really "take hold" of who she truly is.

Part of this development also includes the difficult process of coming to terms with essential identity dimensions such as the following:

• Gender: Who she is as a girl and emerging woman, especially in light of today's cultural expectations for girls (see Text Box 2.2).

WHAT DO I BELIEVE ABOUT THE ROLE
OF GIRLS AND WOMEN TODAY?

In her book *Girls without Limits*, Lisa Hinkelman describes a study performed in 1990 that defined the *feminine role* as having four dimensions:

1. Adherence to fashion and beauty standards
2. Performance of family and domestic skills
3. Satisfaction of the needs of others
4. Acquisition of male attention

In your view, are these the roles that girls should be working toward? Do these roles still fit for today's girls? Are there pressures for a girl to do all of the above plus be independent, accomplished, and competitive? Are these the values that you want your daughter to adopt for herself? Why or why not? Are there more empowering messages about what it means to be a girl?

- Physical characteristics, including her appearance, body weight/shape, physical fitness and agility, and her ability/disability status.
- Sexual identity: coming to terms with her sexual feelings, sexual identity, and decisions around sexual activity.
- Ethnicity, racial background: Developing an appreciation for her cultural background and how this affects her overall sense of self.
- Religious beliefs, as well as her overall value system: She will start to question who she is in terms of her spiritual beliefs and values.

A note about this last area: It is normal for your daughter to begin to question the beliefs held by your family. She may start to ask you questions about what you believe in terms of your religious views. She will question why you believe as you do about what is right and wrong, which may feel as if she were challenging you at the very core of your being. You might feel personally rejected and defeated by this questioning and criticism. Yes, this does hurt, but it helps to know that it is normal. As she starts to think more abstractly and less in black-and-white terms, it is natural that she will start to question what she has been taught. Instead of accepting everything that is handed to her as fact, she will begin to wonder, "Why should I believe this?" She may end up rejecting many of your deeply held values for a time; this is part of the individuation process. Just know that after a time of questioning and experimenting, she will eventually adopt personally meaningful values and spiritual views that are based on her own thoughtful struggle with these questions. As you know from your experience, this takes time, and her worldview will not become consolidated until adulthood. For now she needs your support and guidance, not rejection. Trust that in time she will sort it all out.

To conclude this section, I would like to introduce two activities related to your daughter's gender role development. It is helpful for you to first think through your own views (Activity One, Box 2.2) and then have a discussion with your daughter about what she is learning about being a girl (Activity Two, Box 2.3).

Box 2.3: TO COMPLETE WITH YOUR DAUGHTER

WHAT DO YOU LIKE ABOUT BEING A GIRL?

Author Lisa Hinkelman interviewed girls regarding what they liked about being a girl. Overwhelmingly 85 percent of the responses fell into categories of physical beauty, material possessions, and getting what you want ("I can get my nails done" I can wear frilly dresses," "I can get daddy to buy me things"). Are you interested in hearing how your daughter might respond? Ask her the following questions and try the activity with her.

First, ask your daughter, What do you like about being a girl? What are good things and not so good things about it? Who do you think has it better, boys or girls? Why?

Next, talk to her about how several companies have recently produced videos that ask girls to discuss what they think it means to be a girl today. Watch these powerful videos with your daughter and then ask her opinions about the questions posed in the video. What does she now think about the messages she is hearing about being a girl?

- The "Like a Girl" video (http://www.always.com/en-us/likeagirl. aspx), which asks girls the question "What does it mean to run like a girl?" went viral and was featured as a commercial during the 2015 Superbowl.
- The "Like a Girl" director also released a recent "Voice of Their Own" video for Sheknows.com: http://www.sheknows.com/parenting/ articles/1052621/introducing-hatch-helping-girls-find-a-voice- of-their-own)

CONCLUSIONS

I have covered a lot of ground in this chapter—from examining the physical changes that your daughter can clearly see when she looks in the mirror, to changes in her thinking, feeling, decision making, and identity that don't show up in her appearance but are playing a major role in her attitudes and outward behavior. I also discussed the rewiring of the brain during puberty and adolescence, which make this a challenging but exciting time during which she can develop strong self-regulation skills and lay the groundwork for establishing a healthy identity. As you have learned in this chapter, your daughter needs you not only to offer her knowledge about what is happening to her body and mind but also help her learn the skills needed to navigate these changes; in addition, she needs you to keep setting limits so that she stays safe. In other words, she needs you to be both her guide through this process as well as her protector.

To fulfill these roles, you should know the culture in which she lives and you need to understand adolescent development. Hopefully, after reading these first two chapters, you now feel better equipped in this regard. She also needs skills for resilience, which is what Part Two of this book is all about. But before I move on to resilience building, let's look at what can happen when cultural expectations and developmental transitions become overwhelming, resulting in mental health problems. It is important for you to be able to recognize when your daughter is getting off track so that you can intervene as early as possible to give her the support she needs. In Chapter Three I will discuss common mental health problems that can develop in girls, followed by suggestions for how to respond appropriately in order to help your daughter.

NOTES

1. See Belsky, J., Steinberg, L. D., Houts, R. M., Friedman, S. L., DeHart, G., Cauffman, E., ... Susman, E. (2007). Family rearing antecedents of pubertal timing. *Child Development*, 78(4), 1302–1321; Steinberg, L., & Silk, J. S. (2002). Parenting adolescents. In M. H. Bornstein (Ed.), *Handbook of parenting: Vol. 1. Children and parenting* (2nd ed., pp. 103–133). Mahwah, NJ: Erlbaum; Weisz, J. R., & Hawley, K. M. (2002). Developmental factors in the treatment on adolescents. *Journal of Consulting and Clinical Psychology*, 70(1), 21–43. doi: 10.1037/0022-006X.70.1.21

2. Greenspan, L., & Deardorff, J. (2014). *The new puberty: How to navigate early development in today's girls*. New York: Rodale; Swarr, A. E., & Richards, M. H. (1996). Longitudinal effects of adolescent girls' pubertal timing, and

parental relations on eating problems. *Developmental Psychology, 32*(4), 636–646. Doi:10.1037/0012-1649.32.4.636

3. Parkes, A., Strange, V., Wight, D., Bonell, C. Copas, A., Henderson, M., . . . Hart, G. (2011). Comparison of teenagers' early same-sex and heterosexual behavior: UK Data from the SHARE and RIPPLE studies. *Journal of Adolescent Health, 48*, 27–35; Levine, M. P. (2012). *Teach your children well: Parenting for authentic success*. New York: Ballantine.

4. Graber, J. A., Nichols, T. R., & Brooks-Gunn, J. (2010). Putting pubertal timing in developmental context: Implications for prevention. *Developmental Psychobiology, 52*(3), 254–262; Steinberg, L. (2014). *Age of opportunity: Lessons from the new science of adolescence*. New York: Eamon Dolan/Houghton Mifflin Harcourt.

5. Biro, F. M., Galvez, M. P., Greenspan, L. C., Succop, P. A., Vangeepuram, N., Pinney, S. M., . . . Wolf, M. S. (2010). Pubertal assessment method and baseline characteristics in a mixed longitudinal study of girls. *Pediatrics, 12* (3), E583–E590.

6. Greenspan, L., & Deardorff, J. (2014). *The new puberty*. New York: Rodale.

7. Ibid.

8. Steinberg, L. (2014). *Age of opportunity: Lessons from the new science of adolescence*. New York: Eamon Dolan/Houghton Mifflin Harcourt.

9. Belsky, J., Houts, R. M., & Fearon, R. M. (2010). Infant attachment security and the timing of puberty: Testing and evolutionary hypothesis. *Psychological Science, 21*(9), 1195–1201. Doi:10.1177/09567610379867; Greenspan, L., & Deardorff, J. (2014). *The new puberty*. New York: Rodale.

10. Greenspan, L., & Deardorff, J. (2014). *The new puberty*. New York: Rodale.

11. Blumenthal, H., Leen-Feldner, E. W. Babson, K. A., Gahr, J. L. Trainor, C. D., & Frala, J. L. (2011). Elevated social anxiety among early maturing girls. *Developmental Psychology, 47*(4), 1133–1140. Doi:10.1037/a0024008; Belsky, J., Steinberg, L. D. Houts, R. M., Friedman, S. L., DeHart, G., Cauffman, E., . . . Susman, E. (2007). Family rearing antecedents of pubertal timing. *Child Development, 78*(4), 1302–1321; Graber, J. A., Nichols, T. R., & Brooks-Gunn, J. (2010). Putting pubertal timing in developmental context: Implications for prevention. *Developmental Psychobiology, 52*(3), 254–262; Sontag, L. M., Graber, J. A., & Clemans, K. H. (2011). The role of peer stress and pubertal timing on symptoms of psychopathology during early adolescence. *Journal of Youth and Adolescence, 40*(10), 1371–1382; Nishina, A., Ammon, N. Y., Bellmore, A. D., & Graham, S. (2006). Body dissatisfaction and physical development among ethnic minority students. *Journal of Youth and Adolescence, 25*, 179–191; Steinberg, L., & Silk, J. S. (2002). Parenting adolescents. In M. H. Bornstein (Ed.), *Handbook of parenting: Vol. 1. Children and parenting* (2nd ed., pp. 103–133). Mahwah, NJ: Erlbaum.

12. Steinberg, L. (2014). *Age of opportunity: Lessons from the new science of adolescence*. New York: Eamon Dolan/Houghton Mifflin Harcourt.

13. Piaget, J. (1972). Intellectual evolution from adolescence to adulthood. *Human Development, 15*, 1–12.

14. Steinberg, L. (2014). *Age of opportunity: Lessons from the new science of adolescence*. New York: Eamon Dolan/Houghton Mifflin Harcourt.

15. Steinberg, L. (2014). *Age of opportunity: Lessons from the new science of adolescence*. New York: Eamon Dolan/Houghton Mifflin Harcourt.

16. Greenspan, L., & Deardorff, J. (2014). *The new puberty*. New York: Rodale.

17. Steinberg, L. (2014). *Age of opportunity: Lessons from the new science of adolescence*. New York: Eamon Dolan/Houghton Mifflin Harcourt.
18. Steinberg, L. (2014). *Age of opportunity: Lessons from the new science of adolescence*. New York: Eamon Dolan/Houghton Mifflin Harcourt.
19. Greenspan, L., & Deardorff, J. (2014). *The new puberty*. New York: Rodale.
20. Greenspan, L., & Deardorff, J. (2014). *The new puberty*. New York: Rodale.
21. Institute of Medicine and National Research Council, Committee of Science of Adolescence. (2011). *The science of adolescent risk-taking* [workshop report]. Washington DC: National Academics Press.
22. Taffel, R. (2005). *Childhood unbound: The powerful new parenting approach that gives our 21st century kids the authority, love, and listening they need to thrive*. New York: Free Press.
23. Simpson, A. R. (2001). *Raising teens: A synthesis of research and a foundation for action*. Boston: Center for Health Communication, Harvard School of Public Health.
24. Steinberg, L. (2014). *Age of opportunity: Lessons from the new science of adolescence*. New York: Eamon Dolan/Houghton Mifflin Harcourt.

CHAPTER THREE

Vulnerable Girls

Common Mental Health Problems

To this point you have been whisked into the whirlwind of girlhood. As discussed in Chapter One, a girl learns that to be acceptable she must look hot and sexy, act like a princess/diva, and maintain a hypersocialized online presence; in addition to all of this, she must do everything exceptionally well—school, sports, extracurriculars, relationships. This is a lot to take in and much of it is impossible to achieve, especially all at the same time, often leading to feelings of emptiness, frustration, and even failure. But it doesn't end with cultural pressures.

Chapter Two reminded us that there are also multiple pressures closer to home—girls' bodies are morphing into new shapes, their hormones are surging in peaks and valleys, their brains are being rewired, and they often feel like strangers even to themselves. In this time with exciting possibilities paired with mile-high stress and change, it is no wonder that many girls struggle and develop mental health problems in late childhood and early adolescence. In this chapter, I will explain the ways in which these cultural influences and massive changes can collide, creating a ripe environment for serious mental disorders. Then I will describe some of the most common mental health problems that can occur in the preteen and teenage years.

Before moving on to the next section, however, I would like to put in a word of reassurance: The purpose of the first two chapters was to highlight cultural trends and all of the changes that are occurring for girls. I know that some of this might have been shocking and discouraging for you as a parent. This chapter will focus on how girls respond to cultural trends and pressures and, unfortunately, sometimes these responses can be extreme (i.e., suicide attempts, self-injury, eating disorders). Just like the first two chapters, this chapter might be difficult to read, so be prepared. It is my hope that your daughter will never respond in these ways and will stay resilient throughout the adolescent years. However, this information is vital for parents, as you need to be aware of these potential problems so that you can intervene if you notice early warning signs. I know it may seem daunting at the moment, but keep reading. The rest of the book focuses on strategies for building resilience in your daughter so that she can stand strong against cultural pressures and resulting problems.

SELF-CONSCIOUSNESS VERSUS SELF-OBJECTIFICATION

Of course you have noticed your daughter's increased sensitivity to what other people are thinking or saying about her. She is probably embarrassed about a lot of things, and you in particular, because she is overly focused on an *imagined audience* that she believes is following and watching her at all times. If she makes a mistake, it is amplified 1,000 times because she believes that everyone knows about it and everyone is laughing at her. If there is something wrong with her outfit, she thinks everyone will notice because she believes everyone is watching her, judging her, and whispering negative things behind her back. All of this self-consciousness is a normal part of adolescent development. David Elkind first wrote about the "imagined audience" in his studies of adolescent psychology in the 1960s, and the concept is still quite relevant today.

But one wonders if the "imagined" part of the term is even accurate in our current culture, given that teens are one cell-phone click away from a worldwide audience viewing their every word and move. Say something embarrassing at a party? It will be blasted online in minutes. Make a fashion mistake? Your picture will go as far as social media can carry it. As I reviewed in Chapter One, there truly *is* an audience, and it is hungry for details of your daughter's life. On her end, it causes her to feel that there is nowhere to hide. The *audience* is following her twenty-four hours a day. This can become highly problematic, especially for girls, who are already feeling unsure about how they fit in and whether they measure up to others' expectations.

For girls today there is also an even more insidious process that takes normal self-consciousness into hyperdrive. Your daughter is likely to be asking herself "What can I do to be noticed, accepted, and liked?" If she doesn't find a satisfactory answer, she won't have to delve very deeply into the culture before she learns that attractiveness and sexual appeal will bring her the attention she desires (I discussed this as the sexualization of girlhood in Chapter One). Over time, she will learn to view herself not as a multidimensional person but as an object—an object to be viewed and critiqued by others. If she starts to self-objectify, she will no longer ask herself, "How do I feel about this?" but rather "How do I look to others?" "What are they thinking about me?" In other words, she will be so worried about how she is coming across to others that she won't take the time to consider how *she* feels, what *she* wants, whether or not *she* approves of herself. This process is referred to as *self-objectification*, a much-studied concept that explains how girls internalize cultural pressures specific to appearance and social success. If this happens, she will carry the constant burden of feeling "checked out" by others instead of just going about her day and enjoying whatever it may bring. The problem with this is that it is not only exhausting but also causes her to base her self-worth on whether or not she believes she has secured others' approval. And as we know, this leads to an endless cycle of emptiness and frustration. This self-objectification is linked to the onset of many mental health problems in girls.[1] For example, we know that self-objectification is associated with body dissatisfaction, negative body image, dieting, anxiety, and depression.

Self-objectification can cause a girl to monitor her appearance constantly, check herself repeatedly to see if she looks her best, become preoccupied with others' opinions, and feel shame about her body and appearance if she can't meet cultural ideals for beauty. Because she is so focused on externals—what others are thinking, how she looks to others—she has less energy left for other things. It is harder for her to concentrate in school. It will be harder for her to participate in class if she is worried what everyone will think when they look at her as she raises her hand to answer a question. If your daughter becomes preoccupied in this way, she will be distracted and less able to focus on the moment, potentially affecting both her academic and even future professional performance. Her life becomes a show, and the only thing that matters is the ratings supplied by her audience. But self-objectification is not inevitable; your daughter can learn to resist its pull. Chapters Four through Eight will help you to instill these skills in her so that she can thrive—not just survive—through the adolescent years.

So there is a difference between self-consciousness, which is a normal part of adolescence, and the more extreme self-objectification, which is linked to mental health problems. I present three contrasting examples in Box 3.1.

BEFORE SELF-CONSCIOUSNESS

I love to observe my 9-year-old daughter, Abby, who has not yet developed self-consciousness about her appearance. It rarely occurs to her to look in the mirror; she throws on whatever clothes she finds, and I have to force her to at least occasionally brush her hair. She is simply just not able to imagine that anyone would look at her with a critical eye, and she wastes no time or energy worrying about how she appears to others. She is too busy living her life! She is just herself, without the baggage of others' labels or expectations. I know this won't last, but for now I am in awe of this stage of freedom in her life.

SELF-CONSCIOUSNESS

Rose has only recently started to develop a critical eye. She has started to compare herself with the other girls in her class, questioning whether they are prettier or thinner than she is. For the first time, she is self-conscious about her stomach and how it looks in a bathing suit. She sometimes wonders what other people think about her when she walks into a room, but this mostly bothers her when she is going into an unfamiliar situation where she does not know anyone.

SELF-OBJECTIFICATION

Maggie wakes up early every morning in order to put on makeup to cover any blemishes and to style her hair so it is perfectly in place. She feels frustrated because she still feels she looks ugly. She hates getting dressed, because no matter how many outfits she tries on, they don't seem to fit right and tend to cling in all the wrong places. She gets on the bus for school looking down at her feet, knowing that everyone is staring at her and thinking that she looks hideous today. In class she does not raise her hand to answer the teacher's questions because she does not want everyone to look at her if she speaks. As she walks down the hall, she feels the boys' eyes on her and believes that they are thinking her thighs are too fat. In her mind, she thinks that none of them would ever be interested in her because of her weight and her ugly face. When girls talk to her, she just knows that they are staring at the new zit on her chin. In P.E. she worries so much about her gym shirt and how it emphasizes her stomach bulges that she can't focus on serving the ball during the volleyball unit. Her entire day is consumed with thoughts about how her appearance comes across to others, so that she is not able to concentrate on anything she is doing.

As you can see, the current culture sets girls up for high levels of stress and also disappointment in themselves: how can they ever live up to others' expectations when the bar is set so high? What happens when the pressures become too much? It is to this issue that we now turn.

COMMON MENTAL HEALTH PROBLEMS IN GIRLS

Girls and Depression

It should come as no surprise that depression has become increasingly common in girls. Headlines from 2012 sounded the alarm: "Depression rates triple for girls between the ages of 12 and 15," rising from 5 percent of 12-year-olds to an eye-opening 15 percent of 15-year-olds. It continues to worsen: by age 18, some 20 percent of adolescent girls will have experienced at least one episode of depression and 10 percent will have made a suicide attempt.[2]

Box 3.2 highlights the standard criteria for depression, but the symptoms may look somewhat different in children and adolescents. Instead of the persistent sadness you might see in an adult who is depressed, you might notice some of the following in your daughter:

- Increased irritability and grumpiness
- Low frustration tolerance, even temper tantrums
- Physical symptoms such as unexplained headaches or stomachaches
- Extreme sensitivity to feedback, interpreting comments as criticism

Another difference between adults and children or younger adolescents is that although adults who are depressed fail to find enjoyment in any activities and tend to stay in a consistently depressed mood, children and teens still have the ability to bounce in and out of their depressed moods, even occasionally having fun. In addition, unlike depressed adults who might withdraw from all social interactions, children and adolescents usually keep up with at least some of their friendships. In other words, it is not unusual for teens with depression to undergo a major decrease in the amount of time they spend with others but still be able to have a friend or two. Parents can be on the lookout when they notice any of the listed signs that last two or more weeks and when symptoms start to interfere with your daughter's ability to function at home and at school. The earlier you can intervene, the better the prognosis for recovery, as will be covered later in this chapter.

Before beginning to discuss why depression remains such a significant problem for girls, it is important to note that in writing about depression I am not referring to an occasional bad mood. Having a depressed mood for a few days following a sad event is normal and expected. We all have days when we are grouchy or moody, and girls are certainly not exempt from having a bad day or two. When mental health professionals talk about depression, though, they are referring to a cluster of symptoms that form a major depressive episode, and someone who has had two or more such episodes meets the criteria for major depressive disorder. Here are the signs and symptoms of this disorder, the breadth of which extend far beyond what is typically considered a depressed mood:

- Depressed mood and/or loss of interest or pleasure in life activities for at least two weeks and at least *five* of the following symptoms that cause clinically significant impairment in social, work, or other important areas of functioning almost every day:
  - Depressed mood most of the day
  - Diminished interest or pleasure in all or most activities
  - Significant unintentional weight loss or gain
  - Sleeping too little or sleeping too much
  - Agitation or psychomotor retardation noticed by others
  - Fatigue or loss of energy
  - Feelings of worthlessness or excessive guilt
  - Diminished ability to think or concentrate, or indecisiveness
  - Recurrent thoughts of death[3]

Why should you as a parent be concerned about a major depressive episode or two? Isn't this just part of being a teenager? Can't she just snap out of it over time? The answer is no—there are several significant reasons why we should be concerned about depression in girls:

- Once she has had a depressive episode she will be at extremely high risk of having continued episodes of depression throughout her life.
- Because she is withdrawn and is less likely to interact with others, her development of social skills can become derailed, causing long-lasting problems in relationships.

- She is more likely than nondepressed girls to have school and work problems in later adolescence and adulthood.
- She is more likely than nondepressed girls to have later substance abuse problems, to have criminal offenses, and to have legal problems.
- Adolescent depression is highly associated with suicide risk—both thoughts about suicide as well as actual attempts.[4]

Why Does Depression Affect Our Daughters More Than Our Sons?

Until the age of 12 or 13, girls and boys experience equal rates of depression. This changes dramatically by age 13, as at that point girls are twice as likely as boys to become depressed. This 2:1 ratio is present throughout adolescence and adulthood, so that one of the greatest risk factors for depression is being female! In addition, females are 2.5 times more likely than males to take antidepressants.[5] So what is going on for girls at that time? Or, after reading Chapters One and Two, your more logical question might be "What *isn't* going on for girls as they reach puberty?" Simply put, this is a staggering amount of pressure for anyone to deal with, let alone a 12- or 13-year-old girl.

But why do these upheavals and pressures affect girls so much more than boys, and why do they so often result in depression? The "Why girls?" question doesn't have a simple answer; instead, there are multiple influences that disproportionately affect girls more than boys. Some of these include the following.

Girls Are More Likely Than Boys to Experience Multiple Stressors at Once

It is true that both adolescent girls and boys experience a lot of stress in today's complex world. The difference is that boys tend to react to the stressors differently, often coping by externalizing the pressures. This can cause the problems we see with boys' acting out by fighting, using illicit substances, and engaging in other criminal behaviors. Girls, however, are more likely to internalize the pressures, holding them in and blaming themselves for not being able to cope. So although both girls and boys may experience high levels of stress, girls are far more likely to become depressed in response to stress. An additional consideration, mentioned in Chapter Two, is that girls are more likely than boys to experience multiple stressors all at once—all the changes of adolescence such as transitioning to a new school and new academic expectations, dating, bullying—while also going through puberty. Boys are somewhat protected from this because they tend to reach puberty at a later age. Girls are more likely to be hit with everything at once and to become depressed as a result.

Girls Are More Likely Than Boys to Have Problems With Early Puberty

Boys who reach puberty earlier than their peers are no more likely to develop depression than are other boys. On the other hand, girls who experience early puberty are more likely to have lower self-esteem, to be sexually harassed, and to be pressured into sexual activity. Unfortunately all of these issues are linked with depression, placing early-developing girls at high risk for depression and other problems (as discussed in Chapter Two).[6]

Girls Are More Emotionally Sensitive Than Boys

Studies of girls' and boys' brains show that girls can recognize and read emotions faster than can boys; while that can serve as a strength, this very same emotional sensitivity can also make girls more vulnerable to depression.[7]

Girls Place More Importance on Relationships Than Do Boys

Girls are socialized to base their self-esteem and worth on the success of their relationships and on gaining others' approval, making them more sensitive to rejection by family, friends, or romantic partners. Boys, on the other hand, do not base their sense of self so heavily on their relationships. The more time your daughter spends on her relationships and the more she shares intimate details of her life with others, the more vulnerable she becomes when something goes wrong in a relationship, as it so often does in adolescent girls' tumultuous relationships. Feeling that everyone must like her and approve of her at all times, that *she* is not okay if any of her *relationships* are not okay, can leave her prone to depression.[8] For example, when there is family conflict, girls are more likely to become depressed in response to the conflict than are boys. Some research even indicates that when girls have a negative relationship with their fathers in particular, this tends to affect daughters more negatively than a similar situation would affect sons.[9]

Girls Are More Likely Than Boys to Suppress Their Anger

From an early age, girls are socialized to hold anger inside so that they can keep others happy with them in their relationships. They are told "be nice" and "don't make waves." While this is still the case, the "attention" trend discussed in Chapter One is also increasingly seen in the behaviors of young girls, so they also learn to demand what they want and to be as competitive as possible with other girls in order to get ahead. This is impossibly confusing for girls: "How do I 'play nice' while I am also told to 'play to win?'" "How do I deny my anger at the same time I am encouraged to tell my friend off on Facebook?" While specific strategies for coping with these pressures will be discussed in later chapters, it is worth noting here that whether she suppresses her anger or screams loudly to millions on social media, neither of these methods will be effective for getting her relational needs met, and this frustration can end up manifesting as depression.

Girls Are More Likely Than Boys to Have Excessive Empathy

Girls are also more likely to feel *excessive empathy* in their relationships with others. Girls' use of empathy is positive and empathy should be encouraged in all children. Excessive empathy, however, involves taking on other people's problems as if they were your own and even feeling guilty because other people are suffering when you are not.[10] Just as how your daughter's emotional sensitivity can be both a gift and a risk factor for depression, so is her ability to take on others' feelings and problems as if they were her own; it helps her connect with others but also leaves her vulnerable to depression.

Girls Are More Likely Than Boys to Ruminate With Others

Rumination refers to the tendency to worry excessively about your problems, to blame yourself for every bad thing that happens and to mull your shortcomings and mistakes over and over in your head instead of taking action to make the problem better. Girls are more likely to use this style of thinking than are boys, and rumination is highly linked to depression. Girls, more than boys, also talk about their feelings and problems with their friends. This is called *co-rumination*—ruminating with others, sharing your weaknesses and problems in a way that just fuels negative thinking rather than moving toward positive change. The more that girls co-ruminate with their friends, either in person or online, the more likely they are, over time, to become depressed.[11]

What Parents Can Do to Learn More About Preventing Depression

- All of the resilience strategies presented in this book will help to decrease your daughter's vulnerability to depression, particularly those that help her let go of the need to live up to all the cultural pressures imposed on her.
- If there is a history of depression in your family or if you are depressed yourself, know that this increases your daughter's vulnerability to depression. Growing up in a home with a depressed parent is difficult for children, and they are likely to learn to see the world through the same negative lens that their parent does. Do what you can to get help for yourself. Depression is a highly treatable condition and you owe it to yourself and your daughter to get the help you need.
- For additional information, check out the online resources listed at the end of this book.
- If you believe that your daughter is depressed, first visit your family physician to discuss a diagnosis and get a referral to a mental health professional who can provide appropriate treatment. Even if a doctor offers you only a prescription for an antidepressant, it is highly advisable to seek counseling as well. Best practices in the field recommend psychotherapy such as cognitive behavioral therapy first. Only then, if her condition doesn't improve, should an antidepressant be considered. Even when the depression is severe and medication is recommended as an immediate step, also seek professional counseling; the medication alone won't help her to learn new ways of thinking and behaving; only these new skills can make positive changes permanent.[12] Remember that no matter how well a medication works, she needs a place where she can be heard and where she can learn new ways of coping in terms of her thoughts, feelings, and behaviors.

Girls and Anxiety

Although we can all feel anxiety about an upcoming event (such as public speaking—a very common fear) or experience stress over something that recently happened to us, this does not necessarily indicate a lasting problem. In contrast, consider the array of anxiety disorders, each with different symptoms but all centered around excessive and irrational fear and dread of a real or perceived threat.[13] Just as major depressive disorder involves far more than a depressed mood, the term "anxiety disorder" describes a constellation of symptoms that last at least six months and get worse over time. This is usually not the case for most of us when we say we are "anxious." Here are some common symptoms of anxiety disorders[14]:

- Muscle tension, headaches, stomachaches, unexplained pain
- Heart palpitations
- Sweating
- Dizziness
- Shortness of breath
- Restlessness; difficulty relaxing, falling asleep, and staying asleep
- Pervasive fear that something terrible will happen
- Fear of dying
- Fear of embarrassment or humiliation
- Excessive worry about everyday issues
- Difficulty concentrating
- Being easily startled

Although what follows in Box 3.3 is not intended to help anyone label a child with a particular anxiety disorder, it is helpful for you to know about the different types of anxiety disorders and what they might look like in a girl. Again, this will help you with early detection so that you can get help for any of these problems as soon as possible.

Box 3.3: COMMON TYPES OF ANXIETY DISORDERS[15]

SEPARATION ANXIETY DISORDER

What is it? It is a developmentally inappropriate and excessive fear or anxiety about separation from home or from a parent or other caregiver. It is most commonly seen in children but can be diagnosed in adulthood. The fears must be present for at least four weeks in children and adolescents.

What does it look like? Symptoms might include

- Recurrent, excessive distress when separation from home or caregivers occurs or is anticipated

---

- Persistent and excessive worry about losing caregivers or about possible harm happening to caregivers
- Persistent and excessive worry that a scary event will lead to separation from caregivers (e.g., getting lost or being kidnapped)
- Difficulty leaving home or refusal to go to school or elsewhere because of fear of separation
- Repeated complaints of physical symptoms (such as headaches, stomachaches, nausea, or vomiting) when separation occurs or is anticipated

SPECIFIC PHOBIA

What is it? An intense or irrational fear of an object or event that poses little or no actual threat. The fear or anxiety happens each time the person is around the feared object or situation.

What does it look like? Fears might include:

- Animals (e.g., fear of spiders, dogs)
- Environment (e.g., fear of the water, heights, dark)
- Blood injection fears (e.g., fear of needles, fear of blood, fear of injury)
- Situational (e.g., fear of enclosed spaces such as elevators or airplanes)

Fears often result in physical responses like feeling faint, hyperarousal, increased blood pressure, and can cause problems in overall functioning if the person has to inhibit his or her daily life activities in order to avoid the feared object or situation. Symptoms must last at least six months for a diagnosis of specific phobia to apply.

SOCIAL ANXIETY DISORDER

What is it? Ongoing fear and worry that occurs in many different social situations. This goes way beyond shyness, as the person's life becomes significantly impaired by the fears and resulting behaviors (e.g., difficulty keeping friends, refrains from participating in school or sports activities).

What does it look like? Your daughter might be highly anxious and self-conscious in social situations owing to her fears of how others are evaluating her performance or interactions. She might fear humiliation, embarrassment, or rejection by people she knows or even whom she does not know. For a diagnosis of social anxiety disorder, the symptoms should last at least six months.

What is it? The experience of fear or concern of inappropriate fear responses, including actual physical symptoms that create a sense of panic in an individual; because of the unexpected nature of these symptoms, the person also has great fear of having another attack.

What does it look like?

- Racing heartbeat
- Dizziness
- Trembling or shaking
- Shortness of breath or a sense of being smothered
- Sense of unreality
- Intense fearful that something terrible is happening
- Fear of dying or losing control
- Fear of these unexplained symptoms

Once a person has had a panic attack, she might begin to avoid places where previous panic attacks have occurred or avoid situations in which another panic attack may be triggered. Following a panic attack, the individual will experience persistent worry about having another attack or use significant behavior changes to avoid another attack. These symptoms must last at least one month.

AGORAPHOBIA

What is it? Marked fear or anxiety about being in two or more of the following situations:

- Using public transportation (cars, planes, trains)
- Being in open spaces (parking lots, marketplaces)
- Being in enclosed places (shops, theaters)
- Standing in line or being in a crowd
- Being outside the home alone

What does it look like? The person experiences fear when she has a belief that she can't escape from a particular situation. She also fears that she might experience panic-like, embarrassing symptoms and that there will be no one around to help her. For a diagnosis of agoraphobia, symptoms must persist for at least six months.

GENERALIZED ANXIETY DISORDER (GAD)

What is it? One of the most common mental disorders, GAD includes anxiety or worry that takes place across a number of settings on more days than not for at least six months. A person with GAD will go through her day intensely worried, tense, and bothered about all of her everyday problems. She worries that something terrible will go wrong in most of her life circumstances.

What does it look like?

- Restlessness
- Fatigue
- Keyed up or on edge
- Difficulty concentrating, mind going blank
- Irritability
- Sleep disturbance
- Muscle tension, sweating
- Nausea, dizziness

The person wants to control the worry so that it is not so invasive, but she is usually not able to control it despite all her efforts.[16]

RISK FACTORS FOR ANXIETY DISORDERS

Statistics show that approximately 15 to 20 percent of children and adolescents will develop an anxiety disorder at some time, with the most frequent disorders being separation anxiety and specific and social phobias.[17] With these large numbers it is important to look at the risk factors—in other words, who is most likely to develop an anxiety disorder? Some of the most common risk factors are as follows:

1. **Gender**: Females are two to three times more likely than males to develop anxiety disorders. The potential cultural reasons behind these gender differences are discussed under "Social Factors" section.
2. **Age**: Some of the anxiety disorders are age-specific, showing up in early childhood (e.g., separation anxiety, phobias), while social phobia and panic disorder might not be seen until adolescence.
3. **Personality**: Some children are predisposed to worry and fear, placing them at risk for an anxiety disorder.
4. **Family history**: Genetic factors can be involved, but it is just as important to note that the overall family environment also plays a role. For example, if parents have certain fears, they may pass them along to

their children; that is, the children learn to fear an event or object because they have observed the parents' reactions over time.

5. **Stressors and traumatic events**: A major traumatic life event can trigger anxiety. Although such major events are likely the most observable, an accumulation of minor stressors or daily life hassles can also be a cause.

6. **Medical conditions**: Certain medical conditions such as migraines, chronic fatigue syndrome, premenstrual syndrome, and irritable bowel syndrome are often associated with anxiety, although it is not clear whether one causes the other.

7. **Social factors**: Anxiety disorders are certainly more common today than they were in the past, possibly owing to greater lack of social connections and lack of perceived safety and security among teens. In fact, according to counseling center directors, anxiety is the number one presenting problem for which students seek counseling at university and college counseling centers.[18] Why girls and women in particular, though? I have already introduced ideas behind this in Chapters One and Two; if girls are socialized to be overly worried about others' feelings instead of their own, if they are to keep everyone happy and meet everyone's expectations, it is not surprising that worry, fears of rejection and embarrassment, and an overhanging sense of dread ("Am I doing enough?") might ensue. These issues, as well as strategies your daughter can use to overcome pressures and prevent anxiety, are explored throughout this book.

What Parents Can Do to Learn More About Preventing Anxiety Disorders:

- Mild exercise and stretching is shown to have a calming effect for all girls, as do the relaxation strategies described in Chapter Eight.
- Help her to reach out to others and talk about her worries and fears. Let her know that she is not alone. Be there to listen and encourage her to communicate openly.
- Consult the resources listed at the end of the book for more information.
- If you are concerned about anxiety that already exists, first see your family physician for a diagnosis and referral to a mental health professional. As with depression, it is important not to look only for medications that will simply erase the problem. The medications at best will only keep her symptoms under some degree of control while she works through her real fears. Cognitive behavioral therapy is the most common treatment, helping her to change those thinking patterns that support her fears and to change the way she reacts to anxiety-provoking situations.[19]

While many parents might worry more about their adolescent sons becoming heavily involved with the use of alcohol and other drugs, the reality is that girls' use of illicit substances compares directly with boys' use and in some cases even surpasses it. These numbers may surprise you: ninth- and tenth-grade girls show slightly higher rates of alcohol use than do boys (43 percent versus 41 percent).[20] Almost a quarter—23 percent—of all ninth- to twelfth-grade girls report having consumed four or more drinks in a row within a two-hour period (the definition of what is termed "binge drinking").[21] Not only do girls and boys try and use substances at similar rates, they also experience similar problems from their use. Rates of substance use disorders are roughly the same in adolescent girls and boys (8.1 percent of girls versus 8.0 percent of boys aged 12 to 17).[22] Researchers call this new trend the *convergence effect*, which indicates the narrowing gender gap in substance use that has occurred for people born in the 1960s and later. So yes, parents should be concerned with boys' vulnerability to using and abusing substances, but girls are becoming just as prone to problems.

Parents also need to know that while any girl can develop problems with alcohol and other drugs, it is White and Hispanic girls who have the greatest levels of use and problems. Some recent comparisons are shown in Box 3.4.[23]

What Are the Main Influences on Whether or Not a Girl Develops Problems With Alcohol and Other Drugs?

As reviewed in Chapter Two, part of what your daughter is trying to do is fit in with her peer group while also forming a unique personality. Many girls may experiment with alcohol and other substances as a way to achieve this goal, as it does help them blend in with friends who are also using; it also helps them to feel more independent from parents and authority figures. Many girls try alcohol and other substances during their adolescent years as part of their normal development and experience few or no problems as a result. Other girls, especially those that start using illicit substances at an early age (before age 15), develop problems with usage that continue to plague them throughout their lives. I will discuss some of the reasons why some girls are more likely than others to develop such problems.

Box 3.4: SOME COMPARISONS OF NINTH-
TO TWELFTH-GRADE GIRLS' SUBSTANCE USE BY
RACE/ETHNICITY

Percent of ninth- to twelfth-grade girls who say they currently use alcohol:

White females, 40.3 percent
Hispanic females, 42.3 percent
Black females, 30.5 percent

Percent of ninth- to twelfth-grade girls who report binge drinking:

White females, 21.7 percent
Hispanic females, 22.4 percent
Black females, 10.3 percent

Percent of ninth- to twelfth-grade girls who say they have misused prescription drugs:

White females, 22.2 percent
Hispanic females, 19 percent
Black females, 11.9 percent

Is She Using to Fit in With Her Friends or Dating Partners?

Many girls are so concerned with fitting in with peer groups that they start using illicit substances as a way to belong. When a girl believes that this is the only way she can fit in, she will continue to drink and use other drugs as a way of securing her status in a group of friends or even as part of a dating couple. If this happens at an early age, the only way she might feel comfortable hanging out with friends or meeting new people is when she is buzzed or drunk. Because this is occurring during the developmental window in which adolescents learn to finesse their social and communication skills, she won't necessarily develop the normal but necessary social skills she will need to be successful in life (e.g., how to start a conversation, read social cues, deal with awkward silences, find connections with others, work out conflicts, or start a dating relationship based on mutual interests). Stated differently, drinking will not only limit her relationships during adolescence, but because it will thwart her development of social skills, it can also affect relationships throughout her life.[24]

In addition, when a girl relies on substances to fuel her social life, she will likely remain walled in to hanging out with others who also use substances. It will be much harder for her to branch out and make positive connections that might help her build resilience during these difficult adolescent years. When she is using substances, she is less likely to remain connected to family, school, sports, religious institutions, and other support systems that might help her to thrive. Rather than opening up opportunities (as it might seem to her at the time), her options actually become much more limited.

Girls might also be drawn to substance use as a coping strategy. More so than boys, girls are likely to say that they use illicit substances to increase confidence, reduce or numb negative emotions, calm tension or stress, and cope with problems. Boys, on the other hand, are more likely to say that they use such substances for pleasure (to enhance their emotions or to get high).[25]

What Is Her Family History of Substance Use and Abuse?

It is widely known that children are at risk for substance-use problems when they have a family history of substance abuse or dependence. Genetics does play a role in whether a person will have a problem related to substance use: for example, children of alcoholics are at increased risk for developing alcoholism themselves, even when they are adopted at birth and raised by nonalcoholic parents.[26]

In addition to genetics, children and adolescents are more likely to develop problems with substance use when they grow up in a home where others are heavy users. This is because families with high levels of substance use are likely to:

> Downplay the risks associated with alcohol and drug use
> Have poor parent-child communication if the caregiver is frequently intoxicated
> Have caregivers who provide inadequate discipline and supervision of their children[27]

This underscores the importance of family involvement in adolescent girls' lives. Parental monitoring and limit setting will be highlighted as a cornerstone parenting practice in Chapter Four.

How Young Is She When She First Experiments With Alcohol and Other Substances?

Research clearly demonstrates that the earlier a girl begins drinking or using other drugs, the more likely she will be to develop serious problems later. A major concern is that once a girl starts using illicit substances, she may progress to addiction more quickly than a boy would.[28] In particular, adolescents who start using substances before the age of 15 are far more likely than other teens to:

> *Become involved in the juvenile justice system*
> *Experience school failure and drop out*
> *Have relationship problems*
> *Become involved in risky sexual behaviors, potentially leading to pregnancy and sexually transmitted diseases*
> *Have depression and low self-esteem*[29]

To summarize the research findings, it is crucial to keep in mind the importance of protecting our daughters from alcohol and other drugs, particularly before the age of 15, as it seems that using substances earlier than this sets them up for potentially chronic problems that can significantly affect the direction of their lives. This is especially true for girls who undergo puberty at an early age, sometimes as young as age 9 or 10. As discussed in Chapter Two, young girls who look older than they are will attract an older group of friends and dating partners and will be more likely to be offered alcohol and other drugs when they hang around these peers. Because they are so young, they are unprepared for handling this type of peer pressure, particularly when they want to fit in and to act older than they are. Not only are they vulnerable to the problems associated with early use, described previously, they are also more likely than other girls to become victims of sexual assault and to suffer from depression and anxiety, all of which are associated with a higher risk of adolescent substance use and abuse.[30]

What Parents Can Do to Learn More About Preventing Substance Abuse Problems:

• Self-awareness: Parents can be aware of their own attitudes about the use of alcohol and other drugs and consider what their family values will be regarding their children's substance use.

- Monitoring: As will be reviewed in Chapter Four, a key parenting practice is to monitor your daughter's whereabouts, knowing where she is and what she is doing. This is paramount to protecting her from undue pressure to experiment early with alcohol and other drugs. This might seem like a simple step, but it becomes increasingly difficult as your daughter becomes more independent and spends more time away from home.
- Setting limits: This practice will also be covered in Chapter Four. Parents should decide on their family rules, stick to them, and ensure that there are consequences when limits are violated. This should be balanced with an ongoing conversation about adapting these limits as your daughter demonstrates increased maturity.
- Consult the online resources listed at the end of this book.
- If you are concerned that your daughter may be using alcohol and other drugs at an early age, seek professional help. As girls can progress to addiction much more quickly than boys, the earlier you seek help, the better.

Girls and Eating Disorders

Parents hear a lot about eating disorders in the popular press, and these reports tend to focus on the major ones: anorexia nervosa (AN), bulimia nervosa (BN), and more recently binge eating disorder (BED). See Box 3.5 for listings of the symptoms that meet the criteria for a diagnosis of AN, BN, or BED.

These disorders are very serious, hard to live with and treat, and tend to be long-lasting. Up to 10 percent of adolescent girls have a diagnosable eating disorder.[33] However, when we focus only on AN, BN, and BED, we miss the number of girls who also have problems related to eating, weight, and shape but may not meet official criteria for a formal diagnosis of an eating disorder. We may tend to dismiss these girls' concerns because they do not fit the traditional pattern described by medical professionals (as provided in Box 3.5). However, initial problems like occasional binges, dieting, excessive exercise, and negative body image are very common and cause girls a great deal of distress. Consider the following statistics:

> 61.2 percent of adolescent girls reported that they were trying to lose weight.
>
> 17.4 percent did not eat for 24 hours or more to lose weight or to keep from gaining weight.

Box 3.5: DSM-5 CRITERIA FOR EATING DISORDERS[31]

DSM-5 CRITERIA FOR ANOREXIA NERVOSA

- Restriction of food intake leading to weight loss or a failure to gain weight that results in a significantly lower body weight than would be expected for an individual's age, gender, and height.
- Intense fear of gaining weight or becoming fat.
- Distortions in thinking, such as overvaluing weight and shape in determining her worth, or believing that she is too fat when she is really too thin, thereby denying that there is anything wrong with her efforts to lose weight.

DSM-5 CRITERIA FOR BULIMIA NERVOSA

- Presence of binge eating: consumption of an unusually large amount of food coupled with a subjective sense of loss of control
- Presence of behaviors to compensate for the calories consumed during a binge (self-induced vomiting, abuse of laxatives and diuretics, excessive exercise, fasting)
- Occurrence of both binge eating and compensatory behavior at least once per week over the preceding three months
- Overvaluation of shape and weight in determining self-worth

DSM-5 CRITERIA FOR BINGE EATING DISORDER

- Objective eating episodes (eating within a discrete period of time an amount of food that is definitely larger than most people would eat in a similar time period and under similar circumstances)
- Loss of control during binge eating episodes (feeling that one cannot stop eating or control what or how much one is eating)

Binge eating episodes may also be associated with

- Eating more rapidly than normal
- Eating until feeling uncomfortably full
- Eating in the absence of hunger
- Eating alone owing to embarrassment over how much one is eating
- Feeling disgust, depression, or guilt after overeating

The major difference between BN and BED is that the latter is not associated with any behaviors to purge or compensate for the calories consumed during the binge. The girl with bulimia may vomit, take laxatives, or excessively exercise to burn off calories from a binge, while a girl with binge eating disorder engages in binge eating only. Because she consumes hundreds of calories during a typical binge, eventually binge eating disorder leads to weight gain and is also linked with obesity.[32]

5.9 percent took diet pills, powders, or liquids to lose weight or to keep from gaining weight.

6.0 percent vomited or took laxatives to lose weight or to keep from gaining weight.[34]

In addition, concerns about body shape, image, and weight may begin much earlier; 40 to 60 percent of elementary school girls aged 6 to 12 said they were concerned about their weight and becoming fat; in another study, 63 percent of 13-year-old girls reported that they were afraid of gaining weight or getting fat.[35] As a parent and counselor, it saddens me to think that so many girls are trying so hard to lose weight when they could be focusing on other more important things. I will return to this idea and how to help girls focus on more meaningful pursuits in Chapter Five.

Eating disorders and eating-related problems were once considered a problem for middle-class White girls only. We now know that this is just a stereotype and that prevalence data on eating disorders indicate that they affect increasing numbers of men and women in all westernized racial and ethnic populations.[36] In some studies, for example, African American and Latina women engage in binge eating at rates similar to those found among White women.[37]

We know that there is a continuum of problems, from occasional dieting or body image concerns at one end, to the life-threatening starvation of anorexia nervosa at the other. We also know that girls who develop anorexia or bulimia often start at one end of the continuum and progress to the other end over time. That is why we need to pay attention to early-developing symptoms and address problems before they become entrenched. I will first look at the leading risk factors for eating disorders. Note that some of these are preventable and some are not.

Biological influences. There is a genetic component to eating disorders, as girls who develop them are far more likely than others to also have relatives with eating disorders. Hormonal changes that occur during puberty can also play a role, and puberty generally begins at about the same time that girls are most likely to develop an eating disorder (around age 12).[38] However, researchers agree that biological factors alone can't account for the rates of body dissatisfaction, dieting, and eating disorders found among girls and women in westernized societies. Cultural factors also play a strong role.

Cultural influences—media: It is fairly obvious that there is a relationship between the ideals of beauty that we see every day in media sources (television, movies, the Internet, magazines) and women's feelings about their bodies. The current female ideal is, of course, unattainable for almost all of us, yet that same ideal is held up as the standard toward which girls and women are supposed to strive. It has now become normal for girls and women to dislike their bodies and—because females regard their appearance as a major contributor to how they feel about themselves as people—this explains why their self-esteem tends to be lower than that of boys and men. How, then, do girls become vulnerable to the media messages that scream "You must be thin [as well as hot and sexy] or you will have no value?" The answer is *saturation*. You read this in Chapter One but it is worth repeating: The more media your daughter consumes, the more likely she will be to buy into this ideal. If she spends hours each day watching television, poring over magazines, surfing the Internet, and especially watching music videos (which generally feature highly sexualized women), she will start to view what the culture paints as "reality" as the only form of reality. This process moves the external standard to an internalized standard of beauty and worth and your daughter will come to believe that with enough hard work and effort, she can achieve the ideal. It is the internalization of the cultural ideal that places a girl at risk for an eating disorder.

Family influences: I will reemphasize this in Chapter Five. For now, it is important to consider two types of family influence: How do parents model body image development for their daughters through their own attitudes and behaviors, and what do they actually say to their daughters about their weight, shape, or appearance?

Friends: Do your daughter's friends tend to talk about thinness and wanting to diet? Do they frequently talk about their appearance and worry about their looks? Do they frequently say things like "I'm so fat!"? Do they say mean things about other girls' appearance? If the answer is yes, then this places your daughter at higher risk for the development of an eating disorder. When she is involved with other girls in sports that emphasize thinness and appearance—like ballet, cheerleading, gymnastics, and dance—this can place her at additional risk because she belongs to part of a "thinness subculture" that overly emphasizes the importance of thinness for success. Girls who are the victims of teasing about their weight or appearance are also at risk for eating-related problems. They will feel rejected because of their physical appearance and then focus on changing their appearance through dieting or exercise to become "acceptable." Some girls will instead cope with teasing by eating more rather than less. They may turn to binge eating as a way of coping with their distress at being ridiculed.

Internal factors—social comparison: Girls are at risk for the development of eating disorders when they compare themselves with the thin and beautiful ideal projected by the media and believe that they don't measure up. They may also compare themselves with other girls, constantly asking themselves, "Are her legs thinner than mine? Does her stomach stick out more than mine?" or "Why can't I look like her?" Frequent media ideal comparisons and social comparisons also place a girl at risk for dieting, body dissatisfaction, and the development of an eating disorder.

Body dissatisfaction and drive for thinness: When a girl is dissatisfied with her body and looks to the cultural ideal as her standard, she will develop a drive toward thinness that is fulfilled through dieting. When she diets on a regular basis, she is far more likely to have this develop either into extreme restricting behaviors (self-starvation) or binge eating (when her body fights for food after being deprived from what it needs). Dieting can truly set adolescent girls up for disordered eating behaviors and should be discouraged (unless specifically prescribed by a medical professional for the purpose of weight loss).

What Parents Can Do to Learn More About Preventing Eating Disorders:

- Don't diet and don't encourage your daughter to diet. Ever. As stated previously, this is the number one risk factor for an eating disorder.
- Become familiar with the signs and symptoms of eating disorders but don't emphasize them with your daughter. Many girls with eating disorders report that they started their disordered eating behavior after learning about the disorder and the symptoms through a book or educational presentation (*"Oh, you can make yourself throw up after you eat by sticking your finger down your throat? I can eat what I want and get rid of the*

calories? I'll try it!"). The focus should remain on health and not on the disorder.

- Model balanced attitudes toward your physical appearance and inner beauty and reinforce this attitude with your daughter; help her to value herself for things other than her physical appearance.
- Read Chapter Five for specific strategies you can use to build resilience against eating-, weight-, and body shape–related problems.
- Use the resources included at the end of this book.
- If your daughter is already displaying symptoms of disordered eating, seek professional help right away. A mental health professional will help to determine the level of care that is needed based on your daughter's current symptoms and level of risk.

Girls and Self-Injury

Self-injury is another frightening behavior that parents fear might develop in their daughters. Unfortunately it is a behavior pattern that has frequently appeared in the popular press and most adolescents are familiar with it, even from a young age, as the average age when most teens first try to injure themselves is between 12 and 14 years (i.e., in middle school). It doesn't help that celebrities such as Johnny Depp, Angelina Jolie, Russell Brand, Colin Farrell, Fiona Apple, Demi Lovato, Megan Fox, Courtney Love, Christina Ricci, and even Princess Diana have openly discussed their personal use of self-injury. Self-injury is also commonly featured in television shows, movies, books, music, and Internet sites. A recent YouTube search found hundreds of videos of teens demonstrating how they injure themselves (e.g., cutting their legs, burning their arms), and most of these were accessible to a general audience.[39] Recent studies indicate that 12 to 47 percent of adolescents have engaged in self-injury, and up to 17 to 38 percent of college students report this behavior.[40] This is the shocking reality that your daughter faces as she becomes immersed in today's popular culture. So what do you most need to know about self-injury?

It has become normalized, especially when friends and people at school are trying it. Because it is so pervasive in the media and because it is widely discussed at school, self-injury does not seem as bizarre to today's adolescents as it might to us. However, it is very serious (see below).

It is not just harmless experimentation. Self-injury is related to serious physical harm, as it involves skin cutting with sharp instruments (the most common form), scratching, hitting oneself, inserting objects under the skin, and burning the skin.

It is not a suicide attempt. While it might seem that teens who injure themselves want to kill themselves, most report that they use self-injury for the opposite reason: to stay alive. Research indicates that the self-injury helps users to release pent up emotions or cope with pain so that they can continue to live and not want to die. In fact, the term professionals use for this behavior is "nonsuicidal self-injury," because suicide is not the intention.[41]

It is more likely to occur among teens who are highly sensitive. Adolescents who injure themselves have more trouble tolerating stress than teens who don't do so. They are also likely to report that they feel little or no pain when they injure themselves and that they have a high tolerance for pain.[42]

Self-injury is popular in part because it is readily available and easy to use. If you are a typical 12-year-old girl, you might not have easy access to alcohol or other drugs. You might not even be able to easily hide a habit of bingeing on food. However, you can always find a way of injuring yourself; girls report using paper clips, razors, or pieces of glass to cut or curling irons to burn their skin. For some girls, it becomes their coping method of choice when they perceive that they have no other way of dealing with their problems or feelings.

Although self-injury might sound repulsive to parents, it can serve an important function in a girl's life when she comes to rely on it as a coping strategy. The most common functions include the following:

- Self-injury might be an attempt to control her emotions, release pent-up stress or pressure, and reestablish a sense of control.
- When she is feeling "empty" or "numb," it helps her to feel *something*, even if it is physical pain.
- When she feels worthless and experiences self-hatred, it can become a way of punishing herself. Some people who injure themselves say that they feel "cleansed" after such an episode.
- It might be a way of communicating her pain. It can become a way of letting others know how much she is suffering, It can be a way to get others' attention. It can be related to her relationships—either to connect with others, avoid them, cope with problems resulting from them, or shock them.
- It might be a way of seeking a "high" or the "rush" that comes from the release of endorphins, which occurs along with the pain during a self-injuring episode.[43]

In trying to understand why people would deliberately inflict pain on themselves, remember that self-injury does work in the short term. People who self-injure say it is highly effective, and because of its effectiveness, most girls are not motivated to stop doing it. This makes it hard for girls to actually want to get help—they don't want anyone to take away the one thing that helps them cope with their negative feelings and pain.

What Parents Can Do to Learn More About Preventing Self-Injury

- Provide an environment where your daughter can communicate her thoughts and feelings openly without being judged or silenced. If she is able to process her emotions with a caring adult, she may have less need for using self-injury to express her pain.
- See Chapter Eight for strategies that support active coping: instead of turning to self-destructive coping strategies such as self-injury, a girl can learn to cope actively with her emotions and to solve her problems more effectively.
- See the online resources listed at the end of this book; especially recommended are the Cornell Research Program on Self-Injury and Recovery: Resources for Parents.
- If you suspect that your daughter is engaging in self-injury, seek assistance from a mental health professional as soon as possible.

Girls, Sexual Violence, and Dating Abuse

Sexual violence is another dreaded topic for parents. Unfortunately it is a reality for far too many girls today; national statistics indicate that 12 percent of ninth- to twelfth-grade girls report having experienced forced sexual intercourse and over 50 percent of girls report having gone through some kind of sexually coercive experience (this can include a range of behaviors from unwanted sexual contact or touching to actual rape).[44] This is very concerning for parents, who often do not know when this type of traumatic event may have occurred in their daughters' lives. Because of the stigma surrounding rape and sexual violence, girls are often reluctant to talk about their experience out of fear they will be somehow blamed or judged. When a girl believes that she has to keep her story secret, the problems associated with sexual violence only increase; they don't go away just because she tries to push away the memories and fears. In fact, girls who tell trusted family or friends about an assault within the first month are less likely to develop long-term problems as a result. Sexual violence is associated with many negative outcomes, including:

- Chronic pain, headaches, stomach problems
- Anxiety
- Depression
- Eating disorders
- Substance abuse
- Future sexual victimization and physical violence
- Posttraumatic stress disorder (PTSD)[45]

It should be noted that when a girl is sexually assaulted, she will likely develop PTSD symptoms within two weeks following the assault, and these symptoms may resolve rather quickly. Many girls, however, develop full-syndrome PTSD, where the symptoms are long-lasting and cause problems significant enough that her life will be completely disrupted. Consider the following signs of PTSD:

- Intrusive thoughts—nightmares, flashbacks she can't control
- Avoidance behaviors—fearing and avoiding anything that reminds her of the assault
- Changes in her mood and thoughts—strong negative emotions and self-blame
- Increasingly vigilant behavior—being easily startled, having difficulty sleeping, showing irritability[46]

Although treatment for recovery from sexual assault is beyond the scope of this chapter, there are several things you can do to make the situation better for your daughter if she does come to you for help. First, reassure her that she is not going crazy. If she is having flashbacks and nightmares, she will think that she is totally out of control and is losing her mind. Let her know that this is not the case. Remember that PTSD is the diagnosis generally associated with members of the military who have experienced the trauma of war. These are the same reactions that a girl will generally experience after a sexual assault. It is important for parents to recognize the tremendous impact of this type of trauma on their daughter's functioning and to understand that some of her reactions are normal and natural responses to trauma, just as a soldier might experience flashbacks, nightmares, and hypervigilance after returning from a wartime situation. In other words, anyone who has experienced a highly traumatic event might also have these same reactions.

It is essential for your daughter to know that you believe her and support her, and that help is available. Interestingly, girls are less likely to receive supportive reactions from others when they are assaulted by a friend or romantic partner, even though both types of assaults are traumatic.[47] In some cases it is worse for her because her trust in someone she knows and believes in has been shattered and as a result her sense of security and trust in others will be severely damaged. She needs to know that you believe her and that she is not "damaged goods" but rather worth caring for. You can let her know that you will help her in any way you can as she goes through the difficult process of recovery. Assist her in obtaining professional help. The earlier she receives treatment, the more successful the treatment is likely to be.

It is also important for any girl who has suffered sexual assault to believe that she is not to blame for what happened to her. The vast majority of sexual assaults are perpetrated by someone that the girl knows; this makes it easier for her to reason that she was to blame, as opposed to instances where a complete stranger was the perpetrator. Girls are also more likely to blame themselves when alcohol or other drugs were involved in the assault. They might be less likely to call a situation a "rape" if they were drunk and can't remember clearly what happened or if they somehow acted in a way that indicated an interest in sexual activity. In these situations, a girl will be confused, not knowing how to understand her reactions, especially when her memory is unclear and her tendency is to believe that somehow it must have been her fault because she did a "stupid" thing like getting drunk. Ultimately though, while she might not have made a good choice to drink too much, the perpetrator committed a crime and is legally responsible when a rape occurs. As a counselor, I have always said to clients, "No matter what choices you made at the time, the perpetrator (whether friend or stranger) committed a crime and is fully to blame for what happened." Blaming herself doesn't help things and in fact makes things worse.

What Parents Can Do to Learn More About Preventing Sexual Assault

- As with all of the other issues discussed previously, create a warm, open relationship in which your daughter feels safe in sharing with you. Make time to listen and she will be more likely to open up and talk to you if sexual assault should occur. Be available to listen without judgment or shame.

- Protect her when she is young, no matter how old she looks. Girls who look older than they are and who start dating early are at higher risk for sexual assault because they find themselves in situations for which they are not developmentally ready. It's hard for a 12-year-old girl to say no to a 16-year-old boy who has his own car and convinces her that he loves her. Do what you can to help keep her out of those types of situations.
- Model skills like assertiveness and effective communication strategies in all of your relationships (as discussed in Chapter Six).
- Check out the online resources listed at the end of this book.
- If your daughter has been sexually assaulted, seek professional help as a place where she can begin to work through this trauma.

Dating Abuse

It may seem surprising to see the topic of dating abuse included here. After all, teens are only starting to date and it seems that they could just easily walk away if a relationship became even mildly unpleasant. Instead, we see some shocking statistics: 10 to 30 percent of adolescent girls reported physical, emotional, or verbal abuse from a dating partner, and 25 percent of seventh-grade girls said they had been victims of physical violence from a dating partner in the previous year.[48] Yes, a quarter of young middle-school girls said that they had already experienced some type of physical altercation with a dating partner! It is interesting to note two demographic trends: (1) Teens in same-sex relationships experience very similar levels of violence as opposite-sex couples and (2) African American adolescents are 1.5 times more likely than White teens to have experienced physical violence in the course of dating, so this is a population particularly at risk. I would also like to point out that dating abuse does not always begin with physical violence; it often starts with emotional or verbal abuse and progresses to a physical level when the other tactics no longer work. Some of these other types of abuse might include:

- Spreading rumors about a girl to her friends
- Calling her names, humiliating her
- Destroying her property
- Threatening to hurt her or to commit suicide if she leaves
- Controlling who she talks to, who she can be friends with, where she goes
- Lying to her or threatening to break up in order to obtain sex

- Demanding that she spend time with the dating partner, excluding friends and family
- Pressuring her for her cell-phone and online passwords in order to monitor her texts, calls, and online activity

If you are as alarmed as I was when I read these numbers, what we are seeing is partly a result of the way in which violence has become normalized in our culture for both males and females. If you talk to girls, many say that they are just as aggressive toward their dating partners as boys are, and most say that the violence between them is mutual. In fact, according to the Centers for Disease Control, girls and boys are equally likely to say that they are both perpetrators and victims of dating violence.[49] Parents don't need to look far to see how girls are being socialized to become increasingly aggressive and violent—whether toward dating partners or towards one another.

But is it really mutual? The most concerning thing about viewing relationship aggression as "mutual" is that it is most likely not used for the same purposes by both partners. Boys are more likely to use violence in order to establish power and control in the relationship, while girls fight back out of frustration or in self-defense. They are also far more likely to experience negative consequences from the violence (such as injuries) than are boys. It is important to remember that the teen years are a time for learning what is expected in a dating relationship, and if it is currently filled with controlling and abusive behaviors, it might be harder for a girl to know how to develop a healthy relationship when she is older. Unfortunately girls who are abused by their parents are more likely to end up in violent dating relationships as teens, and girls in violent relationships as teens are more likely to experience intimate partner violence when they become adults.[50] This can set them up for a lifetime of problems resulting from romantic relationships.

What Parents Can Do to Learn More About Preventing Dating Violence

- This issue is discussed extensively in Chapter 6 on building healthy relationships. For now, consider the messages you send your daughter about healthy versus unhealthy relationships; the priority she places on staying in a relationship at all costs, even when it is harmful to her; or even the idea that it is normal and expected to be mistreated in a romantic relationship. Healthy relationships are based on respect and equality. This is not what she will see in the media, so these somewhat counterculctural messages will have to come from you and other caring adults in her life.

- As a visual aid, examine the Power and Control Wheel and compare it with the Equality Wheels found at http://www.theduluthmodel.org/training/wheels.html. Plan how you will share these qualities with your daughter.
- Visit the online resources listed at the end of this book.

Box 3.6: GIRLS AND SUICIDE RISK

I realize this is a sobering topic for many parents, as it should be, but it is important to be aware of the potential warning signs for suicide. It is shockingly common for teens to think about suicide: in a 2013 national study, 15 percent of all girls aged 13 to 18 had persistent thoughts of suicide, 5 percent had made actual plans for committing suicide, and 6 percent had made an actual suicide attempt.[51]

Warning signs for suicide: take note of any of the following risk factors:

- Threatening to hurt or kill herself or talking about wanting to hurt or kill herself
- Looking for ways to kill herself by seeking access to firearms, pills, or other means
- Talking or writing about death, dying, or suicide; preoccupation with death and violent themes
- Making direct statements like "I'm going to end it all," "I wish I were dead," "I've decided to kill myself"
- Making indirect statements like "Everyone would be better off without me," "Pretty soon you won't have to worry about me," "Who cares if I am dead anyway?"
- Feeling hopeless or trapped, as if there were no other options; seeing no reason for living, or having no sense of purpose in life
- Decreased school performance and skipping school
- Lack of interest in self-care
- Feeling rage or uncontrollable anger or seeking revenge; feeling anxious or highly agitated
- Spending increasingly large amounts of time on Internet/TV/videogames
- Dramatic mood or behavior changes, acting reckless or engaging in risky activities seemingly without thinking
- Increasing alcohol or drug use
- Withdrawing from friends, family, and society

- Changes in diet or sleep patterns (e.g., being unable to sleep, or sleeping most of the time)
- Sudden improvement in mood after a period of being down or withdrawn
- Giving away favorite possessions[52]

If your daughter is already experiencing depression (also a risk factor for suicide) and/or displays any of these warning signs, seek professional help as soon as possible. If she is in immediate crisis, take her to a local emergency room for evaluation to see if she needs to be hospitalized until she is stabilized and no longer suicidal. Don't assume that these behaviors are just cries for attention. Do take these warning signs seriously.

CONCLUSION

If you have read this far, you are now through the toughest part of the book. Part One painted an emerging portrait of teen-girl world—a world of which all parents should be aware. I realize that this was likely an uncomfortable reality to face. It is a difficult environment our daughters will encounter, but it is not insurmountable; there *is* hope for the future. The remaining chapters (Part Two) are devoted to strategies for building your daughter's inner strength and resolve. Armed with skills for standing strong and holding on to her authentic self, she *can* be healthy and resilient!

NOTES

1. Frederickson, B. L., Roberts, T. A., Noll, S. M., Quinn, D.M., & Twenge, J.M. (1998). That swimsuit becomes you: Sex differences in self-objectification, restrained eating, and math performance. *Journal of Personality and Social Psychology*, 75, 269–284. doi:10/1037/0022-3514.75.1.269; Lindberg, S. M., Grabe, S., & Hyde, J. S. (2007). Gender, pubertal development, and peer sexual harassment predict objectified body consciousness in early adolescence. *Journal on Research on Adolescence*, 17, 723–742. doi:10.1111/j.1532-7795.2007.00544.x

2. American Academy of Child and Adolescent Psychiatry. (2007). Practice parameter for the assessment and treatment of children and adolescents with depressive disorders. *Journal of the American Academy of Child and Adolescent Psychiatry*, 46(11), 1503–1526. doi:10.1097/chi.0b013e318145aelc; Substance Abuse and Mental Health Services Administration. (2012, July 19). Depression triples between the ages of 12 and 15 among adolescent girls. Retrieved from http://www.samhsa.gov/data/spotlight/Spot077GirlsDepression2012.pdf

3. American Psychiatric Association. (2013). *Diagnostic and Statistical Manual of Mental Disorders (DSM-5)* (5th ed.). Washington, DC: American Psychiatric Publishing.

4. American Academy of Child and Adolescent Psychiatry. (2007). Practice parameter for the assessment and treatment of children and adolescents with depressive disorders. *Journal of the American Academy of Child and Adolescent Psychiatry*, 46(11), 1503–1526. doi:10.1097/chi.0b013e318145aelc; Essau, C.A., & Chang, W. C. (2009). Epidemiology, comorbidity, and course of adolescent depression. In C. A. Essau (Ed.), *Treatments for adolescent depression: Theory and practice.* (pp. 3–26). New York: Oxford University Press.

5. Pratt, L. A., Brody, D. J., & Gu, Q. (2011). Antidepressant use in persons aged 12 and over: United States 2005–008. NCHS data brief, no. 76. Hyattsville, MD: National Center for Health Statistics.

6. Essau, C.A., & Chang, W. C. (2009). Epidemiology, comorbidity, and course of adolescent depression. In C. A. Essau (Ed.), *Treatments for adolescent depression: Theory and practice.* (pp. 3–26). New York: Oxford University Press.

7. Deak, J. (2003). *Girls will be girls: Raising confident and courageous daughters.* New York: Hyperion Press.

8. Essau, C.A., & Chang, W. C. (2009). Epidemiology, comorbidity, and course of adolescent depression. In C. A. Essau (Ed.), *Treatments for adolescent depression: Theory and practice.* (pp. 3–26). New York: Oxford University Press; Hankin, B. L., Wetter, E., & Cheely, C. (2008). Sex difference in child and adolescent depression: A developmental psychopathological approach. In J.R.Z. Abella & B. L. Hankin (Eds.), *Handbook of depression in children and adolescents* (pp. 377–415). New York: Guilford.

9. Commission on Adolescent Depression and Bipolar Disorder. (2005). Defining depression and bipolar disorder. In D. L. Evans, E. B. Foa, R. E. Gur, H. Hendin, C. P. O'Brien, M. P. Seligman, & T. Walsh (Eds.), *Treating and preventing adolescent mental health disorders: What we know and what we don't know* (pp. 3–27). New York: Oxford University Press.

10. Hankin, B. L., Wetter, E., & Cheely, C. (2008). Sex difference in child and adolescent depression: A developmental psychopathological approach. In J.R.Z. Abella & B. L. Hankin (Eds.), *Handbook of depression in children and adolescents* (pp. 377–415). New York: Guilford.

11. O'Keefee, G. S., Clarke-Pearson, K., & Council on Communications and Media. (2011). Clinical report—the impact of social media on children, adolescents, and families. *Pediatrics: Official Journal of the American Academy of Pediatrics, 127*, 800–804. doi:10.1542/peds.2011-0054

12. American Academy of Child and Adolescent Psychiatry. (2007), Practice parameter for the assessment and treatment of children and adolescents with depressive disorders. *Journal of the American Academy of Child and Adolescent Psychiatry*, 46(11), 1503–1526. doi:10.1097-chi.0b013e318145aelc

13. National Institute of Mental Health. (2009). *Anxiety disorders*. Retrieved from http://www.nimh.nih.gov/health/publications/anxiety-disorders/nimhanxiety.pdf

14. American Psychiatric Association. (2013). *Diagnostic and statistical manual of mental disorders (DSM-5)* (5th ed.). Washington, DC: American Psychiatric Publishing.

15. American Psychiatric Association. (2013). *Diagnostic and statistical manual of mental disorders (DSM-5)* (5th ed.). Washington, DC: American Psychiatric Publishing.

16. American Psychiatric Association. (2013). *Diagnostic and statistical manual of mental disorders (DSM-5)* (5th ed.). Washington, DC: American Psychiatric Publishing.

17. Beesdo, K., Knappe, S., & Pine, D. S., (2009). Anxiety and anxiety disorders in children and adolescents: Developmental issues and implications. *Psychiatric Clinics of North America, 32*(3), 483–524. doi: 10.1016/j.psc.2009.06.002

18. Reetz, D. R., Krylowicz, K., & Barr, V. (2013). Association for University and College Counseling Center Directors Annual Survey. Retrieved from http://files.cmcglobal.com/AUCCCD_Monograph_Public_2013.pdf

19. American Academy of Child and Adolescent Psychiatry. (2007), Practice and parameter for the assessment and treatment of children and adolescents with anxiety disorders. *Journal of the American Academy of Child and Adolescent Psychiatry, 46*(2), 267–283. doi: 10.1097/01.chi.0000246070.23695.06

20. Youth Risk Behavior Survey (2011). U.S. Department of Health and Human Services, Centers for Disease Control. Retrieved from http://www.cdc.gov/HealthyYouth/yrbs/index.htm

21. Youth Risk Behavior Survey (2011). U.S. Department of Health and Human Services, Centers for Disease Control. Retrieved from http://www.cdc.gov/HealthyYouth/yrbs/index.htm.

22. Commission on Adolescent Substance and Alcohol Abuse (2005). Treatment of substance use disorders. In D. L. Evans, E. B. Foa, R. E. Gur, H. Henden, C. P. O'Brien, M.E.P. Seligman, & B. T. Walsh (Eds.), *Treating and preventing adolescent mental health disorders: What we know and what we don't know: A research agenda for improving the mental health of our youth* (pp. 391–410). New York: Oxford University Press.

23. Youth Risk Behavior Survey (2011). U.S. Department of Health and Human Services, Centers for Disease Control. Retrieved from http://www.cdc.gov/HealthyYouth/yrbs/index.htm

24. Choate, L H. (2014). *Adolescent girls in distress: A guide for mental health treatment and prevention*. New York: Springer; American Academy of Child and Adolescent Psychiatry. (2005). Practice parameter for the assessment and treatment of children and adolescents with substance use disorders. *Journal of the American Academy of Child & Adolescent Psychiatry, 44*, 609–621.

25. Briggs, C. A., & Pepperrell, J. L. (2009). *Women, girls, and addiction: Celebrating the feminine in counseling treatment and recovery*. New York: Routledge/Taylor & Francis Group; Greenfield, S., Back, S., Lawsone, K., & Brady, K. (2010). Substance abuse in women. *Psychiatric Clinics of North America, 33*(2), 339–355. doi:10.1016/j.psc.2010.01.004

26. American Academy of Child and Adolescent Psychiatry. (2005). Practice parameter for the assessment and treatment of children and adolescents with substance use disorders. *Journal of the American Academy of Child & Adolescent Psychiatry, 44*, 609–621.

27. American Academy of Child and Adolescent Psychiatry. (2005). Practice parameter for the assessment and treatment of children and adolescents with substance use disorders. *Journal of the American Academy of Child & Adolescent Psychiatry, 44*, 609–621.

28. Zilberman, M. (2009). Substance abuse across the lifespan in women. In K. Brady, S. Back, & S. Greenfield (Eds.), *Women and addiction* (pp. 3–13). New York: Guilford.

29. Liddle, H. A., Rowe, C. L., Dakof, G. A., Henderson, C. E., & Greenbaum, P. E. (2009). Multidimensional family therapy for young adolescent substance abuse: Twelve-month outcomes of a randomized controlled trial. *Journal of Consulting and Clinical Psychology, 77*(1), 12–25. doi:10.1037/a0014160

30. Brown, S., McGue, M., Maggs, J., Schulenberg, J., Hingson, R., Swartzwelder, S., & Murphy, S. (2008). A developmental perspective on alcohol and youths ages 16 to 20 years of age. *Pediatrics, 121,* 290–210.

31. American Psychiatric Association. (2013). *Diagnostic and statistical manual of mental disorders (DSM-5)* (5th ed.). Washington, DC: American Psychiatric Publishing.

32. American Psychiatric Association. (2013). *Diagnostic and statistical manual of mental disorders (DSM-5)* (5th ed.). Washington, DC: American Psychiatric Publishing.

33. Hudson, J. I., Hiripi, E., Pope, H. G., & Kessler, R. C. (2007). The prevalence and correlates of eating disorders in the national comorbidity survey replication. *Biological Psychiatry, 61,* 348–358. doi:10.1016/j.biopsych.2006.03.040

34. Eaton, D. K., Kann, L., Kinchen, S., Shanklin, S., Ross, J., Hawkins, J., ... Wechsler, H. (2010). Youth risk behavior surveillance—United States, 2010. *MMWR Surveillance Summaries, 59 (SS05),* 1–142.

35. Micali, N., Ploubidis, G., De Stavola, B., Simonof, E., & Treasure, J. (2013). Frequency and patterns of eating disorder symptoms in early adolescence. *Journal of Adolescent Health,* 1–8. doi: 10.1016/j.jadohealth.2013.10.200

36. Tallyrand, R. (2013). Clients of color and eating disorders: Cultural considerations. In L. Choate (Ed.), *Eating disorders and obesity: A counselor's guide to prevention and treatment* (pp. 116–155). Alexandria, VA: American Counseling Association Press.

37. Alegria, M., Woo, M., Cao, Z., Torres, M., Meng, X., & Striegel-Moore, R. (2007). Prevalence and correlates of eating disorders in Latinos in the United States. *International Journal of Eating Disorders, 40,* 15–21. doi:10.1002/eat.20406

38. Commission on Adolescent Eating Disorders. (2005). Treatment of eating disorders. In D. L. Evans, E. B. Foa, R. E. Gur, H. Hendin, C. P. O'Brien, M. P. Seligman, & T. Walsh (Eds.), *Treating and preventing adolescent mental health disorders: What we know and what we don't know: A research agenda for improving the mental health of our youth.* (pp. 283–301). New York: Oxford University Press.

39. Lewis, S. P., Heath, N. L., St. Denis, J. M., & Noble, R. (2011). The scope of nonsuicidal self-injury on youtube. *Pediatrics, 127*(3), e552–e57. doi:10.1542/peds.2010-2317

40. Whitlock, J., Muhlenkamp, J., Purington, A., Eckenrode, J., Barreira, P., Abrams, G. B., ... Knox, K. (2011). Nonsuicidal self-injury in a college population: General trends and sex differences. *Journal of American College Health, 59*(8), 691–698. doi:10.1080/07448481.2010.529626

41. International Society for the Study of Self-Injury. (2007). *Definitional issues surrounding our understanding of self-injury.* Conference proceedings from the annual meeting. Montreal, Quebec, Canada.

42. Nock, M. K., (2010). Self-injury. *Annual Review of Clinical Psychology. 6,* 339–363. doi:10.1146/annurev.clinpsy.121208.131258

43. Nock, M. K., & Cha, C.B. (2009). Psychological models of nonsuicidal self injury. In M. K. Nock (Ed.), *Understanding nonsuicidal self-injury: Origins, assessment, and treatment* (pp. 9–18), Washington, DC: American Psychological Association.

44. Black, M., Basile, K., Breiding, M., Smith, S., Walters, M., Merrick, M. ... Stevens, M. R. (2011). *The national intimate partner and sexual violence survey (NISVS)*. Atlanta, GA: National Center for Injury Prevention and Control, Centers for Disease Control and Prevention

45. Campbell, R., Dworkin, E., & Cabral, G. (2009). An ecological model of the impact of sexual assault on women's mental health. *Trauma, Violence, & Abuse*, *10*(3), 225–246. doi: 10.1177/1524838009334456

46. American Psychiatric Association. (2013). *Diagnostic and statistical manual of mental disorders (DSM-5)* (5th ed.). Washington, DC: American Psychiatric Publishing.

47. Temple, J. R., Weston, R., Rodriguez, B. F., & Marshall, L. L. (2007). Differing effects of partner and nonpartner sexual assault on women's mental health. *Violence Against Women*, *13*(3), 285–297. doi: 10.1177/1077801206297437

48. Swahn, M. H., Simon, T. R., Arias, I., & Bossarte, R. M. (2008). Measuring sex differences in violence victimization and perpetration within date and same-sex peer relationships. *Journal of Interpersonal Violence*, *23*(8), 1120–1138. doi:10.1177/0886260508314086

49. Youth Risk Behavior Survey (2011). U.S. Department of Health and Human Services, Centers for Disease Control. Retrieved from http://www.cdc.gov/HealthyYouth/yrbs/index.htm

50. Black, M., Basile, K., Breiding, M., Smith, S., Walters, M., Merrick, M. . . . Stevens, M. R. (2011). *The national intimate partner and sexual violence survey (NISVS)*. Atlanta, GA: National Center for Injury Prevention and Control, Centers for Disease Control and Prevention.

51. Nock, M. K., Green, J. G., Hwang, I., McLauughlin, K. A., Sampson, N. A., Zaslavsky, A. M., & Kessler, R. C. (2013). Prevalence, correlates, and treatment of lifetime suicidal behaviors among adolescents. *JAMA Psychiatry*, *70*, 300–310. doi: 10.1001/2013.jamapsychiatry.55

52. Granello, D., & Granello, P. (2010). *Suicide: An essential guide for helping professionals and educators*. New York: Allyn & Bacon.

PART TWO

Parenting for Resilience

Resilience Dimension One

Parenting from Your Inner Core

Your daughter stares at you, incredulous. She screams, "What do you mean, I can't go to the party? You lied to me! Now my friends will never speak to me again! You are just trying to ruin my life!" She stomps off and slams the door to her room.

It's another one of those moments where you are left standing there, paralyzed. Communication has broken down yet again. You are wondering what is the right thing to say and do. Do you apologize, beg her forgiveness, and let her go to the party because she is so upset? Do you follow her into her room and have a shouting match until she backs down? Do you ignore her, refusing to speak to her the rest of the day? Or do you calm down, take a deep breath, and respond to the situation when you are ready?

The point here is that you do have a choice in how you respond. You don't have to become paralyzed or react out of strong emotions that are surfacing in the moment. You can stop and think about what is best for your daughter in the long term. That is the purpose of this chapter—to encourage you to become more mindful of your values as a parent and to give you information to help you make choices that stem from those values. While the subsequent chapters in this book are focused on how you can help your daughter develop resilience, this chapter is dedicated to *you* and how you can build your own resilience as a parent so you can stand against cultural pressures that steer you away from your values. I would like to note here that countless volumes have been written about basic parenting skills, and we are fortunate that there are so many resources available for parents. For the purposes of this chapter, I have distilled many parenting studies and programs into a basic no-frills version that will get you started. I will also recommend resources that can offer additional ideas if you need them. For now, in this chapter I will first address ways in which you can learn to slow down and become more mindful of your choices. Then I present some Parenting 101 basics. Finally, I will turn to some of our current parenting trends that may not fit well with what our daughters truly need.

MINDFULNESS

You are undoubtedly familiar with two of the central tenets of parenting: (1) love and connection paired with (2) limits and consequences. Most parenting approaches initially focus on some variation of these two essentials, and they will be discussed in subsequent sections of this chapter. However, I would like to introduce here yet another skill not usually listed as a foundational element of parenting but one that can greatly help you to learn to implement the other two. It is not hard to understand that kids need warmth and love and it is not hard to fathom that they would be lost without structure and limits. But to apply both in the moment when needed, especially while you are busy, stressed out, emotional, and tired? And to have the wisdom and patience to use both when parenting a preteen or adolescent girl? That is the hardest part.

The good news is that there is an approach that will provide you with some clarity and guidance when you are struggling with these issues. I would like to introduce the concept of mindfulness, a tradition that has become increasingly well known in the medical and mental health fields and which has been successfully applied to parenting.[1] Much has been written about mindfulness, but I will keep it very simple here: in a nutshell, mindfulness refers to our willingness and ability to pay attention to what we are experiencing and what is actually happening in the present moment. It means to notice what is going on in our minds and circumstances and then making a conscious decision as to what will happen next. In a nonjudgmental, nonevaluative manner, we can choose to view our thoughts and experiences for what they actually are and then decide how to respond. We become aware that we don't have to react automatically in anger or fear; we can pause, breathe, and choose to respond in a way that is *congruent with our values and what we want for our children.* Here I will list some practical steps for incorporating basic mindfulness into your parenting.

Practicing mindfulness, step one: Pay attention and identify your core values. First, you have to decide in advance what your core values are; these will not be the same for everyone. You set your expectations about your daughter's attitudes and behaviors and then you encourage her to live up to these expectations. To be a mindful parent, start by making up your mind on several levels. First visualize the end point: What values or characteristics do you want your daughter to have? I, for example, want my daughter to have self-initiative and independence so that she will feel confident in solving her own problems by the time she becomes an adult. Instead, I find my natural tendency as a parent is to do too much for her, to save her from struggling with new tasks, to keep her life as comfortable as possible. So as I think about my core values and compare them with my actual behaviors, I realize that these tendencies are actually leading *away from* rather than *toward* my goals for parenting my daughter. To parent mindfully, in making the countless parenting decisions that I make each day, I have to pause and remember: when my daughter does a task by herself today, she is actually learning to be a more responsible, independent adult in the future. So I try to hold myself back and let her do it herself, whether it is cleaning her room or resolving a problem with a friend. I have to pay attention or this will not happen.

So the ending point is actually the starting point for assessing where you are and where you want to go. Whatever your core values may be, when times get tough and you don't know what to do, you can go back to what you have previously decided is right and true for your family. It cuts down on the confusion. If you have reasoned these issues through in advance, then it is easier to remind yourself, "What do I want for my daughter?" "What are my core values?" Then pause, take a deep breath, and stand by what you believe. See Box 4.1 for an exercise to help you clarify your goals for your daughter.

Don't make these decisions in the heat of battle with your child. You will bend and sway, and you will likely make a decision that you will later regret. This does not lead to mindfulness; it leads to confusion and exhaustion because you are constantly fighting with your daughter or questioning whether you have made the right decision. Instead, use this formula in difficult situations:

• Stop! Pay attention to what is happening in the moment.
• Calmly take a deep breath.
• Reflect on your core values.
• Respond mindfully according to your values.

Box 4.1: PRIORITIZING CHARACTER GOALS

To become a more mindful parent, you must ask yourself what character goals are truly at the foundation of your parenting decisions. This may seem like a simple exercise, but it actually takes a lot of soul searching on your part to identify and articulate your core values and how you would like these to be reflected in your daughter. Spend some time with these questions and discuss them with your parenting partner if possible. It helps if everyone shares the same vision.

1. Take a moment to imagine your daughter as an adult. What character traits do you hope that she will possess? What values do you hope she will have? What helps you to feel confident that she is prepared to navigate her way through the complexity of today's life?
2. List as many of these qualities as you can. Just brainstorm here.
3. Review your list and circle your top five. Now narrow them down to your top three most important character goals for your daughter.
4. Write these three goals on a piece of paper and place it in a prominent place in your home so that you can remind yourself daily.

Practicing mindfulness, step two: Become aware of your cognitive filters. Now that you have identified your core values, it is time to become mindful in using your values when you are making decisions instead of deciding impulsively on the basis of your own emotions, problems, or unresolved issues. Left unchecked, we tend to parent out of our pasts; our previous thoughts, feelings, attitudes, and experiences tend to drive our parenting behaviors. Sometimes we are aware of the emotions behind our parenting decisions but many times we are not. They key is learning to gain awareness of your "cognitive filters"—the blinders we all tend to wear that cause us to interpret our children's behaviors through our own past experiences—either as a result of our previous relationship conflicts with them or because of our own struggles.[2]

An example might be if you tend to react with anger when your daughter brings home a bad grade from school. You can become caught up in your thoughts and emotions, thinking, "My child is failing in school; my child is a failure; I am a bad parent; *I am a failure.*" Without even thinking, you lash out at your child because you don't like feeling like a failure! You aren't even consciously aware of why you are yelling, you just feel bad and start to vent your feelings; then you feel guilty for blowing up at your daughter. If you were to be mindful in the moment, you could pause, breathe deeply, and then possibly realize any of the following:

- The bad grade is just a grade, it does not represent anyone's failure as a human being.
- The grade does not define my worth as a parent.
- I'm angry right now, and that feeling can spur me on to positive action—I can choose to act on this feeling in a way that is not hurtful.
- The grade is a call to action that my child might need to do something different to prepare for tests at school.
- This is my daughter's grade, not *my* grade, and I am not responsible for her grades.

In sum, if you had become more aware of your inner experiences and recognized your choice in how to respond, it is likely that you would not have yelled in anger at your daughter. So mindfulness is learning to be aware of what you are feeling and then choosing not to parent from a place of strong emotion, so that you do not overreact in any given situation. Your feelings are valid, but they are just feelings. *They are not facts.* Your thoughts may helpful, or *they may be irrational and detrimental.* Being mindful means knowing that you have a *choice* on whether or not to react out of pain and fear, to mindlessly act just as you have always done, or to respond in the moment based on your core values.

So our formula for mindfulness becomes slightly more complex, but the additional step is critical. It now includes the following:

- Stop! Pay attention to what you are experiencing in the moment.
- Calmly take a deep breath.
- Examine your feelings and thoughts: where are they coming from? Do you need to remove any filters or blinders that are getting in your way of seeing the situation clearly?
- Reflect on your core values.
- Respond mindfully, based on your core values.

For example, Olivia and her mother get into frequent arguments when her mom asks her to pick up around the house. When she is asked to help, Olivia whines and yells that it's not fair that she should have to stop what she is doing in order to pick up her belongings. Olivia's mom tells me that when she reacts without thinking, she quickly picks up everything herself so that Olivia will stop whining. Even though she knows Olivia's behavior is disrespectful, she figures that it's not worth getting everyone upset. When questioned about this behavior, the mom admitted that she is operating from her own painful past. She is automatically trying to shield Olivia from pain or struggle because she doesn't want her to be as unhappy as she herself was at that age. So out of her own pain (not out of her current need or her core values for her children) she will automatically jump in too quickly to rescue Olivia or will hold back from disciplining her. In looking back on the situation, she recognizes that she responded based on her own "filters" and not what was truly needed in the situation. Once she has this awareness, however, she can be free to make more mindful decisions.

In sum, as you become more aware of what is happening with you in the moment, instead of reacting from your personal feelings, you can learn to respond by pausing, observing the behavior, breathing, recognizing any of your automatic thoughts that might be getting in the way of seeing the situation clearly, and then addressing the issue at hand in a way that is aligned with your core values. Can we stay in this mindful place at all times? I wish that were the case. But the more we practice, the better we get at it. Some days I practice mindfulness just while brushing my teeth in the morning without doing other things (like yelling with a mouthful of toothpaste for my kids to get dressed because they are running late!). When you can practice focusing on one thing at one time in any area of your life, you will be better able to apply this focused approach to your parenting. I will review mindfulness again in Chapter Eight when I discuss coping skills; it is also a great strategy for girls to learn.

Sometimes the idea of mindfulness can be hard to wrap our heads around; it is quite abstract and not easily understood. I have found that different experts describe this approach using different metaphors, which make it easier to visualize what being mindful might look like in practice. I will share a scenario and then some metaphors I have renamed so that they are easier to remember; you can choose which one fits best for you.

> *Example: You find that you are arguing with your daughter regularly. She tends to challenge you on every decision. She wants to spend less time with you and tends to criticize almost everything you do. Your typical reaction to this is anger. You react by yelling and arguing with her until she agrees with you, which almost never occurs.*

The eagle: Take a bird's-eye view. I have found this metaphor to be helpful in learning to step back from arguments with your daughter and to view the situation as if you were a bird flying overhead, observing the interaction between the two of you. You focus in on what your daughter is saying and doing, but you can also consider the big picture that is unfolding.

As a bird, you might view the fighting as reasonable for a child struggling to separate and be independent, even if she is using all of the wrong tactics for doing so. The bird would also notice that from its higher perspective, the intent (separation toward an eventual healthy adulthood) isn't nearly as personal and hurtful as it seems from the ground in the midst of battle. On the ground, you are angry and in fighting mode; in the air, you see the larger view and can choose to remove yourself from the fight.[3]

The photographer: Zooming in and out. As a parent, you can start to view your arguments with your daughter as if you were holding a camera lens that you can zoom in and out. When you are zoomed in, the fighting, criticism, and ignoring seem incomprehensible; why would your child speak and act (or ignore you) in this way? But as a photographer, you also have the ability to zoom out and see the big picture. This is but one stage in your child's overall life trajectory. Your daughter is managing multiple life demands and cultural pressures. She is trying to hold it together and sometimes takes out her frustration on you. When you step back and look at the whole picture, you can take the entire context into consideration and it becomes easier to understand.[4]

The sociologist: Analyzing objectively. As a social scientist, you have the ability to study the situation objectively without taking it personally. You can step back and think clearly. Based on the evidence available to you, you see the relationship for what it is: an adolescent doing what she is biologically programmed to do—testing her limits, experimenting with her identity, pulling back from her parent.[5]

With mindfulness—making conscious, thoughtful choices about how you respond in parenting—as your backdrop, you can remember to live out your values through your parenting and do far less reacting. So now we are finally ready to plunge into a review of the other two essentials of parenting upon which everything else is based: love and connection and limits/structure. If we aren't mindful, we will fall to one extreme or the other. Mindfulness helps us remember to stay balanced.

RESPONSIVENESS AND DEMANDINGNESS

One of the best-known methods for understanding parenting styles is the work of Diana Baumrind, who examined parents' levels of demandingness (e.g., setting limits, structure, and enforcing consequences) and responsiveness (love and connection).[6] Many studies have been conducted using Baumrind's approach, but for now, Box 4.2 offers a brief summary.

Box 4.2: BAUMRIND'S PARENTING STYLES

Authoritarian: This approach pairs high levels of demandingness and control with low levels of responsiveness. This is the parenting approach that lays down the rules, enforces them, and expects the child not to question the parent's authority. There is little concern for the actual parent-child relationship, only that rules are obeyed.

What you might hear from this parent: "Do as I say or else."

Permissive: At the other end of the scale, this approach pairs high levels of responsiveness with low demands or expectations for the child. There is freedom without limits or order. Often parents on this end of the spectrum are afraid that their children will not love them if they say no, so they give in to all their children's demands and thereby avoid conflict.

What you might hear from this parent: "Do what you want as long as you stay happy doing it!"

Disengaged/neglecting: This parent is low on both demandingness and responsiveness. The parent does not set limits, not out of fear of losing closeness with the child but because he or she is too distracted to become involved. Not only is there no concern for limits and structure, there is also little concern for the parent-child relationship.

What you might hear from this parent: "I've got my own life. Kids can figure it out for themselves. Nothing I do makes a difference anyway."

Authoritative: This approach is high in both responsiveness and demandingness. In other words, there is a strong parent-child relationship based on love, support, and connection balanced with limits and control when needed. This parent provides clear limits, but choices are offered within those limits; there is freedom, but the child is expected to obey on bottom-line issues.

What you might hear from this parent: "I will listen to what you want and try to understand your perspective, but in the end I will make the decision based on what I think is best."

As you can probably guess, research indicates that the authoritative style is most effective, as it meets children's needs for both support and challenge, for both structure and freedom. Balance, not extremes, is almost always the goal in our parenting. For example, as you will see throughout this book, girls need a balance of external and internal control in their lives; if they are overly controlled, they won't learn to make choices for themselves (or will rebel against authority). But if they are given too much control before they are ready, they will be easily whisked away by the raging cultural pressures and life demands we discussed in Chapters One and Two.

Authoritative parents base their style on these two foundational tenets: the warm and safe parent-child relationship (responsiveness) and a firm maintenance of structure and limits (demandingness). We start with responsiveness.

RESPONSIVENESS: LOVING AND CONNECTING IN THE PARENT-CHILD RELATIONSHIP

Our primary task in parenting is to love and connect. This is vital to everything else and is the most important gift you can give to your daughter. We are all scrambling around, hungry for advanced techniques and gadgets to try to help our children, when the greatest treasure we can give is our love, validation, and support. Your daughter desperately needs to know that you love her deeply and approve of her, not based on her appearance or accomplishments or anything else, but just because she is your daughter. She needs to know that if you got to choose who your child would be and you could choose from among all of the children in the world, *you would still choose her*. She needs to know that you value her core goodness and that she is acceptable and worthy of love.[7] Let her know that you *like* her, you enjoy spending time with her, you believe in her. If she truly believes that she is valued, accepted, and unconditionally loved by you, you have given her a priceless gift, one that paves the way for a resilient life.

However, loving is not the whole story, and it is certainly not a simple task. The loving part comes naturally to most of us. In contrast with previous generations, today's parents get the message that kids are to be placed on a pedestal and that they should center their lives around them. We learn that we should tell our kids how great they are and shower them with compliments and affection (more about these trends later in the chapter).[8] It seems ironic, then, that today's children say they feel more disconnected from their parents and wish their parents would spend more time really listening to them.[9]

Connecting becomes increasingly complex during the preadolescent and adolescent years in part for two reasons; the first is cultural and the second is developmental.

Obstacle one: It's hard to connect with our daughters when we are plugged in and tuned out.

In Chapter One we discussed girls' relationship with technology and how this affects their relationships with others. Now we shine the spotlight on parents: how does parents' use of screens and devices influence their connections with their children? This cultural phenomenon has crept in so pervasively that few families are exempt from its influence. If our cell phones constantly connect us to phone calls, texts, and e-mails, are we ever really "off" from work? Can we ever really disconnect? Are we ever really fully present with people in real life if we are constantly interrupted by "pings" from our phones indicating new Facebook posts? Are we fully able to listen if we are drifting back and forth between face-to-face and virtual contact? If I check my work e-mail on my phone while I am supposedly spending time with my kids, am I really present with them? Or is my mind floating between worrying about a work situation and occasionally tuning in to what my kids are saying? (Okay, it is apparent I have been guilty of this one.)

I highly recommend Catherine Steiner-Adair's recent book *The Big Disconnect: Protecting Childhood and Family Relationships in the Digital Age* and her discussion of this cultural phenomenon. As Steiner-Adair notes,

> Parents are checking out of family time, disappearing themselves and offering that behavior as a model for their children. . . . parents are virtually missing in action, routinely either engaged in cell phone conversation or texting or basking in the glow of a computer screen with work or online pastimes.[10]

Steiner-Adair points out that in today's busy world, even when we are spending time together, each person might be quite alone in his or her separate virtual world. The formerly comical scenario of a family having dinner together at a restaurant with each member looking down, lost in his or her own device and not speaking to one another, is now unfortunately becoming commonplace. I was struck by Steiner-Adair's observations of how many children say they wish their parent would look up from their phones when they pick them up from the car-pool line after school. Many kids she interviewed said they would love their parent to put the phone down, make eye contact, and offer a smile or wave as their child walked out from school. Instead the kids just see the top of their parent's head.

Children have grown jealous of their parents' devices. One child (age 7) Steiner-Adair quotes in her book said, "My mom is almost always on the iPad at dinner. She is always "just checking." Another quote from a different child (age 7): "I always keep asking her let's play, let's play and she is always texting on her phone." The problem is that once we start checking our devices, we become unavailable. Children need us to be present not just physically but also psychologically. It matters that 92 percent of people in a recent national survey said that they had felt ignored because a household member spent too much time on his or her mobile device. This means that it has become normal to feel ignored in our own homes.[11] To adults this might be annoying. To children, however, the message is *everything matters more than you*—that caller, that texter, that update. The "outsider" intruding through the screen is seemingly more important than what we are doing together or what you are telling me. That physically-there-but-not-really-present mindset creates a barrier to forging strong connections among family members.

Obstacle two: It's hard to connect with your daughter when she is pushing you away.

In addition to the virtual connections that pull us all apart, maintaining love and connection is not easy when your daughter reaches the preteen years and starts pushing you away in all sorts of creative ways. It is not easy to connect when she is rebelling and acting out. When times get tough, hold onto the image of the girl you love and cherish, even if she is staying hidden beneath the surface for the moment. Display photos or mementos of her when she was young, so that you can be reminded daily of who she really is underneath her somewhat prickly adolescent skin. Hold onto your positive expectations for her no matter what, and let her hear often how much you love her, like her, and believe in her.

When she is pushing you away, also remember that this is normal and to be expected. You shouldn't have to tolerate disrespectful behavior, but the underlying drive to separate from you is a biological mandate; she is driven to pull away and show that she is a separate being who is capable of becoming an adult. She needs to know that she is more than just a miniature version of you, so she may sometimes insult you or try to humiliate you in order to create this separateness. Another thing to remember is that in many cases her rejection of you is actually a sign that she feels well cared for and loved! With all of the stresses of adolescence, she might take her relationship with you for granted for a while— "I can ignore Mom and Dad or treat them like dirt for a time because I know that they will hang in there with me and will still be there after I have figured out all of these other relationships." She can relax about putting energy into your relationship and focus on other things instead (like how to form an independent identity).[12] Unfortunately this feels terrible to us as parents, but if you keep these two things in mind (that this is a biological mandate, and because she feels secure she is taking your relationship for granted right now), it can start to take the sting out a bit. It's incredibly hard when she is pushing you away, criticizing you, and constantly fighting with you. But no matter what, you need to hang in there and stay connected the best that you can. Inside, she is torn between letting you go and holding onto you for dear life. Although she says she doesn't want you around, she actually does. When you feel rejected, hold onto the truth that you are needed and that you do have a valuable role to play in her life.

PARENTING STRATEGIES FOR LOVE AND CONNECTION

- *Invest in face-to-face time*. If we want to remain connected, especially through the adolescent years, we have to be willing to unplug and be there for face-to-face conversations at those times when she is most likely to want to talk and share: during transition times such as in the morning (before school), driving to and from school, when she first comes home from school, during family dinners, and when she goes to bed.[13] It is not easy, but it is possible to carve out technology-free zones during the day.
- *Keep pressing forward with family rituals and outings*. Allen and Allen (authors of *The Endless Adolescence*) recommend that even if your adolescent rejects 90 percent of the invitations you offer for spending time together, be grateful for the 10 percent of acceptances you do receive! Keep planning, keep offering, and don't give up on building connections.
- *Listen, listen, listen*. This is so important that I want to expand on listening skills; these will become invaluable in keeping a loving and connected relationship with your daughter:

ACTIVE LISTENING SKILLS

If you are reading this when your daughter is young, start to learn these skills now, but you may not need to use them just yet. Your daughter probably talks a lot, and your focus at this stage is to know what is really important to her and to ask her to wait and talk to you at a time when you can give her your full attention. It is okay to have boundaries and to ask her to wait until an appropriate time when you are best able to listen.

On the other hand, if your daughter is entering the preteen and teenage years and you feel her beginning to pull away, increasingly hiding herself from you, and shutting down more than opening up, effective communication requires a different skill set from you. The following section outlines active listening skills that are based on the premise that you are listening and communicating on *her* terms, not *yours*. The quicker we recognize this, the less frustrated we will be. It is a new way of interacting, but it will serve to keep the door to communication open during this phase of your daughter's development.

- Just because you are ready to have a conversation, accept that she may or may not want to talk with you just then. Don't try to force her to share more than what she is willing to give at a particular time.
- However, when the time is right and she does choose to open up to you, listen with your full attention. Welcome this time of communication and treat it as a precious gift, not to be squandered. As already stated, when she is younger, you are focused more on boundaries ("Wait until I am finished with what I am doing before you tell me your story"). In contrast, now you will be lapping up any of her attempts at communication like you are drinking your last few drops of water after days in a desert. Drop everything else and listen fully, using the skills described here.
- Use attentive nonverbals. When I teach new counselors the basic counseling skills, I tell them to face the client, make eye contact, and never look at their watches (or even worse, their phones) during a session. Why? Because it indicates that you are not fully listening, that you need/want to be somewhere else, or that you are in a hurry. And so it should be with our daughters: silence your phone/tablet/laptop and put it away! Turn off (not just mute) the TV. Convey that having an open dialogue with your daughter is the most important thing in the world to you at that moment! (*But don't overdo this with too much exuberance or your daughter will just roll her eyes and shut down again.*)
- As stated previously, make sure that you spend enough time with your daughter during her prime communication periods in order to maximize

your chances of being there for her when she is ready to talk. This calls for an investment of your time.

- Don't interrupt her. Allow her to pour out her story and, as we know, this can sometimes take awhile. Listen for the purpose of understanding what she is saying, from *her* perspective. Show her that you do understand her thoughts and feelings, and while you may not necessarily agree with them, convey that you do get where she is coming from. Think back to a time when you felt truly understood by someone else; it is a liberating experience. Most likely, it helped you to think more clearly and to move closer to a decision about what you wanted to do about a particular situation. Why not make every effort to provide this experience for your daughter?

- As you are listening, use *door openers*. A door opener is just that, an open invitation to talk more about a specific topic. "Tell me more about . . . ." (the problem with Rebecca, the boys' teasing at school, her feelings about being weighed in gym class). Use door openers to keep her talking so that she can further explore her thoughts and feelings about an issue.

- Don't overdo it with questions, but when you do ask one, use an *open*, not *closed* question. This subtle change in whether you use an open versus a closed question can make a huge difference in the type of response you receive. A closed question can be answered in a word or two, like yes or no, and it makes assumptions about the type of response you want (e.g., "Did you have fun at the party?"). In contrast, a well-timed open question can help your daughter to open up about a subject and conveys no expectation about the type of response.(e.g., "*How* was the party for you tonight?") In the closed example, your daughter could perceive that you just want her to say yes and move on. On the other hand, the open question allows your daughter to explore her feelings about the party, both positive and negative, and does not limit her to only saying "Yes it was fun" or "No it was not." Open questions will usually begin with: *who, what, when, where, how,* and *why*. (Be extra careful with the *why* questions, though, because they tend to elicit a lot of defensiveness. Think back to your own teenage years and how you reacted when your parent asked you "*Why did you do that*?" There is usually a hint of accusation or judgment in a "why" question—whether you intend it that way or not. So use your "whys" sparingly if you want your daughter to keep talking.)

- Once you think you have grasped your daughter's thoughts and feelings about an issue or situation, let her know that you understand. How do you do this? Counselors call this skill *reflection of feeling,* and at first novice counselors are taught to rely on the formula "You feel____because.____" ("You feel shocked and betrayed because you believed Devin was your best friend, but then she spread a lie about you around the school today"). You don't have to remember to follow a formula, you just need to listen closely for *understanding* and then validate her feelings whenever possible. This is a powerful skill that will bring you closer to your daughter if you put it into practice often.

- This might seem obvious given the listening strategies already outlined, but it is worth stating: Try really, really hard not to explode (e.g., "you did *what*???"). Try to listen mindfully without overreacting. Yelling will shut down the communication almost immediately. Again, listen and try to *understand*.

- Try not to go into advice-giving mode. Think of how frustrating it is when you are trying to tell someone an emotional story and he or she interrupts you with pat answers and a quick fix. You probably make a mental note not to open up to that person again because you felt cut off, misunderstood, and probably didn't really want a hastily offered Band-Aid answer anyway. Let's try not to make our daughters feel that way either.

- Ask if she would like your advice: "Would you like my opinion?" *If* your opinion is solicited, keep it short and sweet. As Greenspan-Goldberg wisely advises, "Less is more and don't be a snore."[14] Even when you do offer feedback, do whatever you can to increase her talk time and decrease your own.

- Don't offer generalities like "This too shall pass" or "You'll look back on this and laugh." These are not helpful in the moment. She wants to feel understood, not dismissed.

- Before offering your own advice, use questions to help her to think about how *she* wants to move forward with the situation: "How are you thinking about handling this?" "What are your ideas for solving this problem?" Again, open questions are far more effective than closed ones if your goal is to (1) have your daughter view you as a trusted sounding board for her thoughts and feelings and (2) help her figure out her own ways of navigating problems before she turns to others to solve them for her.

DEMANDINGNESS: SETTING LIMITS, INSTILLING STRUCTURE, ENFORCING CONSEQUENCES

The next parenting practice I will examine is positive discipline: setting limits, structure, and enforcing consequences. This is not to be considered the opposite of loving and connecting; rather, it goes hand in glove: we love our children, and we address their problems through discipline *because* we love them.

Probably more than with any other issue in this chapter, an entire industry has been dedicated to the topic of disciplining children and adolescents, and I certainly don't try cover it all here (see the end of this book for some recommended resources). However, despite the intricacies, the literature on discipline includes a few major themes that are present in most approaches, and I will focus on these in the next few pages. But first, a caveat (see Box 4.3).

Box 4.3: A CONFESSIONAL ON DISCIPLINE

Based on all of my professional and personal experience, parents fall into two camps regarding this topic: One group of parents consider it a no-brainer; they discipline their children with ease and few regrets. I am blessed that I have a husband who is in this group. This stuff is easy for him! He stands strong in the midst of the wailing and crying; he doesn't give in when a consequence is due. The other group consists of parents who seem to constantly struggle with discipline-related issues. I fall squarely into the latter camp. So time for a confession: before I was a parent, I was not a structured or consistent person; I rarely knew what time it was, I didn't stick to schedules, and I often resisted the idea of imposing a routine on myself. I still don't make decisions in a clear-cut manner, as I tend to consider all angles, motivations, and feelings involved. It takes me a long time to decide what is "fair." In my role as a university professor and counselor, that attitude works out just fine because I need a lot of unstructured time in order to think and write, and I need to stay open to my clients' worldviews and display empathy and curiosity. In moving into motherhood, though, this approach has created infinite problems for me because, like all children, my children need a schedule, consistency, rules, order, and clear limits. They crave the security of knowing what to expect if a particular limit is crossed. It takes a great deal of awareness and self-discipline for me to provide these things for them and not to fall back on my natural tendencies. I know what I need to do, and sometimes I fail miserably. But keeping the big picture in mind—knowing what is best for my kids in the long run and not what is easiest for me in the moment—this is what keeps me moving forward, staying focused, being mindful of what I am doing. It is about what they need, not what is most comfortable for me.

I say these things to let you know that I am not writing this section from an ivory tower of perfection but am truly gutting it out at the front lines right along with you. I get it; I know this is easy to say but very hard for some of us to do. There is much compassion here. But setting limits and enforcing consequences is essential, and we need to keep forging ahead.

So now that my confession is out of the way, what type of discipline actually works to fit our daughters' needs and will help them become more resilient adults?

Here are some basics for limit setting, structure, and enforcement of consequences with our daughters.

- **Separate the behavior from the person.**

Start with a philosophical view of your daughter as *separate from her behavior* and that she is *much more than* her behavior in a given moment. Hemmen advises parents to love your daughter *first* and feel concern for the behavior *second*. In other words, *she* remains acceptable, even though her behaviors might not be. Before we swoop in and take disciplinary action, we have to keep in mind that we love her, accept her, and appreciate her, even while we generate consequences to help her decrease her temporary but problematic behavior.[15]

- **Her behavior is biologically driven, not a personal attack on you.**

As explored in Chapter Two, her brain is not fully developed; the engine is firing fast but the brakes are not yet ready. She is feeling biological urges to try new things and take new risks, but she is not yet able to plan for or understand the potential consequences of her actions. She doesn't yet know how to set reasonable boundaries in the face of peer pressure. So when you feel a sense of bewilderment as to *why* she acts in certain ways that don't make sense, stay mindful, zoom out, and view the behavior from a developmental perspective. Second, even though physically she looks more and more like an adult, know that she still needs you to set appropriate limits and boundaries because she is not yet able to do it for herself. She still needs your guidance, protection, and supervision. In fact, she may also need to use you as her boundary (e.g., "I want to hang out but my mom would be furious if she found out, so I really can't!"). Let her use you as an excuse for as long as she needs to until she is ready to stand up for herself all on her own.[16]

- **Decide on and communicate your family values.**

As stated in the section on mindful parenting, decide what your family values and core convictions are, and communicate them explicitly to her. Does she know where you stand on such issues as experimentation with sex, alcohol, and other drugs? It would be nice to not have to deal with this issue until she is 25, but unfortunately we do, and probably much earlier than you think. So stop and do a check on what you expect for her in terms of the following:

> *Will it be okay for her to engage in some experimentation with alcohol, smoking, and substances while she lives at home, or will absolutely none be tolerated? And if okay, starting at what age? Am I okay with some experimentation as long as there are no negative consequences (e.g., lowered grades, legal problems, drinking and driving)?*
>
> *How old will she be when she is allowed to date? To attend parties where romantic interests are present? To date someone older than herself? To go on group dates? One-on-one dating? What are my beliefs about her social media use with boys? What is my stance on joined-at-the hip romances in middle and high school?*
>
> *Do I expect that she will remain sexually abstinent until after high school? Until marriage? Does it depend upon whether she is in a long-term, loving relationship?*[17]

All parents should make these decisions for themselves based on their beliefs and values and communicate these clearly to their daughters. No matter what else you decide, there is one overarching message parents should always convey: "I will always love you no matter what choices you may make. If you are in trouble, call me. I will always be there for you. In that moment, don't worry about getting in trouble with me. I will always come and get you if you need help." If she believes this, it will help her to feel safe and supported even if she makes a mistake. She will know that you will be there for her and will help her deal with whatever issue she may be facing. And, stated bluntly, this could save her life; for example, it could be the difference between her feeling comfortable enough to call you at 2 a.m. for a ride home instead of getting into a car with a drunk driver.[18]

• ***Convey clear limits and deliver consistent consequences.***

Girls need limits and structure in the form of rules with clearly stated expectations and consequences that will undoubtedly occur if the expectations are not met. Your enforcement of the consequence is not being "mean" but just part of a process intended to help her learn that when she makes bad choices, negative consequences will follow. As a parent, don't shield her from experiencing these consequences or from the valuable life lessons she can learn from them.[19] For example, do we want her to think "If I do this, then X *will* happen" or "If I do this, then X *might* happen, but probably Mom and Dad will let it go and they will . . . [pay the fine, clean up the mess, let me have the car, go to the party] anyway." If she believes the latter, why bother to try to do the right thing, especially when it's hard?

The other benefit of using consistent enforcement is the incredible amount of energy it can save you as a parent. If we *follow through* with consequences instead of arguing about them with our children, we won't risk getting angry or out of control. I love this quote from Kenneth Ginsburg: "It may seem harsh to have immediate consequences, but it is far better than wasting so much of your valuable relationship time on nagging, hostility, or empty threats!"[20]

Although this scenario is taken from a childhood example, sadly, it can also be applied to our conversations with our teen daughters:

PARENT: Kayla, don't do that again. *Kayla does it again.*

PARENT: Kayla, don't do that again or you will be in trouble. *Kayla does it again.*

PARENT: Kayla, you know I am trying to work right now, you know I love you. *Kayla does it again.*

PARENT: Kayla, you know if you just stop, then in a few minutes we can get some ice cream. *Kayla does it again.*

PARENT: Kayla, if you will just be patient and stop misbehaving then we can go have some fun really, really soon . . . *Kayla does it again.*

PARENT (exploding in anger): KAYLA, GO TO YOUR ROOM AND NO TV FOR A MONTH! I MEAN IT!

Hopefully it is clear from this example that if we are consistent and enforce the limits we have set from the outset, we can spare ourselves (and our children) a lot of energy, confusion, and anger.

• *Just say no.*

Although you need to enforce consequences when boundaries are crossed, you also need to be able to say no to requests that violate your family's values. It is important to be a positive model for your daughter in learning how to say no and mean it. This is a valuable skill she will need in life as well (more about this in Chapter Six). Saying no never decreases in importance; for example, soon enough you will no longer be saying no to buying her a stuffed animal in Target. Soon you will have to face saying no to parties where there will be drinking or to hanging out with older boys. Practice getting used to it now while the stakes are lower. She can throw a tantrum in Target and you will both get over it fairly quickly.

Part of the problem many parents face in saying no is that they don't want their children to view them as "old fashioned" or, worse, as "uncool." Be that as it may, JoAnn Deak sums it up for us nicely: *We need to learn to be unpopular adults.*[21] It's okay not to be the most cool and hip parent on the block. This may be harder for those who have always tried to be part of the "popular" group and to fit in with what is trendy. Instead, this is a time where you will be best served by going with your instincts and core values. Say no when you believe you need to, and don't compare your decisions with what all of the other parents might be doing.

In addition to worrying about what other people might think about their parenting decisions, some parents worry that if they say no, they will lose their child's approval. The reality is that you don't have to become your daughter's best friend. She likely has many friends but only two parents.[22] In healthy families there is a hierarchy, with the parental system at the top and the children below. It is not in her best interest for you and your daughter to be equals. And unlike a friendship, it is not reasonable to expect her to like you all of the time.

If this hard for you, repeat the following on a daily basis until you believe it:

My daughter needs me to say no because boundaries create a sense of safety and help her feel secure, and sometimes saying no is the best way of showing love to her. I care about her so much that I am going to say no, because I value her safety and long-term character development over everything else, even if she is mad at me for a period of time.

- ### Be flexible within limits.

This subheading does not contradict the previous section. Instead, it means that your limits and boundaries should be a set of evolving guidelines that are matched to your daughter's current stage of development. Although some things are not negotiable, other areas might be open to negotiation as she shows increasing responsibility with the freedoms she is already allowed.

Several authors recommend creating a freedoms wish list: making a list of freedoms that your daughter wishes she could have and listing them in order from lowest to highest level of responsibility. Then you can set goals to let her know what she might need to do in order to move up to the next level of freedom. In this way there would be fewer "nevers" in your conversations as you both work together to come up with a plan for moving up to the next level on the wishlist. Offer as many choices as possible so that you are not always saying no. Let her know what responsibilities would she have to display in order to have her next freedom. This can also help her learn to delay gratification and increase her of self-control because it is she who will ultimately decide when she is ready to put forth the effort needed to increase her freedoms.[23]

• Monitor and network

Parental monitoring is a formal term meaning that you know where your child is and what she is doing—and also that she is well aware that you know what she is doing. This one parenting practice makes a huge difference in whether or not your daughter will be successful in school and in life.[24] The skill in monitoring, however, lies in being able to monitor without being too controlling. When your daughter is in elementary school, you provide a lot of direct supervision. As she gets older, you start to loosen this supervision; for example, you begin to feel comfortable dropping her off at birthday parties instead of staying for the party. Even when she enters adolescence, she still needs to be monitored, although you will be far less directly involved. Monitoring might take the form of frequent communication with her and through networking with other adults. Even though you can loosen the structure as she proves to be responsible, she still needs to be aware that you expect to know who she is with, who the adult caregivers are, and that you might drop in at any given time to make sure she is doing what she says she is doing. She also needs to know that you communicate frequently with the parents of her friends and that you make sure that the stories about their plans are consistent. I know this isn't as simple as it sounds because you need to respect her rights to be an individual and to have some degree of privacy as she matures, but you are also responsible for making sure that she is protected and safe. Again, the question is how to strike a balance between trusting her, letting her explore, letting her learn from her mistakes, and your responsibility to protect, but not control, her physical and emotional safety. This should be an intentional choice on your part; you can ask yourself, "I know I should continue to monitor, but how much monitoring is acceptable to me, based on my daughter's maturity and demonstrated level of responsibility?"

• Use encouragement and praise.

I am discussing this strategy last to help you keep in mind that even when you are doing your best to state your rules clearly and enforce consequences, you still need to make efforts to keep the parent-child relationship intact. For discipline to be effective, you need to keep a focus not only on your daughter's mistakes but also on what she is doing *right*. We all tend to respond best when we receive criticism that is also accompanied by positive feedback. Allen and Allen recommend that you offer genuine praise for at least two things a day that your daughter is doing well or that you appreciate about her. Their analogy of a bank applies here: your daughter needs at least as many positive statements (deposits) as criticisms (withdrawals) in order to feel that the doors of communication with you remain open and inviting. Take a moment to reflect on the tone of your ongoing conversations with her. Does she have an overall sense that you approve of her as a person and that you like having her as your daughter? Or do you spend more time correcting and giving advice? Is there truly a balance between deposits and withdrawals?[25]

So we start with love and connection, and we end there too.

SHIFTING FOUNDATIONS: PARENTING IN TODAY'S CULTURAL CLIMATE

The fundamental tenets to "establish limits and enforce consequences" and "love and connect" are parenting practices backed by years of research findings. However, newer parenting practices that have evolved in recent years are not necessarily grounded in research, nor are they recommended by parenting experts. Despite their popularity, these trends have not really been questioned as to their long-term effects on children. They are merely perpetuated as parents look around and see what others are doing without necessarily asking critical questions.

Therefore I am going to place some of these new parenting trends into the spotlight so that we can determine whether or not they are best for our girls. As we review what is currently viewed as normal, we will see that they have only recently become the norm and therefore remain open to question. As you review the list, ask yourself, "Am I following these evolving norms blindly or am I actively making a choice to opt in or out?"

MYTH: *I have to hover over my child or she will drown in today's ocean of problems and demands.*

Reality: You have probably heard of the term "helicopter" parent—a style that has risen to soaring heights in the past decade. Instead of encouraging independence, many of today's parents are highly fearful for their children's safety and are trying to micromanage their every action.[26] While we do need to be vigilant when our children are very young, they are not served well when we continue to rush in and rescue them from every problem or stressor they might face. At my university I commonly hear stories from academic advisors who receive calls from parents about scheduling their 20-year-old child's college classes or about the parents who accompany their adult children to job interviews. I also regularly hear stories of parents who argue with their children's teachers, coaches, or other authority figures to let their children out of sanctions (e.g., bad grades, missing a game) that might make them feel uncomfortable or embarrassed.

So-called helicopter parents (and I have been known to be one of them, so remember that I am not judging here) are known for fearing for their children's safety in a world of terrorism and violence. And it's true, we need to provide safe limits for our children. But sometimes we don't know when to stop. I laugh when I remember my daughter's 8-year-old Girl Scout troop on an overnight campout with all moms in tow, hovering nearby during every activity. Whenever the girls roamed a bit, we followed. The moms spent the entire time chasing the girls with bug spray, sunscreen, and water bottles, reapplying and rehydrating them every five minutes "just in case." This was an 80-degree April day in flat Louisiana terrain! What message must we have been sending these girls? They just wanted to have fun and play!

But this trend goes beyond fears for physical safety; helicoptering often looks like a 24/7 rescue operation to block any type of pain, be it physical or emotional. Many of today's parents don't want their children to have to struggle, to be disappointed, to or experience feelings of failure. They intervene to rescue their kids from every problem, even though the children could (and should) handle the problem themselves. Perhaps it is because of our feel-good culture, in which we try to access a quick fix for almost every problem. Perhaps it is because we are overcompensating for the way in which we ourselves were parented. Perhaps we are worried about protecting our children's self-esteem at all costs, so we keep them from experiencing any type of failure. Perhaps we have bought into the cultural myth that we owe it to our children to give them an always comfortable, problem-free life when maybe that is not what they need at all. In reality what they need is to be prepared for the real world by the time they leave home.[27]

The trend of hovering is harmful in two major ways. First, this *parenting style harms us as parents*. If somehow parents have grown accustomed to believing that their kids should always be happy and worry-free, they have learned to transfer the worrying to themselves. In her book Levine cites research to support the fact that parents who tend to hover and rescue their kids have more worry, less life satisfaction, and less joy and content-ment regardless of whether their kids are succeeding or failing. When their children do well, parents worry how long it will last. When they do poorly, parents worry even more. It is a highly burdensome way to live, making us less effective as parents and as people.[28]

Second, it harms our children. The main harm that results is that our daugh-ters receive the message that "You are too incompetent to do this yourself." If I rush in and do something for my daughter, then I am in essence say-ing, "You don't have what it takes to do this on your own. Because of your incompetence, I have to do it for you." In the *Myth of the Perfect Girl*, Ana Homayoun bluntly writes that it is actually *disempowering* to micromanage our children, because then they will believe that their own parents think they are incompetent. If that is the case, how will they ever learn to believe in themselves and their abilities? If this happens, she grows up thinking "If my parents don't think I can handle this problem, then I must not be able to handle much of anything."[29] It is a sobering thought to realize that when I bend over backward to rescue my daughter from a problem (as I discussed previously), I am actually contributing to her self-doubt and lack of confi-dence. In reality, this is the opposite of what I want for her!

In addition, if we do everything for our daughters so that they never struggle or fail, they will not develop the skills or abilities they need to succeed in the adult world. If we want strong, resilient daughters, it is especially important that they learn to handle responsibility, think inde-pendently, and have good problem-solving skills so that they won't always need to rely on others to solve their problems for them. As summed up by Anea Bogue:

> Loving your children is about enabling them to become individuals who are no longer fully dependent on us by the time they become adults. This is what it takes to raise an empowered woman, one who is complete, strong and self-reliant because she believes in herself and her own ability to create what she wants and needs in the world.[30]

STRATEGIES FOR SWIMMING UPSTREAM: WHAT CAN PARENTS DO?

• **Let the consequences of her actions unfold.**

I so admire the philosophy in Wendy Mogel's *Blessing of a Skinned Knee* and *Blessing of B Minus* books. Her teachings remind parents that there is much to be gained from allowing their children to engage in healthy risk taking as well as letting them learn to solve their own problems and to find their way through life's typical difficulties when they make a mistake. I know it is frustrating to watch your daughter struggle when you could jump in and do the task for her (or make the problem go away). The next time that you want to do something for your daughter that she can probably do for herself, consider this question: *For everything you do for your child, ask yourself whether this action is going to lead her toward independence, competence, and confidence or if it will actually serve to undermine these goals.*[31] See Box 4.4 for an example.

- **Avoid excessive praise.**

If we want to learn to hover less and promote greater independence, we also need to back off from giving *too much* praise. Studies show that

---

Box 4.4: EXERCISE: WHAT WOULD YOU DO?

Your daughter has forgotten her homework on the kitchen table and you know she will get a zero for not turning it in. Your natural reaction may be to feel sorry for her, worry how upset she will be when she realizes that she forgot it, and stress about her lowered grade. You may want to snatch up the paper and rush to the school with it (or scan it and e-mail it to the teacher!). Or do you leave it there for her to find when she comes home from school?

    Pros of delivering the paper:

Daughter views you as an excellent personal assistant.
Daughter is spared a bad grade.
Daughter deserves a break because she has so much else to remember.

    Cons of delivering the paper:

She will not see the need to keep her homework organized and packed the night before.
She will continue to forget her homework.
She will continue to expect you to rescue her from mistakes.
She will blame you if you don't bring it next time.
She will learn the lesson that her mistakes don't have consequences.

In considering the pros and cons of the situation, which decision will lead your daughter toward greater independence, competence, and confidence?

---

general praise ("You're so smart! You're number one!" despite what she might have actually done) leads children to do three things: (1) They tune it out, questioning your genuineness and judgment. (2) They learn rely on your praise to feel good about themselves and can't function without positive feedback from everyone all the time. (3) Over time, they will learn to put in less effort. So your daughter will not benefit from general and excessive praise. This has crept into our culture as a requirement for parenting, when the reality is that promoting a child's self-esteem is not nearly as important as promoting her sense of connectedness, competence, and confidence.[32] Instead, give praise based on something specific, realistic, and based on her actual performance. Research shows that girls are more likely to receive general positive feedback—the kind that is not helpful (e.g., "What a pretty picture!"), while boys are more likely to receive specific and constructive feedback (e.g., "I like how you drew that dinosaur with such detail"). It is clear that in this scenario, a boy can improve in the future and will be motivated to keep trying because he was given constructive feedback—something he can take to heart, learn from, and implement in future drawings. There is not a lot a girl can learn from "You are the greatest artist ever!" She will wonder if you are really paying attention (she knows that she is not the greatest artist to ever grace the planet) and might not make as much of an effort in the future. Instead, try to offer specific praise for her actual efforts and avoid general labels.[33]

• **Give her ample opportunities to solve problems.**

When your daughter tells you about a problem, don't just jump in with the answer. If you tell her what to do (or even do it for her) she won't learn anything from the situation other than that she is dependent on others to fix things for her (remember the "rescue me" theme from Chapter One?). In addition, she will blame you if she follows your advice and it doesn't work out well for her. Instead, ask if *she* has any ideas for solving the problem. Help her implement problem-solving strategies (a helpful model for this is discussed in Chapter Eight). As hard as it is, deliberately refrain from giving answers but instead ask, "What are you going to do next? What needs to happen for you to solve this problem?" Offer your ideas as suggestions, not commands, but certainly offer direction if this is a scenario that might compromise her health or safety in any way. If it is a problem she should be able to handle on her own, let her test out her ideas. If her ideas do not work out, offer support, but allow her the space to pick herself up, dust herself off, and try again. This is how character and maturity develop.

- **Give her responsibility at home.**

In a recent Pew Research report, when parents were asked about their values, 94 percent named *responsibility* as the most important quality they wanted to teach their children.[34] An excellent way for your daughter to learn responsibility, maturity, and increased autonomy is for you to give her ample opportunities to assume responsibility at home. This means giving her regular chores starting at an early age. It's not just a matter of having an extra set of hands around the house (although that is indeed one benefit). Parents who involve their children in household chores actually help to build their kids' sense of competence. Your daughter will feel capable, as she will know that adults count on her to complete essential tasks for the home and that she is responsible enough to follow through with what is needed. She will also benefit from learning basic life skills that will carry her through to adulthood; she will feel strong as she starts to learn how to care for herself. Further, participating in household chores will help her to feel bonded and connected with her family. She will feel needed and valued when she is contributing to an overall team effort. In short, this will help her to develop a basic sense of security that is so important to overall self-esteem.

Finally, and highly relevant to this discussion, your daughter's participation in household chores will help her to feel less entitled and reduce your tendency to be overindulgent. If you worry that you are doing too much for your children, raising your expectations regarding their contributions at home is a way to begin to correct this problem. You don't want your daughter to learn that she is an esteemed guest in your home while she views you as the indentured servant. Instead, everyone in the home should function as a team and be expected to help out. Your daughter is far more likely to cultivate a sense of gratitude and empathy for others who do things for her when she is expected to contribute regularly to the well-being of others at home.[35]

> **MYTH: I have to involve my child in every enrichment activity in order to ensure her academic, professional, and personal success.**

Reality: This parenting style refers to what can be called "the manager"— where the parent's biggest role becomes managing the child's jam-packed schedule. Although today's girls might experience the "fear of missing something" if they put their phones down for too long, parents can become caught in the "fear of falling behind" if they don't push their kids to take advantage of every opportunity that comes along.

Ginsburg reflects this pressure that many of us feel:

> Unfortunately we may feel like we are swimming upstream because we receive carefully marketed messages that "good" parents expose children to every opportunity to excel, buy a plethora of enrichment tools, and ensure that children participate in a wide variety of activities. As a result, most of parent-child time is spent arranging specific activities or transporting children between those activities. . . . [They] fear they are running on a treadmill to keep up, yet they dare not slow their pace for fear that their children will fall behind.[36]

So we worry, can we be good parents even if we don't have our daughters involved in multiple activities? Even though we are frustrated and overstretched, juggling schedules, don't we owe this to our daughters? Questions whirl through our heads: *If my daughter doesn't do the extra soccer skills clinics, will she fall behind her teammates? Will I put my child at a disadvantage if she isn't in the school's cheer camp that is grooming fifth graders for future high school cheerleading tryouts? Will my daughter be less competitive on college applications if she hasn't excelled in at least one sport for ten years? What if she doesn't participate in traveling volleyball teams in addition to the school team? Is it okay that she missed the out-of-state dance competitions? Will she make the community performing arts shows if she hasn't taken private voice lessons and acting classes? Does she need tutoring over the summer to pull her B's up to A's next year? Does she need to do extra community service hours in order to keep up? Will someone please tell me how much is enough?*

On a personal note, several years ago I sat at a meeting with a group of moms of young elementary-age daughters. One of them suggested that we go around the circle and each name all of the activities in which our daughters were currently involved. I began to squirm in my seat, very uncomfortable with the implications of this discussion: if my daughter's list is short, am I an inadequate parent? What is wrong with her if she isn't involved in as many activities as the other girls? Does the parent with the longest list "win"?

The reality is that there is no real evidence to support the idea that the more time a girl spends in structured activities the more successful she will be.[37] In fact, this type of overinvolvement can potentially be detrimental to her overall development, especially if she is exhausted and your family is stretched to the point of breaking due to maxed out schedules and no free time. If you are feeling this way, be reassured that this pressure parents are experiencing is a relatively new cultural phenomenon that is not based on any scientific research—there is no formula that saying that if one activity is good, then ten must be better. Even while parents recognize that this whirlwind of activities may be causing them stress, it is concerning that the pressures have only worsened in recent years. Over the years that this "hurried child" and "overscheduled kid" trend has evolved (starting with David Elkind's *Hurried Child*, 1981), parenting experts have stressed the potential harms that can arise from pushing too many structured activities and not allowing enough time for unstructured reflection and play.[38]

It seems that there are really two issues operating here: one is related to the intense pressure girls feel to excel and achieve. I addressed this issue in Chapter One and will revisit it in Chapter Seven, as we discuss girls' academic and extracurricular performance pressures. As stated previously, many girls start to believe that with the many opportunities available to them, they must excel at *all* of them. And when parents are pushing this need to excel, it is an uphill climb for all. In some cases, the "manager parent" morphs into the "tiger mom"— a parenting term referring to the mother who places constant pressure on her child to perform at the highest levels despite what the child might actually want or need.[39]

The second and equally important problem to consider regarding the price of overscheduling and managing is the cost to *families (See Box 4.5)*. Jennifer Senior writes about this issue in her book *All Joy and No Fun: The Paradox of Modern Parenthood,* where she considers the impact of modern overscheduling not just on children but also on parents.

Box 4.5: PARENTS AS MANAGERS

As you consider where you stand on this issue, consider the following questions:

As a parent, is one of your most time-consuming jobs keeping up with your child's calendar and driving her from place to place?

Do you have any time at all each day just for yourself, or do your kids' activities supersede your own?

Have you taken the time to consider if this type of schedule is really what you want for your family?

She writes about the mindset of today's middle-class parents:

> As far as children are concerned, there is no such thing as excess. If improving their children's lives means running themselves ragged—and *thinking* themselves ragged—then so be it. Parents will do it. Their children deserve nothing less.[40]

I can identify with Madeline Levine's thoughts: "Being a mom is a tough enough challenge without the added stress of premature concern about college, distress about each and every grade, a calendar of child-centered activities that would challenge any cruise director, and a pervasive sense that one is *still* not doing enough."[41]

I was well aware of these facts about overscheduling when I sat in that "mommy trap" moment describe above, but I still felt the pressure, the questioning, "Are we really doing enough? Am *I* enough?" And of course the answer is yes. I had chosen to limit my daughter's activities both for her sake (so that she could have down time just to play and to relax) and for mine (I wanted my family to have time together each day and I know I can't function well if I am driving frantically across town all afternoon and weekend). But every family is different; I realize that some girls and their parents may thrive on the stimulation that multiple activities can provide. The point here isn't to judge; the point is to stop for a minute and reflect that you *do* have a choice in whether you want to go with this flow or consciously swim upstream against it. It is the process of being mindful—of reflecting on your core values and then choosing—that is most important.

STRATEGIES FOR SWIMMING UPSTREAM: WHAT CAN PARENTS DO?

- **Slow down and let your daughter play.**

Think about all that your daughter is learning about herself, how much she is growing and changing, and how much she has to face in a typical day. Does she have ample time for reflecting on all this, for figuring out who she is becoming? When JoAnn Deak writes about her number one wish for girls, she says that it is for them to have time to slow down, to have time to think, to be, to be heard, and to hear.[42] This slower-paced life can't occur when a girl is too busy and too exhausted. When she is younger, give her time to have unstructured play. When she is a teen, give her a different type of play—give her the space to dream.

- **Honor the gift of family time.**

As you learn to prioritize time at home, try your best to keep family rituals in place (e.g., holiday celebrations, birthdays, attending religious services together, family movie nights). Even though your daughter may try to resist these rituals as she grows older, she will still need and secretly cherishes these celebrations. She needs the structure and consistency that they provide while everything else in her life seems to be changing all at once. See Box 4.6 for ideas about the importance of a family dinner ritual.

SOME FINAL THOUGHTS: PARENT SELF-CARE

As is evident from this chapter, parenting can be exhausting, and although it may be highly rewarding in the long run, it does not provide very many short-term rewards.[44] In fact, a recent Pew Research report indicates that parents say their time caring for their children is much more exhausting than their paid work. On the positive side, when comparing child care and paid work, parents were twice as likely to report that their child-care experiences were very meaningful to them. Mothers

---

Box 4.6: THE FAMILY DINNER

Even if it seems insurmountable to streamline your family life, start with one of the simplest rituals of all: the family dinner. There is so much research to support the importance of having dinner as a family. Case in point: families who have dinner together at least five nights a week are far more likely to have children who have high-quality relationships with their parents and who are more successful (e.g., they are less likely to experiment with cigarettes, alcohol or other illegal drugs, they do better in school, and they have fewer problems in general) than those who eat together only one or two nights a week.[43] Even if five nights a week is out of reach, start where you can. Get everyone involved with the preparation and cleanup. And try to make it fun so that everyone will want to do it again.

As discussed earlier in the section titled Love and Connect, being "home alone" together does not really contribute to the type of family time that is beneficial to your daughter's resilience. As much as possible, family rituals and especially family meals should be unplugged, offline time for all. As discussed in Chapter One, with some planning and self-discipline, it really *is* possible to have some technology-free time together!

are especially likely to wear themselves out with parenting; in the report, mothers were more likely than fathers to say that they were exhausted from spending time with children, housework, paid work, and even from leisure activities (one wonders if moms were counting their own leisure activities and not their chauffeur role in transporting kids from one leisure activity to the next).[45]

Obviously this exhaustion isn't good for us; we are already worn out and tired, especially if we are trying to keep up with current parenting trends, and then our daughters reach adolescence! While it may not be as physically tiring as parenting a younger child, it can be far more demanding in terms of your mental and emotional endurance. The first thing we need to recognize, then, is that *this is hard and we need to take care of ourselves*. We can make choices to simplify our lives, as outlined earlier in the chapter. We can say no to the frenzy of activity, recognizing the difference between what is mandatory and what can be unhealthy for the "hurried child" and her equally hurried parent! As her parent, you need to be the center of stability and consistency in your home, even while everything else is spinning around you.

The second thing we can do is to separate a bit; you are still connected to her, but your daughter is becoming her own person as she grows into adolescence. Really assess how much of your identity is tied up with your daughter; when you step back and look at your own life, how much of how you see yourself is defined by being her parent? If you tend to overidentify with your daughter, her natural drive to pull away from you will be especially painful. She is not doing this to hurt you, she is doing it to create her own identity, but the pain can be searing. It is as if you were losing a piece of your soul as she becomes her own person apart from you.[46]

In response, we have to make sure that we start pouring time and investment back into our own lives or we can begin to feel needy and empty. Instead of focusing on losing a part of yourself, turn your energy toward creating your own fulfilling life that isn't dependent on her moods or performance on any given day. You are now freed up to have interests of your own that you can enjoy. She will see you as someone who has her own life; it isn't all about *her* anymore. Of course this does not mean that you should neglect your daughter. I think it is abundantly clear how much she needs you. What I mean is that as she pulls away, spending more time with her peers, you might experience obvious gaps in your life. You can fill these gaps with self-care routines that make you more content and satisfied, and this in turn enables you to become a more effective parent (see Box 4.7 for ideas on self-care).

This is also essential because, as you will discover in Chapter 8 on coping strategies, she needs coping and problem-solving skills to handle life demands successfully. If she doesn't see you implementing

Box 4.7: PARENT SELF-CARE

"Self-care" is a popular term these days, but few of us really put it into practice. We might have nonwork activities that take up a lot of our time (Facebook, surfing the Internet aimlessly, and so on), but are they truly activities that restore our energy and keep us refreshed and renewed? It is important to try to find some activities that do not drain you further but rather replenish you, where you actually feel better when you have completed them rather than just feeling further behind on your to-do list. These will look different for everyone, but here are a few ideas:

Lunch with a friend
A run or workout
Yoga
A scented bubble bath
A long nap
A quiet time of prayer and meditation
Listening to relaxing music
A date night with your partner
Lessons to learn something new (tennis, photography)

It is important to have a repertoire of self-care activities and to schedule them often. Put them on your calendar much as you would any other important event!

these same skills in your own life, it will be hard to convince her of their benefit. Instead, if she sees you as an adult with healthy coping skills that include restorative self-care activities, she will be more likely to develop them as well. After all, the staggering truth is that *you* are the greatest influence in her life. It is important that we model in our own lives what we hope that our daughters will live out in their own journey.

In sum, remember that you are called to be the stable foundation that your daughter can run to when she feels as if her world is caving in. You are her source of sustenance and nurturance to which she will return again and again. To be this rock of stability, you need to take time to keep yourself well cared for and strong. As we know, no one will do this *for* us; we have to provide it for ourselves. You are worth the self-care, and your daughter's resilience depends in large part upon it.

CONCLUSION

The purpose of this chapter was to review basic parenting strategies that form the foundation for everything else that we do. We discussed three essentials: mindfulness, loving and connecting, and providing consequences and limits. We also reviewed some current parenting trends that tend to knock today's parents off balance. If we don't pay attention, before we know it we'll have become less mindful, too permissive, or too controlling. Therefore the point is that it is necessary to make a conscious decision. As I will continue to emphasize throughout this book, the current culture can often be toxic for our girls, so sometimes you are going to have to decide to go against the cultural grain, to swim upstream, and to make an extra effort not to spend your energies on comparing yourself with other parents. You have to make a commitment to what you want in the long term for your daughter instead of what might be popular in the moment. You can decide to be mindful, to stay in the moment without overreacting. You can choose to do what it takes to love and connect despite today's obstacles to this goal. You can decide to remain diligent in saying no when needed, even if this makes you unpopular with your daughter for the time being. You can decide to be willing to step back and allow your daughter to struggle at times even when you want to rescue her, and you can choose to be consistent in delivering consequences even when it is inconvenient. You can also choose to take steps to simplify your life and your daughter's schedule so that you have room to breathe. This is hard, often countercultural work but well worth it. Keep reading to discover additional parenting strategies specifically tailored to enhancing girls' resilience to the three cultural expectations we covered in Chapter One: appearance (Chapter Five), attention (Chapter Six) and accomplishments (Chapter Seven). Positive coping strategies will also be provided (Chapter Eight).

NOTES

1. Duncan, L. J., Coatsworth, D. J., & Greenberg, M. T. (2009). A model of mindful parenting: Implications for parent-child relationships and prevention research. *Child Clinical and Family Psychology Review, 12*, 255–270.; Tsabary, S. (2010). The conscious parent. Vancouver, BC: Namaste; Shapiro, S., & White, C. (2014). Mindful discipline: A loving approach to setting limits and raising emotionally intelligent children. Oakland, CA: New Harbinger.
2. Ibid.
3. Greenspan-Goldberg, A. (2011). *What do you expect? She's a teenager!: A hope and happiness guide for moms with daughters ages 11–19*. Napierville, IL: Sourcebooks.
4. Hemmen, L. (2012). *Parenting a teen girl*. Oakland, CA: New Harbinger.

5. Levine, M. (2012). *Teach your children well*. New York: HarperCollins.
6. Baumrind, D. (1966). Effects of authoritative parental control on child behavior, *Child Development*, 37(4), 887–907.
7. Hemmen, L. (2012). *Parenting a teen girl*. Oakland, CA: New Harbinger; Oestricher, M., & Lindsey, B. (2012). *A parent's guide to understanding teenage girls: Remembering who she was, celebrating who she's becoming*. Loveland, CO: Simply Youth Ministry; Deak, J. (2003). *Girls will be girls: Raising confident and courageous daughters*. New York: Hyperion.
8. Senior, J. (2014). *All joy and no fun: The paradox of modern parenthood*. New York: HarperCollins.
9. Steiner-Adair, C. (2013). *The big disconnect: Protecting childhood and family relationships in the digital age*. New York: HarperCollins; Taffel, R. (2005). *Childhood unbound: The powerful new parent approach that gives our 21st century kids the authority, love, and listening they need to thrive*. New York: Free Press.
10. Steiner-Adair, C. (2013). *The big disconnect: Protecting childhood and family relationships in the digital age*. New York: HarperCollins.
11. The 2013 Digital Future Report (2013). USC Annenberg School Center for the Digital Future. Retrieved from http://www.digitalcenter.org/wp-content/uploads/2013/06/2013-Report.pdf
12. Allen, J., & Allen, C.W. (2009). Escaping the endless adolescence. New York: Ballantine; Deak, J. (2003). *Girls will be girls: Raising confident and courageous daughters*. New York: Hyperion; Ginsburg, K. (2011). *Building resilience in children and teens: Giving kids roots and wings*. Elk Grove, IL: American Academy of Pediatrics.
13. Straus, M. B. (2006). *Adolescent girls in crisis*. New York: Norton.
14. Greenspan-Goldberg, A. (2011). *What do you expect? She's a teenager!: A hope and happiness guide for moms with daughters ages 11–19*. Napierville, IL: Sourcebooks.; See also Ginsburg, K. (2011). *Building resilience in children and teens: Giving kids roots and wings*. Elk Grove, IL: American Academy of Pediatrics.
15. Hemmen, L. (2012). *Parenting a teen girl*. Oakland, CA: New Harbinger; Deak, J. (2003). *Girls will be girls: Raising confident and courageous daughters*. New York: Hyperion.
16. Greenspan, L., & Deardorff, J. (2014). *The new puberty: How to navigate early development in today's girls*. Emmaus, PA: Rodale; Ginsburg, K. (2011). *Building resilience in children and teens: Giving kids roots and wings*. Elk Grove, IL: American Academy of Pediatrics.
17. Hemmen, L. (2012). *Parenting a teen girl*. Oakland, CA: New Harbinger.
18. Hemmen, L. (2012). *Parenting a teen girl*. Oakland, CA: New Harbinger; Deak, J. (2003). *Girls will be girls: Raising confident and courageous daughters*. New York: Hyperion; Ginsburg, K. (2011). *Building resilience in children and teens: Giving kids roots and wings*. Elk Grove, IL: American Academy of Pediatrics.
19. Mogel, W. (2008). *The blessing of a skinned knee: Using Jewish teachings to raise resilient teenagers*. New York: Scribner; Mogel, W. (2011). *The blessing of a B minus: Using Jewish teachings to raise resilient teenagers*. New York: Scribner.
20. Ginsburg, K. (2011). *Building resilience in children and teens: Giving kids roots and wings* (p. 290). Elk Grove, IL: American Academy of Pediatrics.
21. Deak, J. (2003). *Girls will be girls: Raising confident and courageous daughters*. New York: Hyperion.
22. Ginsburg, K. (2011). Building resilience in children and teens: Giving kids roots and wings. Elk Grove, IL: American Academy of Pediatrics.

23. Hemmen, L. (2012). *Parenting a teen girl*. Oakland, CA: New Harbinger; Ginsburg, K. (2011). *Building resilience in children and teens: Giving kids roots and wings*. Elk Grove, IL: American Academy of Pediatrics.

24. Fosco, G. M., Stormshak, E. A., Dishion, T. J., & Winter, C. E. (2012). Family relationships and parental monitoring during middle school as predictors of early adolescent problem behavior. *Journal of Clinical Child and Adolescent Psychology, 41,* 202–213.

25. Allen, J. & Allen, C.W. (2009). *Escaping the endless adolescence*. New York: Ballantine.

26. Masarie, K. (2009). *Raising our daughters: The ultimate guide for healthy girls and thriving families*. Portland, OR: Family Empowerment Network.

27. Bogue, A. (2014). *9 ways we're screwing up our girls and how we can stop: A guide to helping girls reach their highest potential*. Nashville, TN: Dunham.

28. Levine, M. (2012). *Teach your children well*. New York: HarperCollins.

29. Homayoun, A. (2013). *The myth of the perfect girl: Helping our daughters find authentic success and happiness in school and life*. New York: Penguin.

30. Bogue, A. (2014). *9 ways we're screwing up our girls and how we can stop: A guide to helping girls reach their highest potential* (p. 51). Nashville, TN: Dunham.

31. Allen, J., & Allen, C.W. (2009). *Escaping the endless adolescence*. New York: Ballantine.

32. Masarie, K. (2009). *Raising our daughters: The ultimate guide for healthy girls and thriving families*. Portland, OR: Family Empowerment Network.

33. Deak, J. (2003). *Girls will be girls: Raising confident and courageous daughters*. New York: Hyperion; Dweck, C. (2006). *Mindset: The new psychology of success*. New York: Ballantine.

34. American Trends Panel. (2014). Pew Research Center. Retrieved from: http://www.pewresearch.org/fact-tank/2014/09/18/families-may-differ-but-they-share-common-values-on-parenting/

35. Darling, N. (2011, Feb. 15). Chores are good for kids. [Web blog]. Retrieved from http://www.psychologytoday.com/blog/thinking-about-kids/201102/chores-are-good-kids

36. Ginsburg, K. (2011). *Building resilience in children and teens: Giving kids roots and wings* (p. 50). Elk Grove, IL: American Academy of Pediatrics.

37. Levine, M. (2012). *Teach your children well*. New York: HarperCollins; Ginsburg, K. (2011). *Building resilience in children and teens: Giving kids roots and wings*. Elk Grove, IL: American Academy of Pediatrics; Senior, J. (2014). *All joy and no fun: The paradox of modern parenthood*. New York: HarperCollins.

38. Elkind, D. (2006). *The hurried child—25th anniversary edition*. Boston: De Capo.

39. Chua, A. (2011). *Battle hymn of the tiger mother*. New York: Penguin.

40. Senior, J. (2014). *All joy and no fun: The paradox of modern parenthood*. New York: HarperCollins.

41. Levine, M. (2012). *Teach your children well* (p. 17). New York: HarperCollins.

42. Deak, J. (2003). *Girls will be girls: Raising confident and courageous daughters*. New York: Hyperion.

43. CASAColumbia. (2012). The importance of family dinners, VIII. Retrieved from http://www.casacolumbia.org/addiction-research/reports/importance-of-family-dinners-2012

44. Senior, J. (2014). *All joy and no fun: The paradox of modern parenthood*. New York: HarperCollins Publishers.

45. Wang, W, (2013). Parents' time with kids more rewarding than paid work—and more exhausting. Pew Research. Retrieved from http://www.pewsocial-trends.org/2013/10/08/parents-time-with-kids-more-rewarding-than-paid-work-and-more-exhausting/

46. Hemmen, L. (2012). *Parenting a teen girl*. Oakland, CA: New Harbinger.

CHAPTER FIVE

Resilience Dimension Two

Developing a Positive Body Image

You have probably heard your daughter complain "Why am I so fat?" "Are my thighs bigger than hers?" "Why is my chest so flat?" or "Is my stomach sticking out?" It's often hard to know how to answer these questions to her satisfaction. Although the rapid weight gains of puberty and changes in body shape may be shocking to her, they should come as no surprise to us from a developmental perspective; up to 50 percent of a girl's adult weight is gained during this brief period of time in her life. In fact, the average weight gain during early adolescence is between 30 and 50 pounds—mostly in the hips, thighs, and buttocks (exactly the areas where she does not want to gain weight!). Interestingly, about 40 to 70 percent of adolescent girls say they are dissatisfied with two or more of their body parts (most often the very areas I just listed).[1] So if these changes are normal, why are they so hard for adolescent girls to deal with (and for that matter, for us as parents)? This chapter will help you to explore the answer to this question and offer you a wealth of strategies you can use to help your daughter swim upstream against body dissatisfaction by developing a positive body image.

As we have seen, today's girls are increasingly bombarded with media images of thin-beautiful-hot-sexy women, and girls often hold these images up as the standard they believe they must meet. As reviewed in Chapter Two, just at the time they are facing the physical changes of puberty and comparing themselves with others, they also start to count their appearance, weight, and shape as the most central aspects of their identities. Instead of *having* a body, she *is* her body, so that if she perceives that something is wrong with her *appearance*, she feels that something is fundamentally wrong with her overall *self*. She is always asking herself *"Do I measure up? Am I really good enough?"* Unfortunately her answer to this question is often a resounding no.

THE THIN-BEAUTIFUL-HOT-SEXY IDEAL

Body image experts turn to *sociocultural theory* to explain why girls and women are so likely to be dissatisfied with their appearance, weight, and shape.[2] It is important for us to step back and consider why it should be seen as *normal* for females to be as dissatisfied with their bodies as they are. Take a moment to ask yourself how many women you know who are truly happy with their appearance. This number is likely to be close to zero, because cultural pressures tell us that girls and women should focus their time, energy, and money on achieving the largely unattainable thin-beautiful-hot-sexy ideal represented by media images (magazines, television, movies, the Internet, and ads from the fashion industry). Because many girls look to these images as standards of comparison, they come to believe that (1) they *should* look like this and, if they did, they would be happier and (2) practically any girl can look like this if she works hard enough and buys the right products and merchandise. So these girls believe not only that they should attain the ideal but also that something is wrong with them if they are somehow unable to do achieve this goal.

This is where the problem comes in. The thin-beautiful-hot-sexy ideal does not exist in reality. All images are digitally altered; they are enhanced through lighting and professional makeup techniques, and most models admit that even *they* don't look exactly like the images of themselves that they see in magazines. In addition, today's ideal contains many contradictory features that are virtually impossible for any one person to acquire naturally (see Box 5.1).

Box 5.1: A MEDIA BROWSING EXERCISE

With your daughter, go to a bookstore and browse through popular girls' and women's magazines (or, alternatively, search the magazines' websites). What messages stand out for girls about the way they should look and act? Are these messages limiting for girls? Why or why not? Next, try to locate some resources that have been developed to empower girls (e.g., New Moon Girls, girlsinc-online.org, Discovery Girls) and contrast the differences between the two types of resources. What do you notice?

- She is tall, has white, flawless skin (or is light-skinned for women of color), and is extremely thin.
- She is curvy, has large breasts, and a prominent backside.
- She is muscular, physically fit, and angular.
- She is aloof and sophisticated.
- She is hot, sexy, and flirtatious.

No woman anywhere could meet this standard, but somehow there is pressure for girls and women to try to attain this current ideal. Research clearly shows that the more time girls spend viewing thin-beautiful-hot-sexy media images, the more likely they will be to have negative body image. This is especially true for fashion magazines, as many studies have demonstrated a direct relationship between the time spent viewing thin-beautiful-hot-sexy magazine advertisements and girls' negative views of themselves.[3] Most recently this same effect has also been demonstrated through social media—the more time girls reported spending on Facebook, the more likely they were to have negative body image.[4] It seems that when girls spend hours poring over pictures, comparing themselves with how many "friends" other people have, and obsessing over how many "likes" a particular picture or post has received on Facebook, they learn to feel dissatisfied with themselves. As stated previously, this is of concern because they don't just feel badly about their *appearance*, they feel badly about who they are *as people*.

THE TRIPLE INFLUENCE

Sociocultural theory teaches us that although the media may be like a conveyor belt that never stops delivering the same message, these pressures can be buffered by the influence of friends and family. So there are three primary influences (media, friends, and family) that combine to play a role in your daughter's development, for better or for worse.[5] Consider the following influences that her *friends* could have on the development of her body image:

- Do her friends frequently discuss dieting and weight loss?
- Do her friends consistently compare themselves with others or focus on appearance in evaluating themselves?
- Do her friends make fun of others about their appearance?
- Do her friends often put themselves down and criticize themselves regarding their appearance, weight, or shape?

- Are she and her friends primarily involved in activities that emphasize body shape, weight, or appearance (e.g., dance, gymnastics, cheerleading)?

These types of behaviors reinforce the message of the media that a girl's value will come from her ability to match the thin-beautiful-hot-sexy ideal. Strategies for managing the influences of your daughter's friends will be reviewed later in the chapter.

What *parents* say and do also matters greatly in terms of how your daughter will absorb these pressures. In other words, your influence will be a filter through which she interprets messages from the media as well as from her friends. I will focus on how to promote positive body image in the section on resilience strategies. For now, consider some of the following messages you might be sending to your daughter:

- Are you frequently dieting or talking about the need to diet?
- Do you discuss others' appearance, weight, or shape in front of your daughter?
- Do you say that you have been "good" after a day of restricting your eating?
- Do you confide in your daughter that you need to avoid certain events (like pool parties, etc.) because you have gained weight?
- Do you in any way tie your approval of your daughter to her weight and appearance?
- Do you make comments to your daughter like "Are you sure you should be eating that?"
- Dads, do you criticize women's weight or appearance in front of your daughter?
- Do you ever suggest that you and your daughter should go on a diet together?

It is also important for you to gain awareness of the factors that influenced your own body image development. Until you are aware of the messages you received from media, family, and peers, it will be harder for you to recognize how these factors might also be influencing your daughter. See Box 5.2 for a helpful self-awareness exercise.

To summarize, media, peers, and family all have a strong influence on how your daughter develops her sense of self and how large a role her appearance, weight, and shape will play in determining her overall self-concept. As parents, we need to be aware that the messages we send can buffer any negative pressures conveyed by the larger culture. This is the good news. The bad

Box 5.2: SELF-EXPLORATION

These questions will help you explore the influences that have had an impact on the development of your own body image. This exploration will increase your awareness and help you become a more positive influence for your daughter.[6]

- Family and peer influences
  1. Overall, how did you feel about your body as a child and adolescent?
  2. What are some things you remember about your own mother's attitude toward her body? What were her eating habits like? How did this affect you?
  3. What messages did your mother give you about the importance of appearance, weight, and shape to a woman's worth? How did this affect you?
  4. What messages did your father give you about the importance of appearance, weight, and shape to a woman's worth? How did this affect you?
  5. What messages did you receive from your siblings about your appearance, weight, or shape? How did this affect you?
  6. Do you remember any comments about your appearance, weight, or shape that came from male peers in childhood or adolescence? What about female peers? How did these comments affect you?
  7. Do you remember any comments about your body made by teachers, coaches, or other significant adults in your life? How did this affect you?

- Media and Other Influences
  8. What are some movies or television programs you viewed during your childhood or adolescence that influenced your view of the importance of women's beauty or of a particular type of beauty?
  9. How interested were you in fashion and style during your adolescent years? How did this interest influence what you thought you should look like?
  10. What magazines did you read during childhood and adolescence? What messages did you receive from these publications? How did these messages influence your idea of what you thought you should look like?
  11. What were other influences on your development that might have affected the way you viewed your appearance, weight, or shape? How did they influence your view of the importance of physical attractiveness for women?

news is that we can unknowingly reinforce negative messages, resulting in potential harms to our daughters, as outlined in the next section.

WHAT ARE THE PROBLEMS THAT CAN OCCUR?

It is tempting to think that there is no point in worrying about whether our daughters believe they are thin and attractive enough—after all, if dissatisfaction has become normalized in our culture, what is the harm? However commonplace, girls' dissatisfaction regarding weight, shape, or appearance can be particularly destructive during the preadolescent and adolescent years. As your daughter listens to media messages and has them reinforced through family and friends, she begins to internalize the thin-beautiful-hot-sexy ideal; she adopts it as her own personal standard for her value as a person and then does whatever it takes to try to achieve it.[7] When she internalizes the ideal, research shows the following potential negative outcomes.

- **Negative body image and low self-esteem**

As girls experience weight gain and physical changes during the transition to puberty, their body satisfaction decreases, resulting in overall lowered self-esteem. We know that this happens to boys too, but for them physical appearance affects self-esteem far less than it does for girls; a boy can dislike his appearance but still feel good about himself overall because of other abilities or traits. This is rarely the case for girls.[8]

- **Dieting and unhealthy weight-loss behaviors**

When a girl has a negative body image, she will look for a way to improve her appearance so as to move closer to the thin-beautiful-hot-sexy ideal. Therefore internalization of the thin ideal is a lead risk factor for dieting and other unhealthy weight-loss routines, like fasting, skipping meals, overexercising, laxative abuse, vomiting, and binge eating. In one national study of high school girls, 59 percent reported that they wanted to lose weight and over 50 percent were currently dieting.[9] Dieting is particularly harmful to adolescent girls, who are still growing and may deplete their bodies of needed nutrients just when they are most in need of strength.[10] In addition, research shows that dieting leads to weight gain in adolescence, and girls who diet frequently are far more likely to end up having a slowed metabolism and increased likelihood of binge eating. In fact, a startling 20 to 60 percent of girls report that they have engaged in at least one episode of binge eating.[11]

- **Appearance surveillance**

Girls who have negative body image tend to hold back from fully engaging in life; instead of dancing freely at a school dance, they worry about how others are viewing their bodies. Instead of being excited because they are invited to a party, they worry about how they will look or if anyone will notice that they have gained weight. As reviewed in Chapter Three, this belief in an *imaginary audience (believing that everyone is staring at you and thinking about you as much as you are thinking about yourself)*[12] is normal for preadolescent and adolescent girls, but girls who have negative body image take this fear to the extreme. They may develop anxiety about social evaluation and constantly be concerned that they are being checked out by others. This self-objectification—watching themselves as though they were being observed, evaluating themselves against other girls, looking at their bodies in terms of how they look to others instead of how they feel themselves—can lead to lowered self-esteem, body shame, and a decreased ability to simply enjoy everyday activities.[13] Remember Maggie in Box 3.1 of Chapter Three? Imagine focusing on a blemish on your face while you are having an important conversation. It is nearly impossible to attend to what the other person is saying and feeling when you are thinking about a blemish on your nose, wondering, "Is she noticing my zit? Does she think I have bad skin? Does she think I am ugly?" Girls who have these thoughts running through their heads are not free to relax and concentrate on the task at hand; they are always distracted and self-conscious.

- **Depression, eating disorders, and other problems**

It is no surprise then, that internalization of the thin-beautiful-hot-sexy ideal is also related to an increased risk for depression in girls (see Chapter Three) and has associations with early smoking, elective cosmetic surgery, and full-syndrome eating disorders such as anorexia and bulimia (see also Chapter Three).

WHAT IS POSITIVE BODY IMAGE AND WHY IS IT IMPORTANT FOR GIRLS' RESILIENCE?

Up to this point I have discussed what can go *wrong* for many girls as they receive negative cultural messages about their value. Now I would like to turn to what happens when things go *right*: what are things you can do to help your daughter reject the cultural ideal and to value herself for all of her strengths, not just her weight, shape, or appearance? To be resilient, a girl needs to value herself in all life dimensions, not just on the basis of her physical appearance. She will need supportive people in her life who send positive messages about the person she is becoming. She will also need the tools to understand and resist media messages designed to cause her to feel unhappy with her appearance. To be resilient and have a positive body image, your daughter also needs to develop healthy eating and exercise routines in a culture that sends her messages to constantly diet and exercise primarily for the purpose of purging calories. In the next section, I will build on these goals by providing specific strategies that will better enable your daughter to develop a positive body image.

Strategies for Swimming Upstream: What Can Parents Do?

The safe haven: Make your home a "no-teasing-about-appearance" zone.

First and foremost, a girl needs a family that provides her with a supportive, warm relationship filled with open communication. This is essential during the adolescent period when so many changes are occurring in her life, especially with her body. As reviewed in Chapter Four, with all of the negative influences swirling around her, your daughter needs a place where she feels safe and comfortable. In her book *Odd Girl Out*,[14] Rachel Simmons describes this parenting practice as making your home a *sanctuary* for your daughter, a *safe haven* from the storm around her. To create this haven, your daughter needs caring adults who allow her to talk, provide feedback, and validate her opinions and ideas. She also needs a place where she receives reassurance, affirming reactions, and a sense of approval—one that is not tied to her appearance or accomplishments. To make this happen, make your home a place where there is no teasing about weight, shape, or appearance. Teasing by siblings and especially brothers can have a profound effect on your daughter's perception of her appearance. Even when brothers make fun of other girls (e.g., "Look at those thunder thighs!"), it can cause your daughter to ask "Do other boys think that way about *me*? Should I be embarrassed about how I look?" In fact, many individuals with eating disorders report that they were teased about their weight by family members when they were younger. As much as possible, try to communicate that *negative comments about weight and appearance will not be tolerated in your home*. It will most likely happen elsewhere, but at least let your home be one place where teasing does not occur. With this foundation, a girl can feel grounded and safe to process her feelings and to discuss her concerns about her changing body. This kind of environment is where the sparks of resilience begin to develop and flourish.

Moms, You are your daughter's model: Examine your own attitudes and behaviors.

Mom, your daughter is watching you and will absorb your attitudes and behaviors about your body and appearance. While most of us would not knowingly criticize our daughters' bodies or appearance in a harmful way, many of us don't realize that it can be just as damaging if we do these same things to ourselves. If you are chronically dieting and criticizing your appearance, your daughter will likely do the same. Does your daughter see you looking in the mirror, shaking your head in disappointment? She will learn from you that it is normal to criticize your own body and to be openly dissatisfied with yourself. If you are frequently seeking the next fad diet, she will also learn that the answer to her problems is to diet and that she needs to lose weight to feel okay about herself. On the flip side, if you have a positive attitude toward your body, refrain from overly emphasizing your appearance, eat healthily, and exercise moderately, then your daughter will be far more likely to maintain body esteem and less likely to have problems in this area.

An essential factor to consider is not what you say or even what you do; it is what your daughter *notices* you doing. If you are skipping meals, fasting, or exercising excessively, it is hard for her not to notice. If your daughter observes these behaviors in you, she is far more likely to use these unhealthy weight-loss behaviors herself. This is especially critical during the transition to puberty; she will be more attuned to how you handle changes in your own body. Do you complain about weight gains, wrinkles, or changes in body shape that come with life transitions such as pregnancy or menopause? During adolescence, she too is experiencing weight gains, skin changes, and drastic changes in body shape; she will be particularly influenced by how she sees you handling your personal transitions. It is important for you to speak positively about these changes in yourself. In her book *"I'm Like SO Fat!"* Diane Neumark-Sztainer challenges us to do whatever it takes to have our daughters view us as healthy eaters instead of dieters.[15] Consider the exercise in Box 5.3 to provide some ideas.

Neumark-Sztainer suggests the following exercise: describe your weight, shape, and appearance in three words. Would you want your daughter to describe herself in this same way? Why or why not?

Take a moment to view the Dove video "Beauty Sketches" at https://www.youtube.com/watch?v=XpaOjMXyJGk and further reflect on the way you describe yourself.

Next, to really underscore the power of your attitude about your appearance and how this affects your daughter, see the new video "Legacy," part of the Dove Campaign for Real Beauty: http://www.dove.us/Our-Mission/Real-Beauty/default.aspx?gclid=CN7arfC8kcECFYdlfgodT64AKQ

I would like to conclude this section for mothers with a quote from Robyn Silverman's *Good Girls Don't Get Fat: How Weight Obsession Is Messing Up Our Girls and How We Can Help Them Thrive Despite It*:

> Your daughter needs to hear that you think you believe in yourself, your worth, your body, and your mind. You are modeling the self-image that she will absorb! . . . Commit to saying one thing a day about something you like about your appearance. Even if you don't believe it at first, do it anyway. It will help your daughter, and it may just help you too. (Silverman, 2010, pp. 66–67)

Summary Checklist for Moms

- *Avoid dieting or unhealthy dieting behaviors.*
- *Avoid talking excessively about your weight or appearance; instead focus on other topics.*
- *Avoid talking about others' weight or appearance; instead talk about their other strengths.*
- *Engage in regular physical activity you enjoy.*
- *Let your daughter see you making healthful food choices.*

Dads, you're important too: Stay close and monitor your comments about women.

The preceding section was geared to mothers, but dads are not off the hook in this area. As girls reach early adolescence, many dads who were previously close to their daughters tend to back away, feeling awkward and uncomfortable with the changes in their bodies and not knowing how to respond when they bring up topics like their emerging sexuality or body image. A note of encouragement: Dads, if your daughter has been invited to sit on your lap all her life, now is not the time to push her off just because she has grown a little (or a lot!). She will take this as a rejection of her developing body, and she is looking for your approval particularly during this time in her life. Stay close even though it is an awkward period in your relationship, as she will definitely notice if you seem to pull away. Make a conscious effort to spend one-on-one time with her so that she feels valued and loved. If she doesn't perceive that she has your approval, she will seek it from other men and will try to please them instead. That is not what most fathers want for their daughters. In contrast, consider all of the positive benefits that result when girls maintain a positive relationship with their fathers (see Box 5.4).

Dads can also monitor the comments they make about women in general. These can be negative or positive, but they are harmful either way if they convey the message that the only thing of value in women is their physical appearance. If you make frequent comments about women's

---

Box 5.4: DADS MATTER TOO

Girls who have supportive relationships with their dads report the following[16]:

- Increased self-confidence
- Increased self-reliance
- Assertiveness
- Higher academic achievement
- Better career advancement
- Less likely to become pregnant in teen years
- Less likely to marry early
- Less likely to become involved in physically abusive relationships
- Better able to handle peer pressure
- More confident in taking on new challenges
- Better able to work with others in authority

appearance ("Jane is really showing her age" "Kristin is the most attractive attorney on their staff") but never mention other aspects of who they are ("Jane is so strong in her role at the office" "Kristin is one of the brightest young attorneys on their staff"), your daughter will internalize the message that the most (and possibly only) valuable aspect of a woman is her appearance. Along these same lines, your daughter will also notice the comments you make about attractive, sexy women. What do you say or do when you see a highly attractive woman in public or on television? On hearing your comments, does your daughter understand that you have respect and genuine admiration for women as valued individuals, not just for their appearance? It is important to keep in mind that you are modeling how she will expect to be treated by future boyfriends and men in her life.

Finally, you should make efforts not to criticize your daughter's weight or shape but instead praise her for her many strengths. Even teasing a daughter about having "granny's thighs" can cause her to believe that you think she is overweight (which in her mind means she believes that you don't approve of *her*). Commenting on the fact that she has gained a few pounds can be enough to cause her to feel rejected. This is the last thing she needs from her father at this time. In addition, continue to make positive comments about her appearance but avoid linking your compliments on appearance in any way to her weight. For example, "You look beautiful wearing that dress! It really brings out the blue in your eyes!" versus, "You seem to have lost some weight; that dress looks really great on you now!" Further, while she still needs to hear compliments about her appearance, it is even more powerful to praise her for her strengths and all the things that make her unique: "You are so witty! You have the best sense of humor!" "You are so strong when you run long distances" "You really watch out for your little brother. I appreciate that about you." It is important to take the time to make these types of comments, acknowledging that you see her as more than just her physical appearance, and that you value her many other positive attributes.

Bite your tongue: Provide affirming comments, not criticism.

To echo the advice for dads in the previous section, all caring adults in a girl's life need to be mindful to provide affirming comments about all of her many strengths, including compliments about her appearance. At the same time, it is important to *avoid* critical appearance-related comments about our daughters, ourselves, or others.

It is helpful to first examine any appearance-related expectations you have for your daughter. How are those expectations conveyed to her, either subtly or overtly? Does your daughter perceive that you would like her better or approve of her more if she were to lose weight or look more attractive? Before making any weight-related comments to your daughter, really examine whether your daughter has a problem with her weight and shape or whether you are the one who has a problem with it. Is her weight an issue for you because it does not meet your standards, or is it truly a problem for her in terms of making friends, being teased at school, or not being able to do the things she likes to do? It isn't easy to do, but you have to learn to separate your expectations or preferences for what you *wish* for your daughter from the reality of who she truly is, her natural body shape and size, her appearance, and her developing sense of self.

In our culture, this is difficult because weight and appearance are so tied to a "good/bad" binary—if a person is thin, then she is "good" and rated positively in all life areas, while overweight equals ugly equals "bad"— not just in terms of appearance but also of character. As parents, we need to break this connection because it is not based on reality: the truth is that a person's weight, shape, or appearance has nothing to do with his or her value or character as a person. It is so important that you avoid tying your approval of your daughter to her weight and appearance. The overall impact of your attitudes and comments should be that she feels loved, valued, and accepted just for who she is *now*.

So how do you do this? The simplest (but not easiest) way is to keep weight, shape, and appearance-related comments and criticisms to yourself. As I will state repeatedly, you should avoid making these types of comments toward your daughter, others, or yourself. Your daughter is definitely listening and internalizing any critical comments you may make, and she is ultimately equating them with your overall opinion of her. It is especially important to keep in check seemingly innocent remarks (e.g., "Are you sure you need another helping?" or "These donuts we are eating will go straight to our hips!"). Any girl who is sensitive about her weight or shape will internalize these comments and believe that you think she is too fat or her hips are too big. Remember that when she believes this, she perceives that you believe she *is not good enough*. It is hard to keep these comments in check when you have made a habit of self-criticism or if you are truly concerned about what or how much your daughter is eating, but making comments about her weight is destructive for her developing sense of self. It is safe to say that if you are in doubt about whether your comment could be hurtful, it is best not to say it. Say something affirming instead.

Be balanced: Promote wellness and decrease emphasis on appearance, weight, and shape.

What are the values in your family as they relate to the importance of appearance, weight, or shape? How much do family members emphasize beauty and appearance as the most important source of worth and success, particularly for women? What happens if someone in the family does not happen to live up to cultural standards or expectations in this area? How are they treated within the family? These questions are difficult to answer, but it is important for parents to examine the ways in which they can begin to teach their daughters to value their strengths in multiple life areas and to ensure that their sense of self does not rely primarily on their appearance. This overemphasis is what she will learn from the media and even from her peer group, but your role is to praise her for other life areas that may tend to be underappreciated in the larger culture. When she has balance in multiple life dimensions, she will be less likely to overemphasize any one area. In this regard, it is helpful to encourage her involvement in a variety of activities and see that she has ample opportunities to explore all of her interests.

One exercise that may be helpful in evaluating and improving balance in her life—drawn from cognitive behavioral therapy techniques for decreasing the emphasis on weight and shape—is to construct a pie chart as shown in Figure 5.1. Have your daughter evaluate the categories of her life according to how important they are to her overall sense of well-being

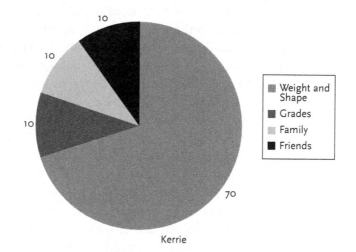

Figure 5.1
Kerrie's self-evaluation pie chart.

(e.g., "If things are going well or not going well in that area, how much does it affect your mood for the day? How much would it disrupt your life?"). In the example shown, Kerrie is currently placing so much emphasis on her weight and shape in determining her happiness that she could easily allow any weight gain to significantly interfere with the way she feels about herself and her overall well-being.

This exercise can also be used as a way to set a goal for improvement: "Draw another graph that represents how you would like your life to be, so the pieces are more balanced." In doing so, Kerrie might see that she has allowed this one life area to supersede all the other areas in her life and that her life is highly limited with only four "slices." How can she decrease the value of the weight/shape slice and at the same time start to increase the number of slices in her pie chart? These are important questions for her to discuss.

In addition to decreasing emphasis on weight, shape, and appearance as the most important aspect of how their daughters define themselves, parents can also encourage girls to adopt broader definitions of what they consider to be beautiful—in other words, that beauty extends well beyond appearance. What are non-appearance-related aspects of a person that are based on character, goals, accomplishments, talents, character, academics, sports, relationships, or her spirituality? Box 5.5 presents a list of just a few strengths you can emphasize. (I will revisit these strengths again in Chapter Seven.)

In addition to a view of beauty as extending beyond physical appearance, also help your daughter to see that beauty comes in all shapes, sizes, and colors. For example, it is interesting to note that African American girls have higher levels of self-esteem, appearance satisfaction, and positive body image than do girls from other groups, in part because they do not limit their view of beauty to a narrow range of weights and shapes.

Box 5.5: STRENGTHS RELATED TO INNER BEAUTY

Kindness	Creativity	Generosity	Patience
Sense of humor	Gratitude	Loyalty	Empathy
Confidence	Assertiveness	Wisdom	Insight
Athletic	Smart	Strength	Artistic or musical talent
Care for others	Self-awareness	Stand up for beliefs	Writing ability

As a group, African American girls are more likely than others to view beauty as much more than being thin; rather, they have a view of beauty as encompassing attitude, confidence, and the creation of an individual, distinctive style. It will be helpful for you to comment on a diverse range of traits and styles that you consider to be beautiful and to introduce your daughter to positive female role models whose bodies come in a range of shapes and sizes.

6. "I am beautiful!" Encourage positive self-talk.

Does your daughter ever look in the mirror and make negative comments about what she sees? Instead, encourage her to try viewing her body and appearance in a positive manner, focusing on her strengths. If you hear her making negative comments about herself, first have her explore how she came to believe in this negative view of herself.[17] For example:

Alyson says "My legs are disgusting. I can't wear these shorts or people will make fun of me." (How she came to believe this: *"My mom thinks her thighs are too big, and she never wears shorts. I have to wear tight shorts in volleyball, and I have started to notice that other people's legs are a lot thinner than mine."*)

Next, she can learn to ask herself the following questions in order to challenge and change the negative belief:

"What is the evidence that this is true about me?" (Answer: *"There really is no evidence. I wear shorts all the time in volleyball and no one has said anything yet."*)

"Would I ever judge a friend as I am judging myself?" (Answer: *"No way, that's too mean to say to a friend."*)

"Is there another way of looking at it? (Positive thought: *"My legs are still growing and changing. They help me when I jump during a volleyball match. I like my new shorts, and I will wear them with a cute shirt today. It doesn't really matter anyway, especially if I can feel strong and confident regardless of what I am wearing."*)

Just as it has become normal for girls to be self-critical, it is also hard for them to accept a compliment. Rather than immediately rejecting a positive comment, as many girls have been socialized to do, teach your daughter to accept the compliment as being true. A common reaction might be as follows:

KELLY: Your hair looks amazing!
KIERSTEN: No, you should see how long it took me to get it this way, and it is still so frizzy!

Instead, teach your daughter how to truly accept a compliment and mean it. The strategy is simple:

KELLY: Your hair looks amazing!
KIERSTEN: Thank you Kellie.

That's it. There is no reason for her to have to take a compliment and turn it around to insult herself.

Have "the talk" about adolescence early and often: Help her understand the normal changes of puberty.

The process of puberty and all its changes is complex, and studies indicate that girls manage these changes better when they are prepared for them.[18] Instead of believing she is the *only* one going through this (as she may often claim), educate your daughter about the changes of puberty, how these changes are normal and expected, and that her weight, shape, and appearance are in flux and will be shifting from one day to the next. For example, if she knows that she is *supposed* to gain weight in her hips and thighs, this will help her feel less isolated and overwhelmed by the experience (see also Chapter 2).

Turn down the volume: Limit her media exposure.

We discussed the importance of generally limiting her media exposure in Chapter One. As stated previously, there is ample research to demonstrate that the more girls view media images of the thin-beautiful-hot-sexy ideal, the more likely they are to have negative body image. A fascinating study of the relationship between television and dieting behaviors by Anne Becker and colleagues examined the introduction of television to the island of Fiji. Just before television was introduced in 1995, researchers examined girls' body-image and weight-loss behaviors; these factors were then measured again three years later. Shockingly, the girls in homes with television were more than three times more likely to have engaged in unhealthy weight-control behaviors like excessive dieting, exercising, fasting, laxative use, vomiting, and purging. These girls reported that they were directly influenced by the characters they saw on television and wanted to look more like them. This dissatisfaction led to a dramatic increase in weight-loss behaviors that are harmful to teen girls.[19] These and other findings indicating a direct relationship between media viewing and negative body image are helpful to us as parents as we make decisions about what and how much media we allow in our daughter's life.

On a practical level, look at the media sources currently in your home. What magazines do you subscribe to? If your daughter subscribes to teen magazines, are the articles and ads mostly about attractiveness and seeking boys' attention? What television shows do you watch while your daughter is home? What movies is she seeing? What sites is she viewing on the Internet? After taking an inventory, what messages do you think your daughter is receiving from all these sources? How can you limit some of the negative messages while increasing the positive ones?

Some tips to try:

- *Monitor your magazines*. If you have fashion magazines on display in your home, consider that for this period in your life it may be healthier for your daughter's development if you cancel your subscriptions. Although fashion magazines might seem an obvious culprit, some research indicates that health and fitness magazines can be just as harmful to girls' body image. Girls who read health and fitness magazines on a frequent basis are more likely to have problems with unhealthy diet strategies like taking laxatives, excessive exercise, or extreme dieting than are girls who don't read these publications. This effect is especially harmful for girls who are already dissatisfied with their bodies.[20]
- *Keep the television out of her room*. Many studies indicate that girls who have unrestricted access to television are more likely to adopt the thin-beautiful-hot-sexy ideal, are more likely to engage in sexual activity sooner, and are more likely to experiment with alcohol and drugs at an earlier age.[21] Keeping television out of her bedroom was covered in Chapter One as a recommendation by the American Academy of Pediatrics.
- *Monitor Internet use*. Although most of us are aware of the potential dangers of the Internet for children and teens, you may not be as aware of the influence of websites and social media on the development of negative body image and even disordered eating patterns. For example, be aware that "thinspiration" websites have become strikingly common, encouraging girls to go on extreme diets, compete with one another, and take other measures to attain extreme thinness. One recent review of these thinspiration sites found over 400 of them, with over 500,000 girls viewing the images and comments in just one year.[22] Many girls meet on the website and then compete with each other to see who can lose the most weight. I have already discussed the study showing that

the more time girls spent on Facebook, the more likely they were to have a negative body image and engage in unhealthy weight-loss behaviors. In general, as discussed in Chapter One, it is good to set limits on the amount of time your daughter can spend online each day, as the more time she spends in the digital world, the more likely she will be to compare herself with the cultural ideal and other girls. As with other types of media, this is likely to result in negative outcomes for her physical self-concept and overall body image.

"I choose not to believe this!": Teach media literacy skills.

While limiting her media use is the most helpful strategy to use while your daughter is younger, as she grows older she will need to learn how to become a critical viewer of the media and to be able to challenge media messages on her own. Media literacy skills promote critical thinking—teaching her not merely *what* to think but *how* to think, how to become an active rather than passive consumer of media. The bottom line is that girls can learn first to understand the message being sent through an image or advertisement and then *make a conscious choice* as to whether they want to believe that message. The idea is that she will recognize that there is indeed a purposeful message being sent and that she has a choice as to whether or not to respond.

As a first step, your daughter needs basic education about the nature of the thin-beautiful-hot-sexy ideal and of the advertising industry. Remind her that the majority of images that represent the cultural ideal have been constructed through multiple strategies designed to enhance the model's appearance—including digital alterations and soft-focus cameras—so that in real life the models themselves do not look like these images of perfection. It is also helpful to provide your daughter with information about the historical nature of the ideal and how it has changed over time. For example, Marilyn Monroe, once considered one of the most beautiful women in the world, wore a size 12 dress, while today's models wear a size 0. It is likely that the cultural ideal will keep changing as it has throughout history. Remind your daughter that the ideal does not represent the average woman in the United States and that beautiful women come in all shapes and sizes.[23] See Box 5.6 for some surprising statistics, and Box 5.7 for some ideas about teaching media literacy skills.

As a next step, focus on some print, television, or Internet advertisements with your daughter and try the steps outlined in Box 5.8 for enhancing media literacy.

Box 5.6: DID YOU KNOW?

Barbie, popular with girls since her introduction in the 1950s, has often been critiqued for her unrealistic body proportions and her negative influence on girls, who believe that they should grow up to actually look like Barbie. The problem is that Barbie's shape is impossible for actual humans to achieve. If she were enlarged to life-size proportions, it would be impossible for her to walk upright! Here are Barbie's human-size measurements compared with those of the average woman in the United States[25]:

	Height	Weight	Waist/Hip Circumference
Barbie:	5'9	110	18
Average US woman	5'3.8	166	37.5

Watch out for "fat talk": Pay attention to her friends' attitudes and behaviors.

As reviewed previously, friends can have a profound influence on the development of a girl's body image. If your daughter's friends talk about dieting in front of one another, your daughter will likely do the same.

Box 5.7: BUILDING AWARENESS THROUGH CO-VIEWING MEDIA

To start, watch a few TV shows and movies with your daughter and have a conversation about the messages the shows might be sending. Ask questions but do it sparingly. When she is ready, have some meaningful conversations with your daughter about the shows. (Helpful hint: Don't overdo this. I know I have already started to annoy my daughter with my questions, and she is only 9. If you are going to allow her to watch a show, sometimes it is good just to let her enjoy it without any commentary from you). Next, focus on the commercials. A fun experiment to try: ask your daughter to guess how many ads she will see during her favorite TV program. Then ask her to count the number of ads she actually sees. Compare her prediction with the actual number. Also, have her note how many times she saw the same commercial. Discuss the pervasiveness of advertising with her.

1. ***Identify the image.*** Media images and messages are not reflections of reality but are constructed for a specific purpose. What is the purpose of this advertisement? Make observations about the image or advertisement. Who is in the picture? What sort of camera angle or lighting is used? What feeling is it intended to evoke?

2. ***Explore and deconstruct the message in the image.*** What are the values embedded in these images? Do real women look like this? Will buying this product help me look like this? Does this model really use this product to help her look like this? If I did purchase this product, would my life really become like the life portrayed in this ad? (See Box 5.9 for more details)

3. ***Resist the message.*** The best way to resist cultural messages is to actively challenge the thin-beautiful-sexy ideal. For example, talk back to the TV when you see an ad or hear a message that makes you question yourself and your confidence. Co-view media with your daughter and model this process for her. With my children, I sometimes ask questions like, "Why is the actress wearing a bare-midriff top while she is discovering the scientific code for a top-secret formula?" "Why are the girls more interested in shopping while the boys are out solving the mystery?" "Do you really believe that this movie star uses that box of hair color? Why does she want to make us believe that the hair color in the box will help us look like her?" This type of modeling will help your daughter form the habit of stopping to think before she chooses to believe a media message.

   Another way to start resisting media messages is to ask her to imagine a warning label on every image she views. Several studies have demonstrated that when women are given a brief warning message before they view media images, they are somewhat buffered from the damaging effects of exposure to the thin ideal. A more recent study found that even a warning label on photos and ads (as simple as "This picture has been digitally altered") seemed to have a protective effect for women who saw labeled images versus women who viewed images with no warning labels. A girl can remind herself that (1) most of us are genetically predisposed to be heavier than these models and (2) all these images of models have been digitally altered. This reminder can help your daughter learn to think through the facts about the image and its message and can help protect her against its negative effects.[25]

Finally, help her talk to herself in a positive, realistic manner in response to these images. For example, "I can choose not to allow this message to influence how I feel about myself." Instead of "I must look like this to be happy," she can say, "I don't have to look like this in order to feel good about myself." She can also keep questioning, "Who really benefits if I believe this message? What will it cost me to buy into these pressures?" All of these strategies will help your daughter to develop resistance to these messages.

4. **Actively work to change the message.** A final step toward media literacy is encouraging your daughter to transcend the problem by becoming part of the solution. Encourage her to write letters to companies that send positive messages to girls and women. Even more important, help her in writing letters of concern to companies that promote the thin-beautiful-sexy ideal and devalue women by equating their worth with their physical appeal. The Media Watchdog campaign at National Eating Disorders.org is a good place to start to locate particular images; it also provides templates for protest letters. For example, one of the targets of the Media Watchdog letter-writing campaign is a diet pill being marketed exclusively for teens. In addition, several years ago a group of girls decided to "Girlcott" Abercrombie and Fitch after that company released a line of T-shirts with slogans that were degrading to women (e.g., T-shirts that read: "Who needs brains when you have these??"). The company pulled the T-shirt line in response to the negative publicity. Activism is very empowering to girls, as they feel they are making a difference in changing the toxic culture for their own benefit and that of other girls.[26]

Studies indicate that friends share similar levels of dieting, desire for thinness, and overall body-image concerns.[27] In addition, if your daughter's friends spend a lot of time talking about appearance and making negative comments about others' appearance, your daughter is more likely to diet and to be overly concerned with her own appearance as well. Overall, your daughter will model what she sees and internalize what she hears. On the other hand, peers can be a positive influence when they are not as concerned about appearance or how much they weigh. Ideally, a girl's friends should help her feel supported and feel good about herself (rather than being competitive or making her feel judged; see Chapter 6).

A note about "fat talk": You might hear your daughter and her friends having a discussion like this:

> *Box 5.9:* A MEDIA LITERACY EXERCISE TO TRY
> WITH YOUR DAUGHTER
>
> First, leaf through popular magazines with your daughter and have her pull some of the advertisements. Answer the questions on this online worksheet with her and discuss her answers: http://www.mediaed.org/ Handouts/DeconstructinganAd.pdf
>
> Next, have her sort through some of the magazines and create two large collages: a "Wall of Shame" filled with negative images that are harmful to girls and women and a "Rave Wall" filled with positive empowering messages for girls and women (this one will take a little more effort and searching in order to fill the page). After comparing the two collages, have her destroy the Wall of Shame in a dramatic fashion, stating: "These messages are not true. I don't have to listen to them anymore."

ANNA: Oh, I feel so fat today. I hate what I am wearing! Why can't I be skinny like Beth?

SOPHIA: Oh you should have seen how much I ate yesterday. I am the one who looks like a pig in these jeans!

What is going on between these friends? First, this common form of communication among girls is not really about a feeling of "fat"; rather, Anna is likely feeling insecure and seeking reassurance from her friend that she really is acceptable. Sophia's reply serves to criticize herself in order to make Anna feel better. But neither friend walks away from the conversation feeling encouraged. To move away from "fat talk" in your conversations with your daughter, encourage her to talk about what is really going on in her life that is causing her to doubt herself or seek reassurance. Then provide her with the validation she needs. When "fat talk" comes up with her friends, tell her to reply with something positive about her *friend* (not negative about *herself*) and then to steer the conversation away from weight and shape altogether.

Promote a positive physical self-concept, not thinness

Instead of viewing her body through a lens of external appearance, help her develop a positive *physical self-concept*. Physical self-concept is broader than just how you feel about your weight, shape, or appearance.

When a person has a positive physical self-concept, she values her body for its fitness, coordination, strength, flexibility, physical appearance, sports competence, and general health.[28] Instead of simply valuing the body for how it appears, people with a positive physical self-concept value their bodies for what they can *do* and how they *function* in terms of overall health and strength. This is critical for girls as they are bombarded daily by messages that encourage them to be dissatisfied with themselves and to focus on how they *look* rather than on how they *feel*. For example, as a girl in our society, your daughter has learned not only that she *should* exercise but that it is an absolute requirement for having a thin and fit physique. Instead of viewing physical activity as an enjoyable way to move the body so that they can experience optimal health and well-being, girls often believe that exercise is simply something they have to do to burn excess calories. The parenting strategy needed here is to deconstruct this myth for your daughter and help her learn to appreciate her body for what it can do and how it feels, not just how it appears to others.

Be free: Encourage movement for her overall health and fitness.

Your daughter has also learned that girls can excel at sports and has probably tried a few sport-related activities throughout her childhood. Many girls emerge from these experiences in a positive manner, whereas others end up developing negative body image and an unhealthy relationship with exercise. It is true that some sports increase a girls' risk for the development of negative body image and even full-syndrome eating disorders. However, it is the *type* of sport that makes a difference in whether or not sports become a risk factor for girls. *Judged* sports that place an emphasis on individual appearance (e.g., dance, ballet, gymnastics, cheerleading) and promote the idea that a thin physique will help a girl excel at the sport (e.g., cross-country track) tend to be more likely to increase her risk for unhealthy eating and weight loss–related behaviors, while *team* sports (e.g., basketball, volleyball) can actually serve as a protective factor against negative body image and other problems.[29] The takeaway from this research is clear: look for teams that have supportive coaches and players that are not competitive regarding physical appearance and that emphasize physical fitness and fun rather than primarily valuing the body for how it looks.

Whether or not she participates in organized sports, her engagement in some type of regular movement will help her feel more strong, healthy, and vibrant. If she chooses to exercise in a structured manner, make sure she has realistic expectations for what exercise can do for her—it is not

> **Box 5.10: AN EXERCISE TO TRY WITH YOUR DAUGHTER**
>
> Discover at least one enjoyable physical activity that you and your daughter can do together and plan it on your calendar. It can be as simple as dancing to music at home or can involve some advance planning like taking a yoga class together.

a panacea for quick weight loss. Exercise will help her feel better, release stress, have more confidence, and possibly contribute to changes in her body shape, but it may not necessarily decrease her body weight. When some girls start exercising, the process actually *increases* rather than *decreases* their body dissatisfaction and their drive to become as thin as possible. It is important, then, to monitor your daughter's goals for exercise and to help her view it as freeing and liberating, not just another form of restriction. You can also model positive behaviors by regularly participating in physical activities you enjoy and inviting your daughter to join you (see Box 5.10). Regularly compliment your daughter on her strength, health, and fitness, not on the weight loss that may result from exercise (e.g., replace "All this working out is helping you to look really thin and great!" with "You look so strong these days!").

Eat together and eat mindfully: Establish family routines to promote a healthy relationship with food.

The first point I would like to make in this regard is to reiterate the harms that can come from encouraging your daughter to diet or lose weight. As reviewed previously, diets only lead to skipping meals, fasting, binge eating, and eventual weight gain in adolescents. We know that girls are more likely to diet when they are criticized about their weight by parents and other significant adults in their lives. Unfortunately research also shows that it is not just your direct comments about dieting but your daughter's *perception* of whether or not you think she needs to diet that is actually related to her use of unhealthy weight-loss behaviors.[30] In other words, if she even *thinks* you disapprove of her weight or that you would be happier with her if she lost a few pounds, she is highly likely to use unhealthy behaviors in an attempt to lose weight, *even if you never directly verbalize these thoughts to her.* It is difficult to control not only our explicit comments but also the messages we send indirectly about weight or shape, but it is important to be aware of both our words and our attitudes.

So why does dieting lead to negative outcomes and weight gain in girls? Research indicates that dieting is generally not sustainable for very long, because when your body experiences deprivation, it responds with a strong urge to overeat, often causing a loss of control when you do start eating again, so that you actually end up eating more than intended. Dieting also puts a girl at risk for binge eating due to the *abstinence-violation effect* (i.e., the view that *"I have blown my diet by eating a slice of cake; I might as well go ahead and eat as much as I want"*). Dieting also leads a girl away from relying on physical hunger as a cue for eating. Instead, she begins to shut out these natural signals and deny herself food when her body asks for it. This can make it very difficult for her to know what her body most needs: when it needs to be nourished and how much fuel it requires at that particular time.[31] Restrictive diets can also lead to eventual malnourishment in girls as their bodies are going through complex changes during puberty. Nutrition experts agree that girls should refrain from dieting during this time as it can compromise their healthy growth and development.[32]

It is clear that dieting can lead to harmful results for our daughters. How can we encourage healthy eating instead? The answer is balance: encourage a positive balance between your daughter's energy intake and energy needs, so that her growing body can function optimally. You can't control everything she eats, but you can have an influence over the foods that are most available to her. Try to provide a home environment that makes it easy for your daughter to make healthy food choices. When she wants to eat, what foods are easiest for her to access? I know that when I am hungry for a snack, I don't search for something that will take a lot of preparation; I tend to grab the first thing I see. Make sure that healthy foods such as fresh fruit or cut up vegetables as well as pure water are noticeable and available around your home so that she will automatically reach for these rather than chips or soda.

Another way to establish healthy home routines is to have regular family meals. In addition to the positive benefits outlined in Chapter Four, studies show that girls who eat regular family meals are less likely to use unhealthy weight-loss behaviors and are also less likely to be obese.[33] Even though we are all very busy and children's extracurricular activities really cut into family time in the evenings, it is worth the effort to schedule several family meals each week where everyone is expected to attend. This will promote better communication, more open relationships, and opportunities to eat a balanced meal with others.

After reading all of these suggestions, you might still be wondering "But what can I do when I see my daughter overeating or making poor food choices?" First, you want to empower her to make the best choices for herself, whether or not you are there to monitor her eating habits throughout the day. Therefore it is best not to shame her in front of others by commenting on her eating or to make a negative remark about her food choices (e.g., "Why would you order *that*? It has the most fat grams of anything on the entire menu!"). It is far better to say nothing at the time. Perhaps at a later time you can bring up the subject of ways she can learn to listen to what her body actually wants in a particular moment and to then feed it exactly the amount that it needs. This will help her develop a healthy relationship with food where she eats not only what she wants but what her body actually needs. This is difficult to do in a culture that encourages us to both restrict our urges to eat as well as to "supersize," indulge, and overeat. It is hard to learn to trust the body's signals for eating, but those who are able to eat in this manner have more confidence and a more positive body image.[34]

Therefore, encourage what is termed *intuitive eating*—the process of learning to eat what you really want and to stop eating when you are full. If your body is craving something salty, then all of the ice cream in the world will not satisfy your craving. In contrast, if you crave something smooth and creamy, a tub of movie theater popcorn will leave you feeling dissatisfied. If your daughter learns to listen to her body, it will tell her what and how much it needs. Here are some steps she can take to learn to listen more closely to her body's signals:

1. **Trust hunger cues to decide when to eat and how much to eat**. Your daughter can begin to listen to her body's signals and know when to eat. She can learn to notice when she is starting to become hungry and respond appropriately to these cues. While eating, she can also learn to notice when she begins to feel full, that satiation point at which she is satisfied but not uncomfortably stuffed. If she eats slowly and deliberately, she can begin to recognize her body's cues for fullness.
2. **Decide what food your body is truly hungry for** (e.g., salty, creamy, sweet, crunchy foods). Intuitive eating means that there are no "good" or "bad" foods but that one can choose foods that give the body what it needs at a particular time. She can learn to pay attention to the type of food her body is craving and to honor that feeling by consuming that type of food.
3. **Pay attention when you are eating when not hungry**. Is your daughter using food to cope with negative emotions? When she is feeling

upset or stressed, it is important for her to deal directly with difficult feelings rather than numbing herself with food. Food can indeed provide some comfort in the short term but it is not a long-term substitute for actual coping or problem solving. Your daughter might find temporary solace in secretly eating candy bars in her room, yet her problem of loneliness and anxiety at school will still be there the next day. Help her to recognize what she is really feeling when she wants to eat as a way to cope. Instead, does she need to find another solution (e.g., by joining a club to meet new friends or developing a better study routine)? Or does she need to use coping strategies to manage situations that can't be changed (e.g., deep breathing to cope with anxious feelings)? Problem-solving and coping strategies are discussed extensively in Chapter Eight.

4. **Finally, eat mindfully**. How often does your daughter eat as she is running out the door or snack mindlessly in front of the television? Encourage her to eat without distractions and to truly focus on the flavor and texture of foods. Try an activity listed in Box 5.11 and review the mindfulness exercises discussed in Chapter Eight.

CONCLUSION

The transition to adolescence is typically a difficult time for girls in terms of their developing body image. In fact, it is more likely for girls to come through this process feeling negatively about their weight, shape, and appearance than it is for them to have a positive outlook about their bodies. Toxic cultural pressures are particularly strong in influencing girls to feel negatively about their appearance while at the same time hammering home the message that looking thin, beautiful, hot, and sexy is the most important aspect of girls' value as a person. It is not easy to

Box 5.12: RESILIENCE STRATEGIES TO PROMOTE POSITIVE BODY IMAGE

PARENTS' SUMMARY CHECKLIST

1. The safe haven: Make your home a "No teasing about appearance" zone.
2. Moms, you are your daughter's model: Examine your own attitudes and behaviors about food and body.
3. Dads, you're important too: Maintain a close relationship and monitor comments about women's weight and appearance.
4. Bite your tongue: Don't criticize weight, shape, or appearance; affirm instead.
5. Be balanced: Promote overall wellness and balance and decrease emphasis on appearance, weight, and shape.
6. "I am beautiful": Encourage your daughter to use positive self-talk.
7. Have "the talk" about adolescence: Prepare her for the normal changes of puberty.
8. Turn down the volume: Limit her exposure to negative media influences.
9. "I choose not to believe this": Teach her media literacy skills.
10. Watch out for fat talk: Pay attention to her friends' attitudes and behaviors.
11. Be free: Promote movement for her overall health and fitness.
12. Eat together, eat mindfully: Establish family routines to promote a healthy relationship with food.

overcome these pressures, especially when they are consistently reinforced by friends and family. Your daughter needs you to take a deliberate stand against this process and instead do what it takes to help her develop a positive image as described throughout this chapter. The strategies reviewed here will enable her to make a strong start in the right direction. Keep in mind the resilience strategies I reviewed in this chapter, summarized in Box 5.12.

NOTES

1. Levine, M. P., & Smolak, L. (2002). Body image development in adolescence. In T. F. Cash & T. Pruzinsky (Eds.), *Body image: A handbook of theory, research, and clinical practice* (pp. 74–82). New York: Guilford.

2. Mussell, M. P., Binford, R. B., & Fulkerson, J. A. (2000). Eating disorders: Summary of risk factors, prevention programming, and prevention research. *The Counseling Psychologist, 28,* 764–796. Rodin, J., Silberstein, L. R., & Streigel-Moore, R. H. (1985). Women and weight: A normative discontent. In T. B. Sonderegger (Ed.), *Psychology and gender: Nebraska symposium on motivation, 1984* (pp. 267–307). Lincoln: University of Nebraska Press.

3. Grabe, S., Ward, L. M., & Hyde, J. S. (2008). The role of the media in body image concerns among women: A meta-analysis of experimental and correlational studies. *Psychological Bulletin, 134,* 460–476. doi:10.1037/0033-2909.134.3.460

4. Tiggemann, M., & Slater, A. (2013). NetGirls: The Internet, Facebook, and body image concern in adolescent girls. *International Journal of Eating Disorders, 46*(6), 630–633. doi:10.1002/eat.22141

5. Thompson, J. K., Heinberg, L., Altabe, M., & Tantleff-Dunn, S. (1999). *Exacting beauty: Theory, assessment, and treatment of body image disturbance.* Washington DC: American Psychological Association.

6. Choate, L. (2008). *Girls' and women's wellness: Contemporary counseling issues and interventions.* Alexandria, VA: American Counseling Association.

7. Bearman, S. K., Presnell, K., Martinez, E., & Stice, E. (2006). The skinny on body dissatisfaction: A longitudinal study of adolescent girls and boys. *Journal of Youth and Adolescence, 35*(2), 229–241.

8. McKinley, N. M.(2002). Feminist perspectives and objectified body consciousness. In T. F. Cash & T. Pruzinsky (Eds.), *Body image: Handbook of theory, research, and clinical practice* (pp. 55–64). New York: Guilford.

9. Eaton, D. K., Kann, L., Kinchen, S., Shanklin, S., Ross, J., Hawkins, J., … Wechsler, H. (2010). Youth risk behavior surveillance—United States, 2010. *MMWR Surveillance Summaries, 59*(SS05), 1–142.

10. Neumark Sztainer, D. (1995). I'm like, SO fat: Helping teens make healthy eating choices about eating and exercise in a weight obsessed world. New York: Guilford.

11. Hudson, J. L., Hiripi, E., Pope, H. G., & Kessler, R. C. (2007). The prevalence and correlates of eating disorders in the national comorbidity survey replication. *Biological Psychiatry, 61,* 348–358. doi:10.1016/j.biopsych.2006.03.040

12. Elkind, D. (1967). Egocentrism in adolescence. *Child Development, 38,* 1024–1034.

13. Stice, E., & Shaw, H. (2003). Prospective relations of body image, eating, and affective disturbances to smoking onset in adolescent girls: How Virginia slims. *Journal of Consulting and Clinical Psychology, 71,* 129–135. Tolman, D. L., Impett, E. A., Tracy, A. J., & Michael, A. (2006). Looking good, sounding good: Femininity ideology and adolescent girls' mental health. *Psychology of Women Quarterly, 30,* 85–95.

14. Simmons, R. (2011). *Odd girl out: The hidden culture of aggression in girls.* Boston: Mariner Books/Houghton Mifflin Harcourt.

15. Neumark Sztainer, D. (1995). *I'm like, SO fat: Helping teens make healthy eating choices about eating and exercise in a weight obsessed world.* New York: Guilford.

16. Silverman, R. (2010). *Good girls don't get fat: How weight obsession is messing up our girls and how we can help them thrive despite it.* New York: Harlequin.

17. Silverman, R. (2010). *Good girls don't get fat: How weight obsession is messing up our girls and how we can help them thrive despite it.* New York: Harlequin.

18. Neumark Sztainer, D. (1995). *I'm like, SO fat: Helping teens make healthy eating choices about eating and exercise in a weight obsessed world.* New York: Guilford.

19. Becker, A., Burwell., R. A., Gilman, S. E., Herzog, D. B., & Hamburg, P. (2002). Eating behaviors and attitudes following prolonged exposure to television among ethnic Figian adolescent girls. *British Journal of Psychiatry, 180,* 509–514.

20. Thomsen, S. R., Weber, M. M., & Brown, L. B. (2001). The relationship between health and fitness magazine reading and eating disordered weight-loss methods among high school girls. *American Journal of Health Education, 32*, 133–138.

21. O'Hara, R., Gibbons, F., Gerrard, M., Li, A., Sargeant, J. D., (2012). Greater exposure to sexual content in popular movie predicts earlier sexual debut. *Psychological Science, 20*, 1–10.

22. Jett, S., LaPorte, D. J., & Wanchisn, J. (2010). Impact of exposure to pro-eating disorder websites on eating behavior in college women. *European Eating Disorders Review, 18*, 410–416.

23. Yamamiya, Y., Cash, T. F., Melnyk, S. E., Posavac, H. D., & Posavac, S. S. (2005). Women's exposure to thin-and-beautiful media images: Body image effects of media-ideal internalization and impact reduction interventions. *Body Image, 2*, 74–80.

24. Center for Disease Control (2012). Body measurements. Retrieved 2013 from: www.cdc.gov/nchs/fastats/bodymeas.htm

25. Slater, A. (2012). Reality check: An experimental investigation of the addition of warning labels to fashion magazine images on women's mood and body dissatisfaction. *Journal of Social & Clinical Psychology, 31*(2), 105–122.

26. Media Watchdog/National Eating Disorders Association. (2013). Media watchdog program. Retrieved from http://www.nationaleatingdisorders.org/get-involved/media-watchdog

27. Media Education Foundation (2005) Deconstructing a print advertisement. Retrieved from http://www.mediaed.org/Handouts/DeconstructinganAd.pdf

28. Dunton, G. F., Jamner, M. S., & Cooper, D. M. (2003). Physical self-concept in adolescent girls: Behavioral and physiological correlates. *Research Quarterly for Exercise and Sport, 74*, 360–365.

29. Zucker, N. L., Womble, L. G., Williamson, D. A., & Perrin, L. A. (1999). Protective factors for eating disorders in college female athletes. *Eating Disorders, 7*, 207–218.

30. Fairburn, C. G. (2008). *Cognitive behavior therapy and eating disorders*. New York: Guilford.

31. Fairburn, C. G. (2008). *Cognitive behavior therapy and eating disorders*. New York: Guilford.

32. Neumark Sztainer, D. (1995). *I'm like, SO fat: Helping teens make healthy eating choices about eating and exercise in a weight obsessed world*. New York: Guilford.

33. Neumark Sztainer, D. (1995). *I'm like, SO fat: Helping teens make healthy eating choices about eating and exercise in a weight obsessed world*. New York: Guilford.

34. Avalos, L. C., & Tylka, T. L. (2006). Exploring a model of intuitive eating with college women. *Journal of Counseling Psychology, 53*, 486–497.

CHAPTER SIX

Resilience Dimension Three

Cultivating Healthy Relationships

Do either of these scenarios sound familiar?

Charlotte, your usually happy and talkative 11-year-old, comes home from school, runs straight to her room, and slams her door shut. Later, when you urge her to come out for dinner, her eyes are red from crying. In response to your questions about what is wrong, she replies "No one at school likes me!" and "I never want to see Katie or Blake ever again!"

After practice, Maria, your 15-year-old daughter, checks her phone as you drive her home from school. She bursts into tears and won't speak during the rest of the drive home. Later, you find out from your son that Maria's boyfriend of three months broke up with her through a text and then posted it on Facebook so that "everyone" would know. Your son's friends saw it on Facebook and told him about it; fortunately he gave you the news. Maria begs you to let her stay home from school so she won't have to face being "humiliated in front of everyone."

THE CENTRALITY OF GIRLS' RELATIONSHIPS

I am certain that these two scenarios sounded familiar to you. A key part of girls' development in preadolescence and adolescence is to create and maintain successful relationships with family, friends, and romantic interests. In childhood a girl first looks to you, her parent, as a source of validation and approval. She reasons that if you think she is a worthwhile person, then of course it must be true! As she reaches adolescence, though, her friends start to displace you as the top priority in her life. Often to your chagrin, she increasingly turns to peers more than to you for support, validation, and information. It is clear that while she will always need her parents' approval, much of the way she feels about herself in adolescence will also stem from her sense that she is accepted and approved of by her peers—first by friends and later by romantic partners. To paraphrase many girls' unspoken thoughts: "*If I am accepted by my friends, only then will I feel that I am okay and that I belong.*" And conversely the indictment: "*If I am rejected by someone, then I have failed as a person; I don't belong; I am not okay.*"

If you keep in mind that these beliefs are at the core of how she sees herself, it is easier to understand why she spends so much energy constantly analyzing and evaluating her relationships—*How are the kids at school viewing me? Is anyone laughing at me behind my back? Have I disappointed my friends? Does Jayden still like me? Am I still best friends with Eva or am I now her second-best friend?*—In other words: *Where do I stand today in this game of approval and acceptance?* She seeks the best way to fit in, and when she finds her way in, she relishes the feeling of belonging but is also painfully aware that this acceptance is only temporary; she has to keep her guard up to make sure she is still "in," as this could change at any moment. In this chapter, I will explore how this plays out in both friendships and romantic relationships. Specifically, I will discuss the nature of girls' friendships—problems within friendships, including relational aggression, and pressures for girls to seek and keep romantic relationships. Finally, I will highlight strategies for resilience that girls need in order to maintain an authentic sense of self while also maintaining healthy relationships with others.

Here Today, Gone Tomorrow

You have probably noticed that your daughter's friendship group preferences have changed over time. According to JoAnn Deak's excellent book *Girls will be Girls: Raising Confident and Courageous Daughters,*[1] girls' friendships tend to follow these patterns:

> Ages 6 to 8: friend clusters, moving around in small groups
> Ages 8 to 10: best friends—the "BFF" era
> Ages 10 to 12: cliques
> Ages 12 to 14: friendship groups based on shared interests

Although each phase has its own challenges, many of the problems discussed in this chapter revolve around the importance your daughter places on obtaining membership in a particular group or clique. But before I review the problems with cliques, it is helpful to remember that friendship cliques can and do serve a vital purpose for girls. Deak offers a beautiful metaphor for the cliques that pop up so dramatically around a girl's tenth birthday: Imagine tweens as wet butterflies. They are coming out of their protective cocoons composed of the family, but because their wings are still wet, they are not yet ready to face the world or to fly on their own. So they need protection so that their wet wings will not be damaged. They create a buffer around themselves, surrounding themselves with other wet butterflies, clustering together in small groups, talking alike, dressing alike, looking alike, all as a form of protective camouflage. Instead of viewing this as "clinginess" (as adults often call it), Deak encourages us to view this process as a survival mechanism for our young butterfly daughters.

Yet these clusters, pairs, or cliques, while always present in some fashion, will likely change membership, sometimes rapidly enough to keep your head spinning. Your daughter is best friends with a girl one day, then enemies the next, then friends again on the subsequent day. For a period of time, then, while your daughter's friendship groups might be vitally important to her sense of belonging, they can also be a highly painful place of chaos and rejection. Take heart during this time; it helps to know that friendships do tend to stabilize by the later high school years.

The Crossroads

No matter your daughter's age, she is in the process of forming an identity: *Who Am I?* This is a big question with no easy answers. As stated previously, an important part of identity formation for girls comes through their feelings of acceptance and belonging to a peer group. However, another huge piece of identity comes from establishing a sense of self that is unique. I discussed this dynamic in Chapter Two, where I described her need to both stand out and fit in. So while she is strongly drawn to blend in with her selected peer group, she is also experiencing a developmental pull toward establishing an individual autonomous identity. How can she manage this balancing act?

Several decades ago, Carol Gilligan[2] and Mary Pipher[3] poignantly identified this highly gendered challenge that girls face as they reach adolescence (See Box 6.1 for other interpretations of this process). In their writings, they describe how many girls choose to hide their true selves in exchange for the acceptance and belonging that comes from blending in with peers. Gilligan termed this choice as a "crossroads" for girls. Because she values her relationships so much, a girl sees how risky it might be to assert her own opinions. If she speaks up about what she really thinks and feels, she believes she might be criticized or even rejected by others she cares about. However, if she hides her true feelings, doing what others want her to do instead, she can make them happy and have reassurance that her relationships will stay intact.

She then stands at the crossroads and must decide

Am I going to go my own way, keeping my own voice?

Or am I going to lose my voice by silencing my true self, so that I don't have to risk rejection?

Is it worth it to me to lose part of myself so that I can belong?

Or do I speak up for myself and risk being alone?

Do I have the courage to say no to my friends and instead express what I truly want?

Exhausting, heavy stuff for a 12-year-old!

So which way will she turn? To hold onto her true self or to go with what is cool and popular? It is not easy, but you can help her find a way to claim her authentic self and hold onto it throughout these years. Your daughter can learn that speaking her truth may not always be popular or easy, but it is essential to her growth and development as an authentic person.[4]

Box 6.1: EXCEPTIONS TO TRADITIONAL SOCIALIZATION

There are two exceptions to the traditional socialization process for girls described here. One is that this process is more likely to be the experience of middle-class White girls. Many authors have pointed out that Gilligan's research from the 1980s does not adequately capture the experiences of girls from other social classes or cultural groups. For example, African American girls do not tend to lose their "voice" at adolescence but are more able to engage in "truth telling" by expressing what they really think. They are less likely to hold back their opinions out of fear of displeasing anyone.[5] Although this protects their self-esteem, it does not always mean that they have developed the skills they need to express negative emotions appropriately, since they are more likely than girls from other groups to get into physical fights as a way of expressing anger.

Second, as mentioned in Chapter Two, in recent years seemingly fewer girls have actually become "silent" (saying "I don't know" or "It doesn't matter to me" to most questions). Instead, you might find that quite the opposite is the case for your daughter: more girls of all ethnicities and social classes are becoming loud, angry, and even physically aggressive. As evidence of this trend, a report by the Substance Abuse and Mental Health Services Administration reveals that 27 percent of adolescent girls had participated in a serious fight at school or work, a group-against-group fight, or an attack on others with the intent to inflict serious harm.[6] Girl-fighting is increasingly common, but the most surprising aspect of this fighting is that much of it is shared with a public audience, often online. I have heard adolescent boys describe how much they like to watch videos of girls fighting one another. Many girls say that they know boys will watch them if their fights are posted online. There is more to this trend, then, than just working out a conflict between girls.

The fighting and aggression do not necessarily indicate that girls are finally able to express their authentic selves. As reviewed in Chapter One, the "act like a diva" trend is a culturally sanctioned way for girls to behave in an edgy, aggressive manner. The question then becomes "Is she acting this way in order to conform to cultural expectations or because it is an authentic expression of who she really is?" Rather than going "underground," is she going "over the top" with her attention-grabbing behaviors? It is important for you to reflect on this distinction. Whether she is acting overly compliant or aggressively defiant, the function of the behavior remains the same: to gain approval and validation.

There are two primary reasons why first *developing* and then *holding on to* her authentic self is so important.

Reason One: You Don't Want Her to Be a "Pleaser"

We have all seen girls (and many adults, for that matter), whether loud or painfully quiet, who could be classified as "approval junkies" (an apt term used by Lucie Hemmen).[7] When a girl doesn't have the internal resources to feel accepted, approved of, and validated *just because of who she is*, she is highly vulnerable to looking to others for reassurance that she is okay. She learns to become overly reliant on the success of her relationships. And this is exactly the way many girls are socialized: "If I keep you happy and do what you want, then you will like me more and feed my need for approval."

The problem with this, of course, is twofold: first, she will need to keep seeking this approval from others because she won't have the ability to supply it for herself. Second, when she relies too much too much on peer approval to feel okay about herself, she will be less likely to speak up for herself in relationships. She will be highly vulnerable to going along with whatever risky behaviors her friends (and increasingly her romantic interests) might pressure her to do. Research clearly shows that if we want to predict whether or not your daughter will take part in high-risk behaviors (substance use, smoking, early sexual activity, breaking the law), the strongest predictor will be whether her friends first take part in these behaviors.[8] Most teens don't do these things alone but as part of a group. So if she can't say no out of fear that she will lose her friends (and future romantic relationships), she is at higher risk for caving in to peer pressure. Unfortunately in most cases this will have a negative outcome for her.

You might be wondering at this point "How can my daughter learn to stand up for herself when I also want her to be nice, not to be selfish, not to argue to get her way, to get along well with others?" I have already discussed how girls learn that keeping others happy is an essential part of being a female in our culture. Lyn M. Brown terms this the "tyranny of kind and nice"—many girls feel caught in the cultural bind that to have value, you must keep your relationships intact, and to do this, you must please others first and foremost. As Carol Gilligan writes, girls learn the cultural imperative to "be nice and don't cause any problems."[9]

Of course you want your daughter to be nice to others. Of course you want her to have basic respect for others and to treat them in a moral, ethical manner. What we are concerned with here is the pressure girls feel to be "pleasers"—not because they *want to* but because they fear that they *have to* or they might put a relationship in jeopardy and therefore cause damage to their sense of identity as "someone who belongs." She feels she *has* to say yes and to please everyone in order to gain approval—*because being herself is not good enough.*[10]

To help us understand the difference between being kind (which we generally want) and conforming (which we generally don't want), Rachel Simmons in her book "*Curse of the Good Girl*" distinguishes between a "nice girl" and a "real girl," one who stays connected to her strong inner core of thoughts, feelings, desires, and then is able to act from this core. "A real girl does not ignore others' needs but can manage the needs of others without sacrificing the integrity of her own. She can defend her interests in a relationship or advocate on her own behalf."[11] She is respectful of others but does not avoid conflict, being able to speak up for her own needs when she believes it is necessary. Of course this isn't easy and takes a lot of practice. I will discuss how to encourage these "real girl" qualities in the boxes appearing throughout this chapter, starting with Box 6.2.

Reason Two: You Want Her to Be Able to Express Anger in a Healthy, Direct Manner

The second reason that you want her to be able to claim and hold onto her authentic self is so she can learn to effectively express her negative

---

Box 6.2: WILL THE REAL GIRL PLEASE STAND UP?

According to Ana Homayoun in her book *The Myth of the Perfect Girl*, "The key to social wellness for girls is to help them develop self-awareness and break free of the compromises they make to fit in."[12] As parents, we should do what we can to provide our daughters with ample opportunities to develop a sense of self—to know who they are, what they believe in, and who they want to become. This cannot happen if they are plugged into their phones or computers during most of their waking hours. This also cannot happen if they are involved in a whirlwind of activity that leaves no room for unstructured downtime. What will benefit them most are occasional times to be "off"—times when they are not "performing" for a social audience, worrying about how others are judging them, and conforming to others' expectations. They need time to reflect on some of the following big-picture questions:

- *Who am I? What do I believe and value?*
- *What do I like? Dislike?*
- *What are my standards for friendships? For romantic relationships?*
- *What are my strengths? What am I good at?*
- *What are my areas for growth? Things I want to get better at?*
- *What are my dreams? What do I want for my future?*

Encourage your daughter to keep a journal about these questions and talk about them with you or with another trusted adult. She will grow as she develops an authentic, solid core from which to blossom. I will revisit these questions in more depth in Chapter Seven.

---

feelings, including anger. From a very early age, girls are socialized to suppress their anger. Studies of preschool children show that girls are more likely than boys to be rejected by their peers if they directly express their angry feelings.[13] Girls learn the confusing message that it is okay to be emotionally expressive—for every emotion, that is, except anger. As a result, many girls never learn the skills they need for open, assertive communication or for effective conflict resolution. When a girl is forced to silence her anger, she might turn her negative feelings inward, leading to self-destructive behaviors such as eating disorders, self-injury, substance abuse, and depression (see Chapter Three). Pushing her negative feelings underground can also lead to forms of indirect aggression that are not only harmful to herself but to others (see the following section on relational aggression). By helping your daughter to learn and practice the appropriate expression of anger, you will be giving her a great gift. For now, let's spend some time exploring the consequences that can result from girls' lack of direct communication regarding their anger.

THE MEAN GIRL: RELATIONAL AGGRESSION

When asked "If your friend makes you mad, do you tell her about it?" many girls say no—which is no surprise given the pressure girls feel to keep others happy with them, no matter what it takes. But of course girls do get mad and of course they have negative feelings. What can they do instead? If Brittney believes that she can't tell Marissa she is mad at her or doesn't like something Marissa has said, what could Brittney do? *Lots of things. Talk about Marissa behind her back. Tell Marissa's friends to ignore her. Spread a rumor about her. Send her a mean, anonymous text.* The list goes on. *Make Marissa's life miserable without ever saying a word to her about the conflict. Brittney can retaliate most effectively by harming what is most important to Marissa: her relationships.*

By now, most parents have heard the term *relational aggression* (RA) and have probably seen the movie *Mean Girls* (which is a humorous but accurate portrayal of RA in girls[14]). RA is typically defined as the act of hurting others by manipulating or harming their relationships.[15] I have already discussed the importance of relationships in girls' lives and how they learn to maintain these relationships at any price. They know that expressing their anger or offering opinions that go against the group might jeopardize these relationships. So they learn to use RA against their friends instead of directly confronting them over disagreements. (Interestingly, girls are most likely to use RA against friends *within* their friendship circles rather than those outside of their circles. It is no surprise that the term "frenemies" has surged in usage in girl culture!). It is almost considered normal for the distinction between friend and enemy to be blurred: One study found that up to 70 percent of third- through sixth-grade girls said that their friends had been mean to them. In a national study of high school girls that included both relational and physical aggression, the Centers for Disease Control reported that 22 percent of girls had been the victims of bullying on school property.[16] Regardless of how it is measured, it is hard to disagree that there is virtually an "epidemic of meanness" and a "cool to be cruel" attitude among girls directed at other girls in our current culture.[17]

Some common examples of RA:

1. Gossiping about another girl behind her back
2. Writing notes about her and passing them around at school
3. Excluding her from your group (e.g., not letting her sit with you at lunch)
4. Revealing her secrets to others
5. Stealing her friends or romantic interests
6. Telling your friends not to be friends with her
7. Making fun of her and then saying "Just kidding!"
8. Cyberbullying: using text messages or social media (e.g., Facebook, Instagram, Twitter) to spread negative messages about her, often anonymously.

Of these, cyberbullying has gotten the most attention in recent years due to the rapid increase in the use of technology among teens and the ease with which RA can be perpetrated electronically. We know that girls are emboldened to be even more aggressive and cruel online, when they feel that their identity will not be known, and we also know that victims are even more negatively affected when they don't know the identity of the originator of the cruel messages. So why do girls do these things to their own friends? Why would friends become frenemies, seemingly overnight?

From research studies, we know that girls who use RA typically use this behavior for the following reasons:

- *I could never tell her that!* They might use it when they don't have the skills for assertive communication and conflict resolution.
- *I feel good when you feel bad.* They can briefly feel better about themselves through downward comparison ("At least I am not as fat as Megan!" etc.). They can experience what Carol Dweck terms a "brief self-esteem rush" by judging and demeaning others.[18]

- *"I will do whatever it takes to make them like me."* They might not have a well-defined beliefs and values system to guide their behavior, so they act in mean or manipulative ways to please those within their desired social circle and to keep others out.
- *"It was only a joke!"* They might not have well-developed empathy skills; that is, they are not able to see things from another person's perspective and to realize the negative impact of their words or actions.
- *"Don't challenge me!"* They might use RA to maintain their social status and power in a clique; others will be less likely to challenge them if they fear they will become the next victims of RA.
- *"Let's stir up some drama."* They might use it to provide relief from boredom, thereby creating some excitement and drama in their lives. According to Marwick and Boyd, girl drama not only involves interpersonal conflict but is intensified when it is played out in front of a networked audience, as on Facebook, Twitter, Tumblr, or Instagram.[19]
- *"I want to see her fail."* In Lisa Hinkelman's book *Girls without Limits*, the girls she interviewed reported that they often felt like they were in competition with one another and said that they often like to see another girl fail.[20]
- *"What else am I supposed to do?"* They might see RA modeled by others in the media and in their peer group and also by adults they know (yes, they are watching us to see how we handle conflict too; See Box 6.3). A quick glance at popular media shows a portrayal of female friendships as comprising backstabbing women who vindictively betray one another without a moment's thought. For parents to consider: From their vantage point, what are our daughters learning about how they should expect to be treated (or expect to treat others) in relationships?

What's the Harm? Can't "Girls Just Be Girls"?

RA may have become mainstream among today's girls, but this doesn't mean that we should dismiss it as merely expected or harmless. Girls are indeed harmed by these behaviors—and RA does not just affect the victims of the aggression. The girls who use RA against others learn manipulative ways of getting their needs met, which can harm them in their own development. Many more girls live in dread that they will say or do something that will land them in the outsider role. The presence of RA in a social setting, therefore, affects all members of that community. You should be aware of some of the possible consequences.

Research indicates that mothers who use RA in their own friendships have daughters who engage in these same kinds of behaviors.[21] This may sound outlandish; after all, what adult will admit that she uses RA? However, consider things like these scenarios:

- You talk about your friends behind their backs because you don't want to hurt them in person.
- You spread rumors or gossip that you overheard from a friend.
- You openly tell someone who made you mad that what she did didn't bother you at all, yet you repeat what she did to multiple acquaintances so that they will think less of her.

If you are like me, you are at least occasionally guilty of several of these things. But rather than condemning ourselves, we need to consider that in order to move forward, we can decide to take steps to become the best role models possible for our daughters. They are watching to see if *we* are able to be assertive in letting others know how we feel, to stand up for ourselves when needed, to express anger appropriately with assertiveness and not aggression, to say no, and to refrain from gossip. Your daughter will learn best when she sees these attributes in you.

So do a gut check and ask yourself the following questions:

- Honestly, what role did you play in the popularity web at your school? Did you use RA behaviors toward others? How does this still play into your social interactions today?
- Do you tend to overstretch yourself to please everyone, or are you able to say no when you need to?
- Are you able to tell someone when you are angry with her about her actions? Are you able to let her know how you feel? If not, what do you do with these angry feelings?
- Are you able to stand up for yourself in a conflict by expressing clearly what you want and need? Do you express yourself assertively?
- Do you assert your own rights without trampling on the rights of others? In other words, can you keep your cool in a conflict and express yourself without screaming and name calling?
- What do you do when faced with gossip? If someone makes fun of an acquaintance in front of you, what do you do?
- Are you an ally for other women? Do you criticize other women or gossip about their flaws? If your daughter overhears you talking on the phone, what would she learn about female friendships?

Consequence One: Pursuit of Popularity Overrides Healthy Social Skills

You can probably recall the most popular children from your daughter's younger years; they were the ones who were kind, helpful, and well liked by other children as well as by adults. As your daughter moves toward early adolescence, however, this dynamic changes drastically. The term "popularity" means a very different thing to a teen versus an adult. We adults might assume that teens who are generally nice and well mannered are still considered popular. Teens view it differently: there are kids that *grownups* like and then there are the *real* popular kids, those who are popular not because they are well liked but because of their social status. These teens may have an air of sophistication or glamour about them, and they are intimidating to others who are outside of their circle. And yes, they often use RA behaviors to help maintain their power. As Rosalind Wiseman writes in her book *Queen Bees and Wannabes*, the queen bee maintains her status as queen because no one will challenge her—from of fear of what she might do in retaliation. Because they want to remain in the queen's circle of friends, those surrounding her (the wannabes) also use RA behaviors to please the queen and keep others out of their social circle. So meanness to other girls is part and parcel in *becoming* popular, and it is an important element of *staying* popular.[22]

It will be helpful to you to understand this dynamic because it will make you stop and think before you steer your daughter toward the pursuit of certain cliques. Do you want her to have to strive to be a queen bee or a wannabe? Again, it is important to remember that being popular does not necessarily mean being well liked, and the best-liked teens are not usually the popular kids once they reach the middle school years.

Another recent study also sheds light on whether you want your adolescent daughter to become "cool" and popular. A group of researchers at the University of Virginia followed a group of 11- to 13-year olds over a ten-year period (into early adulthood). They found that the preteens who were most concerned about being popular tended to use "pseudomature behaviors"—that is, they were trying to act older and more mature than they actually were, trying hard to impress peers with their coolness. It was this group of students who were more likely to have boyfriends/girlfriends at an earlier age, to seek out friends who were also cool or attractive solely to impress others, and to get in fights, use aggression, and experiment with alcohol and other drugs. In middle school, they were already worried about hanging out with others who made them look good rather than seeking out true friendships. These pseudomature behaviors, however, got them what they wanted; the research shows that these were indeed the most popular kids in middle school. They were definitely cool in middle school!

But what do we see ten years later? Did these same kids maintain their popularity and become social stars as adults? Not at all. Of all of the preteens studied, this group of "cool kids" was actually the least socially successful in early adulthood. They were the ones most likely to have problems developing close relationships with friends and romantic partners; they also had problems with alcohol and substance abuse and had elevated rates of criminal activity.[23] The message seems to be that maintaining concern with impressing others and seeking out shallow friendships simply does not bode well for a middle schooler's future. The bottom line, then, is this: if a girl use pseudomature behavior such as RA to pursue popularity, it will likely work for her—but only in the short run.

On the other hand, if a girl is authentic, free from pressures to impress others in order to maintain social status, and uses good social skills such as those outlined in this chapter, she will have a better outlook for the future. True, she probably won't become popular in middle school. Yet research shows that it is not popularity but rather authentic relationships and good social skills that lead to future success and happiness in life. She may not be able to appreciate this yet, but this is where you come in. With your life experience and wisdom, you can help her to see that seeking out quality friendships within which she is able to *be herself* is the key to resilience in the long term.

Consequence Two: She Won't Trust Other Girls

It doesn't take much of a leap to see how girls can grow weary of the popularity treadmill yet still feel trapped in its endless cycle. Over time, girls learn not to trust each other, even those with whom they claim to be close friends. If they are concerned about popularity, they quickly learn that friendships can be simply conditional—"I will be friends with you only if nothing better comes along." Rachel Simmons (in her book *Odd Girl Out*) writes about the way girls use gossip as currency to buy their way into cliques.

To illustrate how this unfolds, consider Maya and Jenna, two close seventh-grade friends. Maya tells Jenna some secrets in private that Jenna promises not to repeat (e.g., that Maya likes Luke and that she doesn't like certain girls in the class). Jenna, in an effort to impress the popular girls at lunch one day, tells the other girls that Maya has a crush on Luke and thinks the other girls in the class are stupid. The popular girls devour this gossip and welcome Jenna to sit with them at lunch. In a matter of minutes, Jenna has sold out her friendship but has bought her way into the clique. Maya is devastated that other girls have found out her secrets, but she is also bewildered that Jenna is now ignoring her and that she would betray their friendship in this way. A few days later, after the popular girls have started to grow tired of Jenna, Jenna starts to show interest in Maya again. Jenna texts her about getting together after school. Maya is relieved and they resume their friendship as usual, until the cycle happens again. Maya learns not to trust Jenna but stays in the relationship because she does not want to be without a close friend.

This should set off an alarm: doesn't this sound awfully similar to the dynamics that many women endure in abusive romantic relationships? Part of a woman's willingness to tolerate abuse—to go back to a relationship again and again even after being treated cruelly in order to keep a romantic

---

Box 6.4: FRIENDS AS SUPPORT, NOT AS ENEMIES

Make sure your daughter knows that an authentic friend is someone who supports her and looks out for her best interests. This may seem obvious, but there is a big difference between being friends with someone in order to gain popularity and social status versus seeking out a true friend who is loyal and kind. Make sure she knows what she is looking for in a true friend so that she can evaluate her current friendships accordingly.

Ask her to complete the following exercise:

1. What are five things you want in a good friend?
2. Next, list your current friends. Do your closest friends have these qualities? If not, what draws you to these friends? Are you getting what you need from these relationships?
3. Do you yourself have the qualities you listed? If not, how can you work to build these qualities in yourself?
4. In examining your friends, do you have someone who meets your needs for support in the following ways?
   - Someone you can tell difficult things to
   - Someone who makes you laugh
   - Someone who believes in you
   - Someone you can trust
   - Someone who really listens to you
   - Someone who protects you[24]

Encourage your daughter to seek friendships that will enable her to say yes to all of these questions.

---

relationship going—can actually stem from what she learned to tolerate in her friendships when she was young. Instead of this dynamic, help your daughter learn the qualities of authentic relationships that enable her to be herself and support her in both her successes and struggles. See Text Box 6.4.

Consequence Three: She'll Learn to Question Her Own Perceptions

Imagine how confusing it must be for your daughter to hear "I am your best friend" from a girl one day and then to be ignored by her the next. To wonder whether others are sincere when they pay her a compliment or say they want to spend time with her. To believe that she is part of a friendship group and then learn that the girls are spreading rumors about her online. To be totally thrown off when a friend says, "Your outfit is hideous!" and have everyone laugh at her while the friend then exclaims, "Just kidding!" Your daughter is stuck. She wonders, *"That really hurt my feelings . . . But did she mean it or not? Is my outfit ugly? Or do they like it and they are just jealous? Why would she say it if she didn't think it? Or is it really just a joke and I am being too sensitive?"* Even though her feelings are hurt, she may try to laugh it off, all the while learning that she can't trust her own judgment.

It is also harder for her to trust her own experiences because much of her communication occurs online, without the face-to-face contact that could help her better determine someone's actual intentions. As we have all experienced, it is so easy to miscommunicate online or through texting! Use of ALL CAPITAL LETTERS, commas, and exclamation points (!!!!!!) can make all the difference in how a message comes across:

No way Nikki is not sitting with us at lunch today.
Versus
NO WAY!!! Nikki is NOT sitting with us at lunch today!!!!

Her immersion in social media can certainly contribute to her lack of knowing what is real and what is not, again causing her to question whether she can trust her own judgment. As she looks at others' pages, posts, tweets, and pictures, she sees a carefully edited version of what is going on, not a portrait of the reality of others' lives. She can come to believe that everyone else has more friends than she does, that everyone has a cool, sophisticated life, and that everyone is out trying risky things—and having lots of fun doing it. She looks to social media as a representation of the social scene, and this strongly influences what she comes to see as "normal."

In a recent national survey of 12- to 17-year-olds, 75 percent said that they had seen social media pictures of teens partying with alcohol and marijuana, and they agreed that seeing these pictures would make other teens "want to party like that." When asked about how they personally felt about the pictures, about half of the teens who had seen pictures of other teens getting drunk or using drugs agreed that the kids in the pictures "were having a good time."[25] In response to these kinds of findings, do everything that you can to help your daughter trust her fragile but slowly developing judgment. Help her pose critical questions such as *"Is everyone in school really getting drunk and using drugs all the time? Are they really having fun or could they be just posing for a picture? Are these people really my friends just because they have "friended" or "followed" me? If they are friends online but ignore me in person, do they like me or not? Why would my friend make fun of me if she is really my friend? And if Hayley has 600 Facebook friends and I have only 200, does that mean I am three times less likeable than she is? What does my number say about me?*

Consequence Four: She Might Limit Her Potential

Elise, a sixth grader, raises her hand in science class to say how much she loves dinosaurs and how great it was when her family went to New York for the first time, because she got to see the dinosaur exhibit at the Museum of Natural History. She hears some snickers from around the room. In the hall after class, another girl rolled her eyes at her and laughed, *"What, are you some kind of dino-freak? Just kidding!"* Embarrassed that she had broken some unspoken rule, Elise never again spoke in class about her interests or opinions. Elise, like so many girls, is caught in a bind: she wants to form her own identity ("I am passionate about studying dinosaurs") while at the same time she also wants to blend in and not call unnecessary attention to herself. Along these lines, Simmons writes about girls who are ridiculed because they seem to think too highly of themselves: "She thinks she is *all that.*" If she stands out too much, if she appears too confident, or seems to think she is *"all that,"* a girl puts herself at risk as a potential victim of RA. Because she fears stepping out of line, as Elise seems to have done in the previous example, a girl who is overly concerned about fitting into a popular clique may learn to stifle her creativity and to avoid pursuing her passions all in order to blend as seamlessly as possible into what is deemed acceptable by the in-crowd.

How Do Girls Respond?

The unthinkable has happened: your daughter has become a victim of cruel and mean behavior, and these acts are being committed by her perceived friends. Girls can react in a variety of ways. Some of them want to avoid or escape the RA by staying home from school, changing schools, or avoiding activities where it occurs. They want to hide. Others seek revenge. They get back at the perpetrators by playing their own game, becoming relationally or physically aggressive in return. Still others, desperately wanting to remain in a clique, accept the mean behavior as inevitable. They simply endure the abuse. Finally, some girls choose to step off the treadmill. They opt out of trying to fit into this particular clique of girls and try to move on to other friendships and activities. Although we know that this is usually the healthiest option, we also know that this is extremely hard for girls who have so much invested in obtaining the approval of a popular clique. The strategies listed in the following paragraphs are designed to help *you* to help *her* in this regard: to learn to *decrease* the importance of popularity in her life and *increase* her opportunities for authentic relationships that help her grow and develop into the unique person she is becoming.

WHAT TO DO: RESILIENCE STRATEGIES FOR PARENTS

RA is very hard to change within any setting (school, sports team, group) because it works so well to get girls what they want (popularity, status), and it continues because girls who are not in the inner circle of popularity are fearful to challenge the RA perpetrators out of fear that they too will become the next victims.[26] Another reason it is hard to change is that it often goes undetected in schools and is usually unreported to adults because girls say that they doubt the adults would do anything about it, or if they did take action, it would only make the problem worse (see Box 6.5).

You might be thinking that this issue sounds somewhat insurmountable. Rather than throwing up your hands in defeat, however, consider some of the following strategies you can use to decrease the chances that your daughter will become entrenched in a web of relationally aggressive relationships:

- **Do your part and stay aware.** Do seek to understand your daughter's position in the social hierarchy at her school. Does she aspire to be popular? Help her explore why popularity is important to her? Without overly intruding in her life, be involved enough that you know what she is doing with her friends and the kinds of things she does online. Another part of your responsibility is to become a positive role model, as previously discussed. You will have a great influence on how she interacts in her relationships.

- **Educate.** She is probably informed about the topic of bullying, but she might not know what RA in particular looks like and how damaging it can be. Make sure she knows that it is actually a harmful form of bullying and is *not* an expected part of friendships. When you see her acting in relationally aggressive ways, point it out to her and her friends. In this way she can start to become more aware of what it is and what she can do differently.

- **Shape her view of other girls.** Help her view other girls as allies, not as competitors.[27] Instead of taking pleasure in seeing another girl fail, help your daughter to support other girls and to cheer them on in their successes.

- **Encourage her to speak up.** Help her know that while it may feel risky, it is important to express her opinion clearly and directly. She doesn't have to couch her sentences in "I am not sure, but . . ." or to always speak in questions ("Could it be that . . . ?"). I work with many female graduate students in their mid- to late twenties who regularly mumble ". . . but I don't know" after every comment they make in class. Clearly this can become a habit that will cause others to take young women less seriously as they progress through school and into their careers. As promoted in recent materials from BanBossy.com, encourage your daughter instead to speak up with no hedging.

- **Teach her to demonstrate empathy.** Empathy is different from sympathy, which means you are sad or feel sorry for someone. The definition of empathy is that you can see beyond your own viewpoint and are able to take on the perspective of another person. It is like momentarily crawling inside another person's skin and imagining what it would feel like to be *her* in this situation. What is the other person feeling? What is she experiencing? Why might she be acting in this way?[28] If Casey is angry at Mauri because Mauri has not returned her texts in several days, she can try to take Mauri's perspective for a moment. Maybe Mauri is preoccupied with her mom's upcoming surgery. Maybe Mauri is so worried about her mom that she is not devoting any time to her friends right now. Casey can start to understand that Mauri has emotions too and that her actions don't necessary reflect any negative feelings toward Casey. Instead of anger or retaliation, Casey can realize that perhaps Mauri could use a good friend and some kind words right now. Bottom line: encourage your daughter to use empathy in her relationships before jumping to negative conclusions.

- **Help her to become a "girl in the middle."** Rosalind Wiseman describes a Girl in the Middle (GIM) as someone who is free to float in and out of several friendship circles and is not overly concerned with fitting into one particular group just because it will help her to look popular. Wiseman reports that it is the GIMs who feel most empowered to voice their own opinions and needs in relationships. According to Wiseman, they are also the ones who are most likely to choose to intervene on behalf of victims by standing up to girls who use RA. Because they are not trying to please a particular clique, they do not fear what might happen if they challenge the leader's treatment of others.

- **Grow a leader.** I am often amazed at the energy and creativity that many girls put into their relationally aggressive behaviors. I am also impressed with the leadership abilities that some girls can use in rallying their troops into action when needed. If a girl tends to be a leader within her circle, instead of putting her skills into devising schemes to maintain her power, help her pour her energy into a broader social issue that captures her interest—perhaps one that sparks her indignation (e.g., maybe get her interested in protesting advertising campaigns that are degrading to girls and women, or the maltreatment of children in poverty; the list of social causes is endless). This will help her spend her time on something that has meaning and purpose, and she can rechannel her anger into a cause that will have a productive outcome. According to Ana Homayoun, if your daughter is actively engaged and feeling purposeful, she won't feel that it is necessary to compromise herself for the quick fix of self-satisfaction that comes from meanness.

- **Diversify.** When things are not going well in her friendships at school, it makes it easier for a girl to have friendship groups outside of the school setting. Without overscheduling her life, make sure that your daughter is involved in a variety of activities—both sports and extracurricular activities outside of school—that help her stay balanced and not overly focused on the approval of a particular friendship group.

- **Provide reassurance.** Girls' friendships are both a wonderful source of support as well as a painful cause of frustration and sadness. This is not an easy time and you won't always be invited in, but stay close and offer ample reassurance. In doing so, try to communicate the following messages drawn from *Raising Our Daughters: The Ultimate Parenting Guide for Healthy Girls and Thriving Families*[29]:
  - Hold onto your real voice in relationships.

- Risk losing the relationship when it asks you to be less than your true self.
- Face up to the fear of displeasing others.
- Be willing to have disagreements with your friends. It's okay to disagree, debate, negotiate.

Box 6.5: IF YOU SUSPECT THAT YOUR DAUGHTER IS A VICTIM OF RA[30]:

- **Be an active and patient listener.** If she is reluctant to share her experiences with you, remember that she might find it humiliating to admit her problem. Ask some leading questions about girls in general to help her open up. Simmons suggests the following questions:

  When girls want to be mean in your class, what kinds of things do they do?

  Are some girls more secret than others about their meanness? How?
  Can friends be mean to each other? How?

- **Empathize with what she is going through.** Don't, however, relive your experiences through your daughter. In other words, remember what it was like for you but don't overdo it. She doesn't want to worry you, and this will only make the experience worse for her.
- **Make your home a sanctuary.** The most important thing that helps girls get through difficult times at school is the "refuge" of home and family. Create a home with unconditional love and support.
- **Get your daughter's opinion before taking action.** Help her to feel empowered by respecting her wishes as to what to do. It is generally not helpful to call the perpetrator's parents. Listen, reflect, and validate her story *first*, then ask your daughter to think of what she would like to say to the girls who are bullying her.
- **Some action steps you can consider**:

  1. Listen to the whole story and get the facts (e.g., "Who is doing this to you? When does it occur?"). Paraphrase and reflect what you heard. Validate and give her praise where appropriate.
  2. Find out what she wants you to do (e.g., "Do you want me to talk to the teacher or someone at the school?").
  3. Help her to plan her day to minimize the effects of the bullying.
  4. Encourage her to role-play how she will respond to bullies in various situations at school.

- Accept that not everyone is going to like you and that's okay.
- Accept criticism without it diminishing your sense of self.
- Learn to say no and expect your no to be honored.

After considering these resilience strategies—which are intended to both prevent RA as well as to soften its impact on your daughter—consider teaching her some specific social skills. Have her practice the exercises in Box 6.6 and 6.7 with you and have discussions about the results.

Box 6.6: FOR YOUR DAUGHTER: STOP THE GOSSIP!

Help your daughter practice what she would do in scenarios like the following:

> *Your friends are sitting around the lunch table at school. One of them says, "See Mackensey over there? I heard that she stole Lauren's boyfriend!"*

What do you say next? Three things to try:

1. **Stop and think**. Take a deep breath and pause before you say anything.
2. **Try to be the first one to respond**. You can make a real difference in whether the gossip is spread or if is stops then and there. Research shows that if you speak up first and you *agree* with the gossip (such as, "Yes that's right! I heard that Mackensey is a real backstabber"), your friends will likely join in and add comments of their own. Instead, if you are the first to speak and you *challenge* the gossip (such as, "I really like Mackensey. I would be surprised if she did anything like that!"), the gossip will usually stop; no one else is likely to say anything.[31] Try it and see if this research finding is true in your friendship group.
3. **Answer three questions**. Later that day, after you hear the gossip about Mackensey, you are hanging out after school with another friend. It enters your mind that your friend might like to hear this piece of gossip.

Before you say anything, try to answer these three questions:

1. Who will benefit if I repeat this gossip? Who will be hurt by it? (*Answer: probably no one will benefit; my friend will be interested, but Mackensey will definitely be hurt.*)

2. How would I feel if this was said about me? (*Answer: I would be horrified! I would want change schools!*)
3. Would I repeat this gossip if Mackensey were standing right here listening to me? (*Answer: No way! I would never say it in front of Mackensey!*)

After you have asked yourself these questions and considered your answers, you can make a good decision about whether or not you want to repeat the gossip.[32]

Box 6.7: FOR YOUR DAUGHTER: UPSET WITH SOMEONE? SPEAK UP AND HAVE A SANDWICH

This strategy is called the *sandwich technique*. It is very effective when you need to confront someone about something they said or did. I know it is hard to speak up directly about what you need and want from someone, but practicing these skills leads to resilience and strong self-esteem. It is also helpful for the other person because she will have a chance to change her behavior. It might make a big difference in her life—all because you were willing to speak up!

Here is your sandwich:

Layer one: Say something positive. ("I want you to know that I think you are a good friend and I want to stay friends with you.")
Layer two: Let her know what it is that you don't like, ask that she stop the behavior, and then tell her what you would like her to do. ("I heard from Danielle that you were making fun of me and that you said in front of a bunch of kids in our class that I needed to go to Weight Watchers. I am really hurt that you would do this. I would like you to stop making fun of me.")
Layer three: End with something positive. ("I normally think of you as someone I can trust. You have always stood up for me in the past.")[33]

In this way, you start with something positive, so you have her attention and she won't tune you out. Then you say what you want and need in a direct manner and end with something good, so that she won't be as defensive. This may not resolve the problem, but at least you will have done your part and will have practiced assertiveness!

GIRLS' CRUSHES AND ROMANTIC RELATIONSHIPS

Okay, steel yourself: I have talked about the complex world of girls' friendships; now it is time to dive into even deeper waters—their romantic relationships. It is normal for girls to be driven toward romantic relationships starting in early adolescence. Remember, as reviewed in Chapter Two, part of this need for a relationship stems from an awakening physiological drive for relational closeness.

Does this mean that she is biologically driven toward romance craziness? In a way, yes. But if biology is what lights the match, it is cultural, media-driven messages that fuel the spark that then causes a wildfire. Cultural pressures are quite strong in this life dimension: Consider the fact that girls regularly receive the following messages: (1) romantic relationships should take precedence over friendships, (2) other girls are competitors in the serious game of finding a romantic partner, and (3) most important of all, your success and worth as a person is tied up in finding and keeping a romantic relationship.

If she buys in to these cultural messages, a romantic interest can supersede her priorities in all other areas, including her friends, interests, and personal goals. How ironic that when girls need true, supportive friendships the most, they often drop their friends at the first sign of male or female attention. Sadly, girls become distrustful of other girls who might potentially "steal" a boyfriend or girlfriend. Being "in a relationship" becomes intertwined with self-worth; it is a status symbol that is seen as worth almost any sacrifice.

It should be acknowledged from the outset that although all girls receive cultural pressures about prioritizing romantic relationships and most are starting to explore their emerging sexual identities during this developmental period, their experiences in this area are not at all uniform. Although many girls are drawn to heterosexual relationships, others are questioning and exploring their identities as individuals who might be lesbian, bisexual, or transgender. I certainly do not want to ignore their particular concerns and challenges. Although specific parenting strategies for girls who are exploring same-sex romantic attraction is beyond the scope of this chapter, some recommended readings to help you and your daughter are included at the end of this book. Because cultural messages primarily revolve around the importance of girls' success in seeking and maintaining attention from a romantic partner (whether male *or* female), many of the issues discussed throughout this chapter apply regardless of a girl's sexual orientation. For ease of discussion, though, I will sometimes use the term "boyfriend" or use a male pronoun in referring to a romantic interest while remaining aware that it does not apply in every case.

If a girl soaks in the cultural pressure that she must be in a relationship, it follows that she might compromise her beliefs and values in order to stay in that relationship. If she is looking to others for approval, trying to grasp a sense of being affirmed and valued, she will be vulnerable in the relationship and will have trouble saying no to the person who is providing that affirmation. As an obvious example and one that many parents fear is that in order to maintain their relationships, some girls engage in sexual activity only because they believe that their partner will break up with them if they say no. Many girls say that they regret their first sexual experience and report that they had sex only because they didn't want to upset their boyfriends (saying things like "I didn't want my boyfriend to be mad at me"). Others have sex in order to try to obtain a relationship in the first place, mistakenly believing that this will make the other person like them. A girl may be so in need of validation that she would rather accept brief sexual attention rather than feel alone, empty, and unworthy of acceptance. Unfortunately the very feelings she is trying to avoid are only intensified when the sexual encounter does not bring her the lasting acceptance she craves.

A Word About Sexting

These concepts and statistics help us better understand a current phenomenon sweeping through middle and high schools today: sexting. In a recent national study, 22 percent of middle schoolers (yes, that is ages 12 to 14) admitted to sexting. If you are like me, at first thought it is hard to imagine why a girl in middle school would send someone a partially nude picture of herself via cell phone, knowing that it would likely be shared with others around the school (and even the world) within a matter of seconds. After reading these paragraphs, however, you grasp the context in which this happens. For example, Whitney has a boyfriend and feels that she has finally obtained the approval and status she was searching for, but then he asks her to send some pictures. She doesn't want to, but he threatens to go find another girl who *is* willing and *promises* that he won't show the pictures to anyone else. She wants to please him, to make sure he likes her. And so she sends the pictures.

Other girls sext in order to get others' attention in the first place. They believe it is the price they have to pay in order to get the attention they are seeking. We know that if a girl is unable to say no to sexting, she is also less likely to say no in real life, and surveys of students bear this out. Studies of middle school students who sext found that these students were four to seven times more likely to be sexually active (this includes kissing, having oral sex, or sexual intercourse) than those who did not participate in sexting. In particular, girls who sext are more likely to have multiple sexual partners and to use illicit substances. Heavy cell phone use is also related to sexting and sexual activity: those students who text 100 or times per day are more likely to have sent or received a sext and to be sexually active than those who text less frequently.[34] Again, this is happening regularly in the world of *middle schoolers*. The numbers are even higher for high school students. To be able to swim upstream, your daughter clearly needs your support and guidance in this area; consider the resilience strategies that follow.

What to Do: Resilience Strategies for Healthy Romantic Relationships

Love, approve, validate. As discussed extensively in Chapter Four, it is vitally important for your daughter to feel loved and accepted just for who she is. When she believes that she has your approval, she won't feel desperate to seek out others' validation to prove that she has value. She will not *need* the validation that comes from romantic attention or from having a boyfriend (or girlfriend) in order to feel good about herself. She won't be as vulnerable to losing herself in a romantic relationship.

Dad, you are the model. A girl's relationship with her father is generally the first one she has with a male, and it sets the standard for how she will expect to be treated by boys and men (or any romantic interest) in the future. First, observe your interactions with the women in your life; your daughter is watching you, her father, to see how you treat women and especially how you interact with her mother. Next, consider your current relationship with your daughter. She wants to have a special relationship with you, one in which she knows she has your approval. She needs to hear you say you love her, but she also needs to see it through your actions. She feels valued when you spend time with her. This occurs when you clear your calendar to take her on a father-daughter outing, when you hug her and show her affection, when you listen to her problems, when she knows without a doubt that you are on her side and that you are her biggest fan. When she feels that you *love* and *like* her, she will feel less need to frantically search for validation from other males.

Make space for conversation. The stereotype of having "the talk" with our adolescents is one of mumbling, awkwardness, and relief when it is over. In reality, what our daughters need is not a one-time lecture about relationships, sexuality, and sexual pressures but an open atmosphere of trust characterized by ongoing conversation. Madeline Levine writes that we as parents are responsible for being the sex educators of our children, for "if we don't discuss the most critical issues our kids will face—new bodies, sexual choices, intimacy—then the information is likely to come from their equally confused peers."[35]

Therefore, as uncomfortable as it may feel, you have to deal with reality: Your daughter will be faced with sexual pressures, and probably a lot sooner than you think. Rather than ignore it and wishing it would go away, you need to clarify certain issues for yourself: What are your expectations and standards in this regard? What are your values? (Revisit the list you created in Chapter Four).

Second, once you are clear on where you stand, you need to communicate your values to your daughter in multiple conversations and over time. You should communicate your expectations in a clear manner, but you also don't want to become too dogmatic so that your daughter will be reluctant to ever approach you with questions. Instead, she needs to know that you want her to come to you when she is confused or feeling pressured; she won't do this if she fears that you will demean or punish her in some way. As Kathy Masarie recommends, *be an askable parent*; demonstrate that you are open to questions.[36] Your goal should be to make your daughter feel comfortable in coming to you when she is actually facing a dilemma or decision.

Some parents mistakenly believe that talking about sexuality and relationships will encourage their daughters to actually engage in sexual activity. Instead, research shows that girls who have had ongoing conversations about sexuality and dealing with sexual pressures are more resilient and make better choices than other girls when actually faced with pressures in these areas. This is because they have information, they know how to assert their boundaries, and they are able to make informed decisions grounded in their parents' belief systems.[37]

Establish rules for dating. As already stated, decide in advance how old your daughter should be in order to be allowed to go on group dates and then one-to-one dates (see Box 6.8). Many experts recommend the age of 16 as a safe age to begin one-to-one dating. They also recommend that you should have a rule against dating someone who is more than one school grade above or below her. In this way she is more likely to be on an equal footing psychologically and mentally with her romantic interest when inevitable sexual pressures do arise. Meg Meeker—pediatrician, parenting expert, and author of the blog "Family Matters"—claims that teen dating should be discouraged until the later years of high school;

even then, she says that it is rare for anything positive to come from exclusive dating relationships. Studies show that early romantic involvement (even relationships that do not involve sexual intercourse) is linked with future psychological and social difficulties for girls because the time invested in these relationships replaces energy that would otherwise be spent in developing healthy friendships.[38] It is the social skills that develop through friendships that are linked to success and happiness in later life. Further, girls who date earlier are more likely to have sex earlier, and a strong line of research indicates that girls who have sex before the age of 16 are at far higher risk for significant problems, including unwanted pregnancy, HIV, and other sexually transmitted diseases [39]

You might be thinking that a rule of "no one-to-one dating until age 16" sounds like a throwback to the 1950s courtship era. If you look at current cultural standards, it does indeed sound old-fashioned. To be clear, I am presenting the facts here so that you can be the one to make informed decisions for your family. In general, the earlier she goes on one-to-one dates, the earlier she will face pressures for sexual activity and the more at risk she will be for problems. It is far better to encourage friendships with both boys and girls so that she can develop the communication skills

---

Box 6.8: DATING VERSUS HANGING OUT AND HOOKING UP

Note that "dating" is an antiquated word among teens today and even more so among college students, who report that dating has become officially dead on campus.[40] Instead, students rarely go on traditional dates but rather hang out in groups and then pair up at some point. This is what teens mean by the terms "hanging out" and "hooking up" with friends (and resulting in the additional term "friends with benefits" or FWB—a hookup that has no stated expectation for a subsequent relationship). I've worked with many college women who say they go along with this arrangement because it is the norm on their campus but they really desire more than this; they hope that the "benefits" will ultimately lead to a relationship. I am reminded of a university student client who regularly received what she called "booty call" texts from guys at 2 a.m., asking if she would come over to their apartment. She complained, "I knew all they wanted was to have sex with me, but I thought it was better than nothing, so I always went. I thought one of them might actually turn into something more, but they never did."

This is an example from a college student, but parents should be aware that even middle-school girls talk about having to participate in the FWB culture, especially being pressured to offer oral sex to boys, in order to be part of a popular group. Therefore, even if your daughter isn't dating in the traditional sense, she may be hanging out in groups where the expectation is that hookups will occur. Remember that hooking up can mean a broad range of things, from kissing to oral sex to actual intercourse, which makes it a vague and confusing term for parents. Parents should ask their daughters what they mean when they say a girl is "hanging out" with someone, and what they mean when they talk about "hooking up." It is likely that you will be surprised by the answer!

she will need when she is older and better able to assert her boundaries in romantic relationships.

It's okay to have "single" status. We have already discussed the pressures girls feel to be in a relationship. The message is pervasive in her life at school, and she will certainly pick it up from social media, books, television, and movies. We have also already discussed the harms that can come from early dating. She will need reassurance and encouragement to believe that *it's okay not to be in a romantic relationship*. Provide her with as many opportunities as possible to learn that being in a relationship is not a requirement for childhood and adolescence.

Teach Your Daughter to Be Assertive in Relationships

Step One: Decisions First

We have discussed all of the reasons why it is hard for girls to say no to someone they care about. That is why your daughter's assertiveness skills need to be particularly strong. Prior to discussing the nuts and bolts of assertiveness, however, a focus on her values is necessary. She can't be assertive about what she wants and needs unless she knows at her core what she really wants and needs! What are her core convictions regarding her own social and sexual limits? What kinds of boundaries does she want to put in place that will help her stay true to herself? These are issues that you can help her think through well in advance of her first social experiences.

Girls will be far more successful if they have a trusted adult with whom they can talk about their social/sexual boundaries. It doesn't have to be you, but you can certainly be instrumental in helping her find an adult mentor whose values are aligned with your own. These discussions will help her sort through all of the pressure and media messages in order for her to get to the foundation of who she is and what her standards will be in a relationship. Help your daughter practice the exercise presented in Box 6.9.

Step Two: Practice the Art of Saying No

Unfortunately, despite our advances in education on this issue, many boys are immersed in a culture that still encourages them to believe that if a girl says no, she probably means yes. So they don't listen to the first few attempts at no. At the same time, girls witness a myriad of examples of women in their lives who use wishy-washy no's that often

---

Box 6.9: FOR YOUR DAUGHTER

In my presentations to groups of teen girls, I encourage them to think about their sexual limits. I tell them:

Don't try to decide what your sexual limits will be while you are in the heat of a romantic moment. You will almost always make a poor decision, based on emotion, that is not in your best interest. Decide in advance what you are going to do, why you have made this decision, and stay mindful of these values when you know you will be in a high-risk situation. Don't wait until it happens. Decide now.

In light of this advice, take some time to answer the following questions:

- What are you looking for in a romantic relationship?
- What are the qualities you expect of the person with whom you are in a relationship?
- When you are alone with a person you are really attracted to, what are your personal limits as far as what you are willing to do?
- What is the line you won't cross? What are the limits you want to put in place so that you will feel good about yourself and your decisions?

sound as though they could mean "maybe."[41] I have worked with many girls who say they remained in situations when they knew something wasn't right when they were alone with a partner, but they stayed in the situation because they didn't want to say no out of concern that they would hurt his feelings or come across sounding mean. For girls to be resilient, they need to learn that they have a right to trust their instincts, to say no and to mean it. Help your daughter practice the exercises listed in Box 6.10.

• Step Three: Watch for red flags

If your daughter is in a relationship and starts to feel uncomfortable with how much her partner is trying to control her life and she feels that she can't be herself while she is in the relationship, help her to evaluate the relationship by comparing it with these warning signs (see also Chapter Three).

• Examples of Controlling Behaviors
  Does her partner display any of the following?:
  • Tells her how to dress and act
  • Tells her who she can see, where she can go
  • Isolates her from her support system; discourages her from seeing friends and family
  • Tells her to stay home while he goes out with friends or family
  • Threatens to hurt her (or himself) in some way if she breaks up with him
  • Causes her to feel afraid to bring up certain subjects that might upset him
  • Causes her to feel tied down, as if she has to stay in contact at all times
  • Examples of Digital Abuse
  • Uses excessive texting to track her whereabouts
  • Pressures her to provide her online or cell phone password
  • Looks through phone her frequently; checks up on pictures, texts, outgoing calls
  • Tells her who she can or cannot be friends with on Facebook
  • Sends negative or even threatening e-mails, Facebook messages, tweets, or other messages
  • Puts her down in status updates

Box 6.10: FOR YOUR DAUGHTER

- Practice saying no. Use this checklist:
  - Use a direct, short message, using an "I" statement: "No, I am not OK with that."
  - Use a clear, even voice tone. Do not waver.
  - Make direct eye contact with the other person.
  - Make sure your facial expression matches what you are saying.
  - Maintain a confident body posture.
- Now role-play these skills with a partner. Pretend that you are saying no to someone you have a crush on. Don't worry about sounding mean or hurting the other person's feelings. Say no because you are being asked to do something that you do not feel comfortable doing.
- Keep saying no. When someone is pressuring you, he or she won't often stop after only one no. You will have to keep repeating your no until the other person gets the message. What would you do in the following scenario?

    You are attending a party with your friends and you see a person that you really like. After talking for a while, he decides that you should leave the party together so that you can be alone together. You don't feel right doing this. When he says, "Let's get out of here. I really want to be alone with you."
    What is an assertive response you can make?

    Next, he says, "What's wrong with you? I thought you were cool!"
    What can you say in response?

    Next, he says, "I guess I'll go back to the party. I know Sonia won't be a big baby. I'll see if she wants to go with me."
    What would be your next response?

    Remember, it is best to be prepared to have multiple assertive responses you can use. If a person you like doesn't listen to and respect your first assertive response, it is a clear sign to you that the person isn't concerned about your needs. If you are in a truly caring relationship, why would this person force you to do things you don't want to do?

- Pressures her to send explicit pictures or videos (sexting) and then shares the pictures with others

- Examples of Stalking
  - Waits for her at places where she says she is going
  - Follows her when she goes places with friends and family
- Examples of Sexual Abuse
  - Pressures her sexually, calls her "immature" or "babyish" if she won't engage in sexual behaviors
  - Threatens to break up with her or spread lies about her if she will not cooperate sexually
- Examples of Emotional Abuse
  - Manipulates her in ways that cause her to believe that she is responsible for unhealthy or abusive behaviors
  - Ignores her, gives her the silent treatment, or frequently hangs up on her
  - Spreads rumors about her in an attempt to humiliate her
  - Threatens to expose her secrets
  - Calls her names, puts her down in public
  - Compares her negatively to other girlfriends from the past[42]

In contrast, the following qualities should be part of any healthy relationship:

- She should be treated with respect.
- Her partner should not make fun of things she likes or wants to do.
- Her partner should not get angry if she spends time with friends or family.
- Her partner should listen to her ideas and compromise at times.
- Her partner should share some of her interests and activities.
- Her partner should be comfortable around her friends and family.
- Her partner should be proud of her accomplishments and successes.
- Her partner doesn't pressure her to do things she doesn't want to do.
- Her partner doesn't threaten her or make her feel scared.
- Her partner enables her to express how she feels so that she can speak up for herself in the relationship.
- Her partner is caring, honest, and doesn't constantly accuse her of cheating or being unfaithful.
- Her partner respects her right to set limits and boundaries in the relationship.[43]

If this is not the case, help her express her fears and talk about your concerns with her. Encourage her to seek adult help and guidance when she finds herself in this type of relationship.

CONCLUSION

After reading this chapter, it is my hope that you have now gained some valuable insight into the importance of girls' relationships. You learned that girls are encouraged to base their overall sense of worth on the success of their relationships. This, in turn, places girls in a bind: *"Do I follow what I want for myself, in order to be true to my authentic self, or do I do what is needed in order to be accepted by others? Do I choose to please others at the expense of myself?"* This is a balance your daughter must achieve in order to be resilient: to hold on to who she is at her core while also maintaining close and healthy relationships. For you as her parent, the purpose of this chapter has been to help you help her find this balance. She needs to develop a core identity so that she can be confident in standing up for what she believes and values. Help her to find friends that respect her for who she is, not how well she conforms to what is popular. Teach her that being in a romantic relationships is not a requirement for success. Empower her to be empathic, a person who cares about others' needs, while also having the freedom to speak up and assert her own needs. Finally, remember that one of the most important things you can do is to continually provide her with a sense of love and validation. When she feels accepted by you, she will be less driven to seek excessive attention and acceptance from her peers in order to define her worth and value.

NOTES

1. Deak, J. (2003). *Girls will be girls: Raising confident and courageous daughters*. New York: Hyperion.
2. Gilligan, C. (1982). *In a different voice: Psychological theory and women's development*. Cambridge, MA: Harvard University Press.
3. Pipher, M. (1994). *Reviving Ophelia: Saving the selves of adolescent girls*. New York: Random House.
4. Silverman, R. (2010). *Good girls don't get fat: How weight obsession is messing up our girls and how we can help them thrive despite it*. New York: Harlequin.
5. Buckley, T. R., & Carter, R.T. (2005). Black adolescent girls: Do gender role and identity impact their self-esteem? *Sex Roles, 53,* 647–661; Basow, S. A., & Rubin, L. R. (1999). Gender influences and adolescent development. In N. G. Johnson,

M. C. Roberts, & J. Worell (eds.), *Beyond appearance: A new look at adolescent girls* (pp. 25–52). Washington, DC: American Psychological Association.

6. SAMHSA, Violent behaviors among adolescent females. Available at www.samhsa.gov/newsroom/press-announcements/201001131245

7. Hemmen, L. (2012). *Parenting a teen girl: Crash course on conflict, communication, and connection with your teenage daughter.* Oakland, CA: New Harbinger.

8. Miller, S., Loeber, R., & Hipwell, A. (2009). Peer deviance, parenting, and disruptive behavior among young girls. *Journal of Abnormal Child Psychology, 37*(2), 139–152.; Sontag, L. M., Graber, J. A., & Clemans, K. H. (2011). The role of peer stress and pubertal timing on symptoms of psychopathology during early adolescence. *Journal of Youth and Adolescence, 40*(10), 1371–1382.

9. Gilligan, C. (1982). *In a different voice: Psychological theory and women's development* (p. 19). Cambridge, MA: Harvard University Press.

10. Deak, J. (2003). *Girls will be girls: Raising confident and courageous daughters.* New York: Hyperion.

11. Simmons, R. (2009). *The curse of the good girl: Raising authentic girls with courage and confidence* (p. 11). New York: Penguin Press.

12. Homayoun, A. (2013). *The myth of the perfect girl: Helping our daughters find authentic success and happiness in school and life* (p. 174). New York: Penguin.

13. Underwood, M. K. (2003). *Social aggression among girls.* New York: Guilford.

14. Messick, J. (Producer), & Waters, M. (Director). (2004) *Mean Girls* [Motion picture]. Paramount Pictures. Note: The screenplay by Tina Fey was adapted from Rosalind Wiseman's *Queen Bees and Wannabes* book, also recommended reading for parents. *Mean Girls* is celebrating its ten-year anniversary as I write, and pop culture critics are still commenting on its application to the experiences of teen girls.

15. Crick, N. R., & Grotpeter, J. K. (1995). Relational aggression, gender, and social-psychological adjustment. *Child Development, 66,* 710–722; Underwood, M. K. (2003) *Social aggression among girls.* New York: Guilford.

16. Eaton, D. K., Kann, L., Kinchen, S., Shanklin, S., Flint, K. H., Hawkins, J., . . . Wechsler, H. (2012). Youth risk behavior surveillance—United States, 2011. *MMWR Surveillance Surveys, 61*(4), 1–168.

17. Homayoun, A. (2013). *The myth of the perfect girl: Helping our daughters find authentic success and happiness in school and life.* New York: Penguin; Steiner-Adair, C. (2013). *The big disconnect: Protecting childhood and family relationships in the digital age.* New York: HarperCollins.

18. Dweck, C. (2006). *Mindset: The new psychology of success.* New York: Ballantine.

19. Marwick, A., & boyd, d. (2011). The drama! Teen conflict, gossip, and bullying in networked places. Paper presented at *Oxford Internet Institute's "A Decade in Internet Time: Symposium on the Dynamics of the Internet and Society,"* September 22, 2011. Oxford, UK.

20. Hinkelman, L. (2013). *Girls without limits: Helping girls achieve healthy relationships, academic successes, and interpersonal strength.* Thousand Oaks, CA: Corwin.

21. Ibid.

22. Wiseman, R. (2009). Queen Bees and Wannabes: helping your daughter survive cliques, gossip, boyfriends, and the new realities of girl world. New York: Three Rivers Press.

23. Allen, J. P., Schad, M. M., Oudekerk, B., & Chango, J. (2014). Whatever happened to the "cool" kids? Long term sequelae of early adolescent pseudomature behavior. *Child Development, 85,* 1866–1880.

24. Hinkelman, L. (2013). *Girls without limits: Helping girls achieve healthy relationships, academic successes, and interpersonal strength.* Thousand Oaks, CA: Corwin.

25. CASAColumbia. (2012). *National survey on American attitudes on substance abuse xvii: Teens.* Retrieved from http://www.casacolumbia.org/addiction-research/reports/national-survey-american-attitudes-substance-abuse-teens-2012

26. Simmons, R. (2002). *Odd girl out: The hidden culture of aggression in girls.* Boston: Houghton Mifflin Harcourt.

27. Underwood, M. K. (2003) *Social aggression among girls.* New York: Guilford.

28. Kottler, J. (2010). *On being a therapist* (4th ed.). Hoboken, NJ: Jossey-Bass.

29. Masarie, K. (2013). *Raising out daughters: The ultimate parenting guide for healthy girls and thriving families.* Portland, OR: Family Empowerment Network.

30. Simmons, R. (2002). *Odd girl out: The hidden culture of aggression in girls.* Boston: Houghton Mifflin Harcourt; Adapted from Choate, L. H. (2008). *Girls' and women's wellness: Contemporary counseling issues and interventions.* Alexandria, VA: American Counseling Association.

31. Dellasega, C., & Nixon, C. (2003) *12 strategies that will end female bullying: Girl wars.* New York: Simon & Schuster.

32. Ibid.

33. Adapted from Dellasega, C., & Nixon, C. (2003) *12 strategies that will end female bullying: Girl wars.* New York: Simon & Schuster; Choate, L. H. (2008). *Girls' and women's wellness: Contemporary counseling issues and interventions.* Alexandria, VA: American Counseling Association.

34. Houck, C. D., Barker, D., Rizzo, C., Hancock, E., Norton, A., & Brown, L. K. (2014). Sexting and sexual behavior in at-risk adolescents. *Pediatrics, 133*(2), e276–e282.; Rice, E., Gibbs, J., Winetrobe, H., Rhoades, H., Plant, A., Montoya, J., & Kordic, T. (2014). Sexting and sexual behavior among middle school students. *Pediatrics, 134*(1) e21–e28; Temple, J. R., Paul, J., van den Berg, P., Le, V., McElhany, A., & Temple, B. (2012). Teen sexting and its association with sexual behaviors. *Archives of Pediatrics & Adolescent Medicine, 166*(9), 828–833.

35. Levine, M. (2013). Teach your Children Well: Why Values and Coping Skills Matter More than Grades, Trophies, or "Fat Envelopes". Page 101. New York: Harper Perennial.

36. Masarie, K. (2013). *Raising out daughters: The ultimate parenting guide for healthy girls and thriving families.* Portland, OR: Family Empowerment Network.

37. Ibid.

38. Allen, J. P., Schad, M. M., Oudekerk, B., & Chango, J. 2014 Whatever happened to the "cool" kids? Long term sequelae of early adolescent pseudomature behavior. *Child Development, 85,* 1866–1880.

39. Levine, M. (2012). *Teach your children well.* New York: HarperCollins.

40. See Sessions Stepp, L. 2008. *Unhooked: How young women pursue sex, delay love, and lose at both.* New York: Riverhead.

41. http://www.BanBossy.com, 2014

42. Masarie, K. (2013). *Raising out daughters: The ultimate parenting guide for healthy girls and thriving families.* Portland, OR: Family Empowerment Network; Choate, L. H. (2008). *Girls' and women's wellness: Contemporary counseling issues and interventions.* Alexandria, VA: American Counseling Association.; Choate, L. H. (2014). *Adolescent girls in distress: A guide for mental health treatment and prevention.* New York: Springer.

43. Ibid.

CHAPTER SEVEN

Resilience Dimension Four

Keeping Success in Perspective

If you had to guess, who do you think would have higher overall grade point averages in high school: boys or girls? Who would have the highest test scores on achievement tests? Who would be more likely to go to medical school? Law school? The answer to all of these questions is: Girls. It is true that girls as a group are outperforming boys in terms of school performance. They get better grades (about a half-grade higher GPA than boys) and they earn higher scores on achievement tests (tests that measure what they are actually learning in school). Women go on to graduate from college and graduate schools at higher rates than men, and there are now more women than men enrolled in law schools and medical schools.[1]

If girls as a group are doing well, why do so many still seem to be struggling? In Chapter One I introduced the cultural imperative that tells girls to do it all and be perfect. I explored how hard-won educational and career opportunities for girls have indeed produced spectacular results, resulting in these kinds of academic successes. However, a surprising consequence of these open doors is that the bar keeps being raised higher and higher. *Opportunities* have now morphed into *obligations*. Pressures for excellence loom as girls receive messages like these: *It's not that you can do it all, you are expected to do it all. Excellent grades. Sports. Extracurriculars that help you stand out on college applications. Oh, and don't look like you are trying too hard. This should all come effortlessly and naturally if you really have what it takes.* Girls absorb these messages and many run with them.

According to a Girls Inc. study, 75 percent of girls say that they are under a lot of pressure to please everyone and that they feel stressed most of the time; 84 percent say that they dislike feeling this way.[2] In a recent survey reported by *Girls' Life* magazine, more than half of the girls surveyed said that they felt as though they had to succeed at everything, "from school to sports to fitting in the right-size jeans to having a BF [boyfriend]."[3] According to one girl interviewed for the survey, "All of this pressure makes me feel like I can't have a life." "Everything needs to be perfect."

As exemplified by this quote, the problem occurs when girls feel overwhelming pressure not only to meet cultural expectations for *achievement* but also for *perfection*. Ana Homayoun writes about this problem extensively in her book *The Myth of the Perfect Girl*, warning us that this pursuit of perfection does indeed come at a price.[4] Many girls are struggling as they feel incredible pressure to run with a sprint-like pace through childhood and adolescence, frantically checking off boxes on a to-do list of things they must accomplish if they want to be viewed as successful.

Girls respond to these cultural pressures in different ways. As you think about current pressures placed on girls, start to ask yourself where your daughter falls on the continuum described here. Also start to consider how much you might be contributing to any pressure your daughter is experiencing.

- At one end of the continuum, your daughter might be one of the girls who places undue pressure on herself to win the "race," believing that nothing but perfection will enable her to feel she is good enough to meet societal expectations. As a result, she might push herself to extremes, always studying, always practicing, and always striving.
- Your daughter might be someone who experiences the pressure to achieve but instead feels paralyzed by it; she procrastinates and lacks motivation because she fears that even if she gives her all, it still won't be good enough. So she holds back.
- At the opposite end of the continuum, your daughter might be starting to drift and then drop out of the race altogether, performing poorly in school, neglecting her talents and interests. She might choose to pursue validation from other external sources, often related to her appearance, popularity, or male approval.
- In the middle of the continuum, perhaps she is a girl who is in the process of creating a life that is leading to the development of her fullest potential while also leaving room for exploration, fun, and enjoyment. The goal of this chapter is to provide strategies to help her find the balance needed to pursue this kind of life.

In our coverage of these issues, I will address the following: In the first part of this chapter, I will discuss cultural pressures for girls to do it all, especially when it comes to high achievement in academics, sports, and other activities that are culturally deemed important for their "success." In turn, I will explore ways in which you and your daughter can learn to broaden your vision of success and to help your daughter to identify, develop, and appreciate more of her strengths and talents. Later in the chapter I will address a different angle on the problem: as already described in the continuum, instead of pushing forward, some girls respond by holding themselves back or by choosing another path entirely, pursuing external validation through their attractiveness, popularity, or romantic relationships. I will provide guidance as to how parents can respond to these particular types of challenges. Finally, I will present parenting strategies that can help all girls become resilient to extreme cultural pressures around performance and grades in the hope that they will be able to anchor themselves in the middle of the academic continuum. I will start with a spotlight on girls who are pushing themselves too hard in their pursuit of perfection.

THE STRESSED AND PRESSURED DAUGHTER

Because it is harder than ever for students to gain admission to a top college, to secure a slot in graduate school, and to win a well-paying job, many parents now fear that there are just not enough "resources for success" to go around: they believe that success is scarce, so you have to do what it takes to secure it. Therefore parents are told that unless their children perform at extraordinary levels, they just won't be successful in today's competitive world. Parents are indoctrinated to believe that "only the hyperaccomplished will survive."[5] And part of that survival stems from the ultimate goal: admission to the "right" college.

In the past, parents were told to encourage their children to go to college, but today's parents are warned about the critical importance of having their children graduate from a high-ranking, highly selective (usually highly expensive) college. Just any college won't do. So the college admissions pressure is on, and because only a select few are admitted, the competition begins earlier and earlier in our daughters' lives.

For many girls, this means not only earning top grades throughout middle and high school, including advanced placement (AP) classes, but also having specialized achievements that show that they are not only well rounded but also "angular"—they stand out in some exceptional way that distinguishes them from the rest of the competitors.[6] She comes to believe things like *I can't have "A's" with a few "B's" sprinkled in along the way. Only straight "A's" will count. I have to take all the AP classes that are offered, even if I don't know whether I can handle all of the homework. I have to stay busy and* take advantage of every opportunity. I can't just be in orchestra for fun, I have to be first-chair flute. I can't just be on the soccer team, I have to be a member of an elite traveling squad and be part of a championship team. I can't write for the yearbook; I have to be the editor. If I am to win in this frenzied college admissions contest, I have to do it all and I have to be the best. According to one girl quoted in a recent *Girls' Life* magazine article, "If you're not busy, you're losing precious time to build up your college application and you're falling behind the ones who participate in more activities" (Isabelle K., age 16).

Although boys also feel the pressure around these issues, girls experience them differently and more intensely. A girl is more likely to be socialized to please everyone and to find her identity in winning others' approval. As discussed in Chapters Five and Six, girls also receive the message that they must not only do well in school and in multiple activities but also maintain their relationships, attract romantic partners, and be as attractive as possible while doing so. These expectations accumulate, and for many girls they become translated into a requirement for perfection in all areas.

Succeeding in School but Failing in Life[7]

Buying into this belief system becomes highly problematic because your daughter will start to equate her worth as a person with her accomplishments. Just as it is easy for girls to get caught up in believing that their worth is equated with their appearance and their relationships, this pressure is also very real for a girl when she starts to believe *My worth is based on my numbers and my credentials.* If she is in tune with cultural pressures, she can have thoughts such as *My value is based on how high my GPA is, how strong my SAT scores are, how many lines I have on my resume. I am only acceptable if my "numbers" are good. It doesn't really matter whether I like any of the things I am doing. I just go through the motions in order to reach this goal that I have been assigned.*

You can probably see how a girl with this attitude might feel—as if she were dutifully checking off the boxes for success. *What do the admissions officers want? I will satisfy them whether I like it or not. I will do what it takes to make sure the box is checked. I will stifle my own passions and dreams (or never learn what they are) in order to appear as "hyperaccomplished" as possible. I may not take any risks to try anything outside of my comfort zone, in case I am not good at it, I might not make a good grade in it, or it may not look good on my college application.* Homayoun refers to this process as "box filling"— that is, a girl's tendency to meet others' expectations even if they don't fit with who she is and what she wants (see Box 7.1). According to Homayoun:

As you read this, you might be wondering whether your daughter is indeed spending too much time in academic "box filling" rather than enjoying her life, discovering herself, and exploring her interests.

To help you with this, can you answer yes to any of the following?

_____ 1. My daughter is involved in many activities and sports but seems burned out on them and doesn't seem to enjoy them anymore.

_____ 2. She has no real free time to just relax or to have fun.

_____ 3. She puts off important projects until the last minute and then claims that she didn't do well on them because she didn't have enough time.

_____ 4. She stays up late on school nights finishing homework and does not get enough sleep.

_____ 5. She consumes a lot of caffeine to carry her through the day.

_____ 6. She is on the go so much that I feel like I only see her when I am driving her to and from events.

_____ 7. She is hesitant to try classes or activities in new areas because fears she might not excel (or make an "A") in them.

_____ 8. If she had an afternoon "off" with no activities or school-work, she would have trouble knowing how to fill her time.

_____ 9. She seems as though she were walking around in a fog because she is consistently sleep deprived and exhausted.

_____ 10. She is focused on being admitted to a highly selective university (or on winning a scholarship) and won't really consider other options.

_____ 11. She seems competitive with her friends and feels disappointed in herself when a friend is more successful than she is.

_____ 12. She is not involved in anything just for fun; everything she is enrolled in is to help her chances for college admission (or it is just done out of obligation).

_____ 13. She feels like a failure if she makes a low grade or doesn't win a competition.

_____ 14. She would say that she is "stressed out" much of the time.

If you said yes to several of these items, this might be an indicator that your daughter is experiencing too much stress and pressure in her life and that she is placing too much emphasis on achievements and accomplishments in determining her value. As you read the following resilience points, try to identify ways in which you could help her change her beliefs around the importance of perfection so that she can start to be comfortable with doing her personal best. It is also helpful to consider ways in which you could work with her to find more balance in her life; she needs time to learn about her true interests, talents, and goals and to develop character qualities that she will carry with her throughout her life.

Despite widespread advances, both girls in school and women in the world are confronted by a paradoxical consequence ... even though they are moving forward in all sorts of measurable ways, they often feel, when they stop to consider their accomplishments, that their outward successes are not matched by a sense of inner fulfillment. Girls and young women feel that they are succeeding in school and failing in life for the same underlying reason—they are all too good at becoming who they think others want and need them to be.[8]

No matter where they look to find external approval, girls end up with a sense of emptiness when they don't develop an authentic identity and become dependent on others to validate their worth and value. Conversely, resilience occurs when your daughter can take the risk of creating *her own version* of success and fulfillment. This chapter is dedicated to highlighting strategies that you can use to help your daughter develop the resilience to explore her passions and dreams so that her drive for achievement and accomplishment will stem from a desire to learn and to develop her true potential, not just from her need to prove her worth or meet an external standard of success.

RESILIENCE STRATEGIES FOR REDEFINING SUCCESS

The First Step: It Starts With You

As with the other parent self-awareness questions throughout this book, the following are questions that ask you to reflect on what you truly want for your daughter (see Box 7.2). It is important to take time to examine your parenting values and then to consider what it might mean to live according to those values. Instead of blindly accepting today's pressured, perfectionistic trend for girls, you can make a thoughtful and deliberate decision regarding what it is that you really want for your daughter's

Take some time to reflect on, write about, and discuss your answers to the following questions:

- What is the image of success that you have for your daughter? In future years, my daughter will be a "success" in my eyes if she is _____ (fill in the blank)
- Is your vision of success narrow (about admission to a certain college, an athletic scholarship) or broad?
- Is it based on your own goals or does it also include your daughter's passions and talents?
- Does the vision require perfection and extreme busyness if success is to be achieved?
- Does your daughter's current schedule reflect your definition of success?

After completing this exercise, do you see areas where your vision for success needs to change? Are there expectations that you might be placing on your daughter that need to be refined? Do you see where your family's expectations and schedules might need to be revised so that they are better aligned with this vision? It is my hope that this chapter will provide you with ideas that will enable you to broaden your view of what "success" is really about so as to free both you and your daughter from societal pressures that might actually be limiting her potential.

future. Is this vision also aligned with your daughter's strengths and with what she also wants for herself?

Broaden Your Definition of Success for Your Daughter

If you are like many parents, your vision of success for your daughter might initially involve specific goals like admission to a certain college or winning an athletic scholarship. As you begin to think about it more broadly, however, you might recognize that that her future success will not be based solely on her middle and high school achievements. Rather, in examining the big picture, it will become clear that success can be attained though a variety of life pathways. Success is not based on specific accomplishments, but stems from a person's character and her ability to craft a meaningful, purposeful life. This usually involves characteristics such as the following:

- Building a strong character steeped in integrity and compassion for others
- Finding meaningful work
- Creating loving relationships
- Participating in an array of activities that promote her growth and learning
- Forging an authentic identity
- Believing that she is capable of handling life's demands

If you are a parent who is currently caught up in the pressure of the college admissions race, feeling that you have no other option but to push your daughter toward hyperaccomplishment, try to give yourself permission to envision your daughter's future in a different light, one that is preparing her not just for the *college* of her choice but for the *life* of her choice.[9] The question then becomes not *What will this test score/accolade/ extracurricular program do to increase her chances for college admission* but rather, *What can it do for her character development? To enhance her love of life-long learning? To prepare her for a meaningful life?*

Does this mean throwing up your hands, giving up, and allowing your daughter's grades and aspirations to plummet? Not at all. When she is given the opportunity to discover her unique strengths and then pursues these talents to the best of her ability, she *will become free to excel*—not necessarily in meeting narrowly defined societal standards for success but rather she will excel in reaching her own unique potential.

Appreciate Your Tree

Building on your answers in the Self-Awareness Check exercise, dig a little deeper. Maybe your dream for your daughter is that she becomes a corporate attorney, but she is artistic and quiet and wants to work behind the scenes. Maybe you want her to be a surgeon, but she wants to be a family counselor. Maybe she wants to be a stay-at-home mom, while you always hoped that she would have a highly paid career. The challenge for parents is to recognize that even though we are the greatest influence in our children's lives, we are not really in control of who they will become. Consider the following metaphor:

You have been given a seedling for a weeping willow tree, but maybe you always wanted an oak tree. Every day you treat your young willow tree like it should be an oak tree, just hoping that it will somehow become the mighty oak tree of your dreams. In some seasons you deprive your willow of what it needs most because you are feeding, watering, and caring for it as if it were an oak tree. You spend a lot of time looking at oak trees, hoping to coax your weeping willow to look more like an oak. The years pass quickly, and one day you open your eyes to see the beautiful weeping willow tree in front of you, its graceful branches swaying in the wind. You realize how much you missed of its beauty by refusing to appreciate the tree you had been given instead of trying to force it to be the oak you thought you wanted! [10]

As hard as it is, we have to separate our daughters' dreams from our own. We can truly hinder their development when we spend our efforts forcing them to fulfill the expectations *we* have set. It takes some work to disconnect our dreams from who our daughters really are because this process often occurs outside of our awareness. Talk to some trusted adults in your support system and ask for their honest feedback. Do what you can to recognize whether you are having trouble accepting the tree in front of you. When your daughter is very different from you, it is very difficult to accept her as she is and allow her to grow into a tree that might look very different from your own. However, even when your daughter is very similar to you, it is just as difficult and perhaps even harder to separate *your* dreams for her from *her* dreams. Parents have a tendency to want to force their children to become different from them in areas that were particularly painful in their own development. For example, I once worked with a mother who was very shy as a child and was quite lonely at times; now she has a daughter who is quiet too. Because she does not want her daughter to feel the same loneliness she experienced, she finds herself pushing her daughter to be more social than the daughter might prefer. The problem is that, despite their similarities, her *daughter's needs* are not the same as *her mother's*; she actually enjoys being alone and doing her own thing. The daughter is doing well and is not at all uncomfortable with her need to be alone. The mother doesn't have to push her in a different direction out of her own fear. With this awareness, she can work harder to accept her daughter for who she is.

After you have done some soul searching to consider the ways in which your dreams might have become intertwined with your daughter's actual gifts and talents, examine the expectations you might be conveying to her through your words and actions. Does she perceive that she can never measure up to your expectations because you want her to be someone she is not? As you examine the messages you are sending, consider how often you compare her with others, including her siblings or peers. When you consistently compare her with other girls, she can feel that what she is doing is never good enough. For example, Asha shares how much she hated those times when her mother compared her with her older sister when she was that age:

> My mom would say things like, "When Anya was your age, she had already been nominated for the outstanding middle school student award!" or "I talked to Kimberly's mom and she says that Kimmie just made all-state choir and got straight A's this semester! She is just thrilled about it!" My mom never directly says that she is disappointed in me, but what else am I supposed to think? Obviously she is telling me these things because she wishes that I would be more like these girls!

Asha's mother may or may not have told her about other girls' accomplishments because she was disappointed in her own daughter. The intention doesn't really matter; what matters is that this is how Asha perceived the comments. When you casually mention what other girls are doing, your daughter hears it as a bar you are holding up for her: "This is what I think is important, and this is the standard you should reach." The bottom line is this: we have to be willing to take a long hard look at what our expectations really are and then make sure that these are accurately reflected through our words and actions. Because you want her to know that her worth is not based on earning your approval, help her to know that she is loved, valued, and worthwhile because of *who she is*, not because of her *abilities or accomplishments*.

Discover Her Strengths and Talents

I have already discussed the need to change our own vision for our daughters' success. In turn, we also have to help our daughters learn to broaden this vision for *themselves*. As stated previously, it is clear that all children are unique, so it is really difficult for them when our society expects everyone to conform to a limited and confining idea of success.[11] To be resilient, our daughters need us to help them broaden that vision so they are free to develop their talents, whatever they may be. According to Lucie Hemmen, resilient teens are those who flourish because they know the adults in their lives will recognize and honor their individuality as well as validate and nurture their talents.[12] Although your daughter's talents might not lead to accomplishments that are touted as necessary to win awards or scholarships, they can become an invaluable part of your daughter's potential contribution to the world. See Box 7.3 to assist you as you start to identify and appreciate your daughter's unique gifts and talents.

Box 7.3: AN ARRAY OF GIFTS

In current culture, it is clear that certain gifts are valued while others are easily overlooked. In fact, some parents might claim that pursuing certain talents is a waste of time because they won't be valued by college admissions officers. Although it might be true that highly selective colleges look for students who fit within a certain formula, what about everyone else who doesn't fit within these limits? Instead, what if you chose to validate your daughter's individuality rather than her conformity? You can seek to identify and then nurture her unique gifts.

Here is just a sampling of strengths to consider as you begin your search. Ask yourself if your daughter possesses any of these gifts and then make a concerted effort to validate any of these often unappreciated talents that you identify in your daughter.

Remember, this is a sample list of potential strengths that are often overlooked in our girls; it is not another checklist for success, so don't feel that you have to work to promote any or all of these areas in your daughter in order for her to be a "success." Please also note that traditionally praised talents like sports, academic prowess, attractiveness, and popularity are not listed here.

A SAMPLING OF STRENGTHS AND GIFTS

- Is she creative and imaginative? Does she express this through her dialogue or through writing, art, drama, or music?
- Is she drawn to spiritual pursuits? Is she seeking to develop her spirituality? Is she interested in actively cultivating a compassionate spirit?
- Does she possess an appreciation of beauty? Does she seem to notice and appreciate details in the world that others might overlook?
- Is she a visionary? Does she seem to possess the ability to see the big picture and imagine not just what is but what might be?
- Is she a good listener? Does she possess the willingness to listen to others and consider their ideas? Is she someone with whom

---

others feel comfortable sharing their thoughts and feelings? Is she empathic, able to understand others' perspectives?

- Is she a motivator and encourager of others? Does she take leadership in connecting people with similar interests?
- Does she have strong friendship skills? Is she a loyal, committed friend?
- Does she possess a love of learning? When she learns about an issue, does she usually want to learn more about the topic? Does she like exploring new areas of knowledge?
- Does she love to read and learn about the world through books?
- Is she a strong problem solver? Is she known for getting things done? Does she tend to be active in planning and executing her plans?
- Is she a natural at organizing her world? Is she logical, pragmatic, and orderly in arranging her schoolwork, her room, and her activities?
- Does she have a sense of humor? Does she seem to have the ability to find humor in most situations? Does she often make others laugh?
- Does she have a desire to care for others (e.g., siblings, grandparents, babysitting)? Does she have a nurturing spirit?
- Does she love to explore and appreciate nature? Love to be outside, dig in the dirt, care for plants?
- Does she have strengths in the areas of manual dexterity and mechanical abilities? Is she interested in assembling Legos, building or repairing things, working with her hands?
- Does she possess a love of scientific discovery? Does she love to discover how the body or certain objects work?
- Does she possess an appreciation for animals? Is she drawn to nurturing and caring for animals?
- Does she have other strengths that are not listed here? Please brainstorm and consider all of the ways in which your daughter shines!

Help Your Daughter to Reexamine Her Own Vision. Perhaps you are now thinking that you might want to change some of the expectations you have had for your daughter. Maybe you are working with her to recognize some of her previously unappreciated strengths and gifts (as identified in Box 7.3). The next step in the process is to help your daughter reexamine and change some of her own perfectionistic beliefs (even if these haven't come from you, she will certainly have been affected by pressures from the culture around her). What does she say when you ask her "What makes a girl successful?" Does she conjure up an image of a hyperaccomplished girl with a jam-packed schedule? Does she believe that her worth is based on whether she is admitted to a particular college or whether she wins a scholarship? Or even whether she makes an "A" on today's chemistry test?

Help her to relax a little, take a deep breath, and recognize that she can be a high achiever without being perfect in every area of life. If she begins to recognize that she is more than her "numbers," she will be free to identify and then explore what her strengths and talents truly are. She will be able to define herself on her own terms, not by external standards. This process takes time, so give her the gift of downtime so that she can discover those areas that truly bring her a sense of fulfillment. What if instead of busyness, stress, and striving, your daughter could begin to view her childhood and adolescence as an exciting time of learning and discovering who she is?

Provide her with the following questions for exploration and encourage her to discuss her answers with you:

- Share the array of gifts presented in Box 7.3. What areas does she identify? Compare your lists and share those strengths you see in her that she might not be able to identify in herself.
- Ask her to explore the following:
  - What is my passion? What are things I do that give me energy rather than draining me?
  - What do I actually like to do? Do I do it because my parents want me to do it, because it will help me get into a good college, or because I actually find it rewarding and fun?
  - What am I naturally good at? What do I love but find I might need more practice in order to enjoy the activities more?
- Map out her calendar.
  Map out her schedule and, as you review her activities and school commitments, help her to evaluate what is most important to her. Is there anything that could be dropped, reduced in frequency, or added? In light of your values, how could her schedule better reflect your family priorities? Does her schedule allow her enough time to get adequate rest and sleep? Help her make these important decisions by using some of the tools provided in this chapter.

- To assist your daughter in trying out new things and discovering her gifts and talents, try this activity, suggested by Ana Homayoun.[13] Ask her to make three lists: (1) three things I enjoy doing, (2) three things

I want to do more of but haven't been able to, and (3) three things I would like to try but haven't yet. After she has made these lists, ask her to choose three activities and commit to making time for those at least three times over the next three months!

If your daughter is spending too much of her time forcing herself to be all things to everyone yet not really knowing who she is or why she is feeling so much stress and pressure, this exercise can help her to learn to view her life as a time of self-discovery. She will become resilient to these pressures when she knows who she wants to be and is able to pursue her dreams with passion.

THE OTHER END OF THE CONTINUUM

So far I have primarily reviewed ways in which you can help to reduce some of the pressure and stress your daughter might be experiencing if she is overly invested in high achievement. You now have a few ideas about how to reevaluate your definition of success, and you can begin to help your daughter identify her unique talents and gifts. You are thinking about ways she can begin to let go of the pressure she might be placing on herself to achieve perfection in academics. In time, she can start to recognize the difference between living her life in ways to meet external (e.g., college admission) standards versus creating an internally derived vision for her life.

But you might also be asking: What if this is not my daughter's experience at all? What if, despite her potential, she just doesn't seem to care about whether she does well in school? What if she is more concerned about other things, like looking and acting a certain way to gain popularity or male attention? We focused on these concerns in Chapter Five (attractiveness) and Chapter Six (popularity and romantic relationships); I encourage you to revisit those strategies and acquaint yourself with the coping skills introduced in Chapter Eight. If this is more of your experience, you are probably looking for answers as to how to get your daughter to study and focus more. You probably want to be able to hand her a set of study skills and tell her to get to work! As you have probably already noticed, though, this book is not written with the intention of being an academic skills handbook designed to deliver specific study strategies such as note taking, test-taking skills, and so on. There are plenty of excellent resources for you to use in this regard, and I recommend a few at the end of the book. These skills are invaluable, but they are helpful only once you have first taken a step back and examined the *reasons* behind her lack of commitment to school.

If it is just that she doesn't know how to study, then yes, she needs some tools. But for most girls the issue goes much deeper. There are strong cultural influences that can chip away at her confidence, causing her to question herself, struggle, and even quit trying. Until you understand the cultural influences and then work to challenge these myths with her, she will not likely be able to take action in this area. So for the purposes of this chapter, I would like to address some of the stereotypes that linger in our current culture, surprisingly still alive alongside the culture pressures for perfection already discussed. As you read the following section, ask yourself whether some of these stereotypes about girls might be undermining your daughter's confidence and therefore her actual performance in her academic endeavors.

Toxic Cultural Stereotypes About Girls and School

In this section, I will explore two stereotypes that serve to undermine girls' confidence and their performance.

Stereotype One: Romantic Relationships Are More Important Than Academic Achievement

Despite girls' and women's many advances in academics and careers, it is shocking that the myths "smart is not sexy" or "boys are intimidated by girls with brains" are still hovering around. While girls clearly see and hear that they are expected to be high achievers, they also remain exposed to the message that they should stifle their intelligence and not to stand out as a "brain" or they just won't fit with the "in" crowd. The message continues to be "Don't show a boy up, because boys don't like feeling outdone by a girl." Or even worse, they hear the message that intelligence in girls isn't valued. Recall the popular Abercombie and Fitch T-shirts for girls with the slogan "Who needs brains when you have these?" And there was also the popular Diesel clothing line advertising campaign telling girls to "Be Stupid."

As a result, some girls feel they have to make a choice between popularity and high achievement, since they discover that doing too well in school can result in a lack of acceptance by their peers. They believe that being smart is intimidating, and they should tone themselves down in order not to intimidate others around them. It is a sad reality that many girls struggle with questions like "Should I dumb myself down to be popular with boys?" "Should I act like I am too cool to care about school, not raising my hand in class?" and "Should I pretend that a boy is smarter than I am so that he won't feel threatened and will like me more?" Lisa Hinkelman quotes sixth-grade girls saying such things as "'Cause if you seem like you are smart, the boys will say, 'Oh you are too smart for me, you can't be my girlfriend.' They think you are a geek." Another sixth-grader she interviewed said, "Guys don't want a girl who is smarter than them. They want to be in control."[14] Note that these are beliefs of sixth-grade girls who have already learned what is expected of them in early middle school!

As an example of how this message is broadcast even in children's early years, I almost jumped out of my chair about a year ago when I was watching some of the new episodes of *Scooby Doo* with my children. In this series of episodes, Velma got rid of her glasses, began to wear bows in her hair, started deferring to Shaggy, and no longer asserted herself in solving the gang's mysteries because she wanted to become Shaggy's girlfriend! Instead of using her intelligence, she was spending her energy on playing down her strengths and trying to please Shaggy. You can find many similar examples in the media if you start to look for them.

A related issue is one explored in Chapter Six regarding girls and the priority they are taught to place on their romantic relationships. Many girls believe that if securing and maintaining a romantic relationship is supposed to become their top priority, everything else should take a back seat to that relationship. If keeping her crush/boyfriend/partner happy and close is her priority, she will be in danger of losing touch with her own values and interests, letting go of all of her friendships and activities outside of what this other person wants and needs. This often includes her commitment to academic achievement. She might stop caring about school, and her grades can suffer when she is overly enmeshed in a relationship. This can also increase her vulnerability to staying in an unhealthy relationship; she might perceive that even being in a relationship that causes her to give up part of herself is still better than having no relationship at all. Further, when her entire identity becomes tied up in her relationship, she can feel "devastated, lost, and completely worthless"[15] when the relationship ends. The resulting grief and loss can also contribute to her diminished focus in school.

Resilience Strategies: What Can Parents Do?

- **Assure her that it is possible to have balance in her life**. It is fine to have a boyfriend, to have friends, to love makeup and clothes, but it is also okay to apply herself in school, have talents, and pursue other interests. She doesn't need to overextend, but she does need to find a healthy balance among these often opposing interests.
- **Co-view media with your daughter**. Point out examples when girls play down their intelligence or talents in order to keep the boys around them happy. Help her question why this needs to be the case for girls.
- **Ask her questions**. If your daughter is in middle or high school, ask her if she thinks that girls in her school have to choose between being smart or pretty and popular. Does she know girls that "play dumb" in order to please boys? If so, what does she wish those girls would do instead?

Stereotype Two: "Girls Are Not Good at Math and Science"

Despite all their successes in academics overall, this stereotype is still alive and well and is perpetuated by media, parents, and, sadly, teachers. After teaching college women over the past fifteen years, I am still shocked at the number of those who report that a teacher downplayed their potential in math or that their school counselors discouraged them from taking advanced math and science classes even though they had excellent grades in these subjects. They tell me, "I could tell that they didn't think I was smart enough to take those classes." So they didn't take the classes that would prepare them to choose a wide range of science, technology, engineering, and math-related careers (i.e., STEM careers), and their options became more limited. They also said that they became less interested in these areas overall, even though they had always liked them prior to high school.

Research bears this out. Even when girls have good grades and test scores in math and science, compared with boys of equal ability, they have lower *expectations* to do well in math, and have lower *confidence* in their math skills. It is noteworthy that girls' *beliefs* about their math and science abilities tend to fly in the face of their *actual abilities*. When their confidence is low, they are less likely than boys to believe that they can be successful. In addition, parents are more likely to say that they place a lower priority on math and science success for their daughters than for their sons. So on the one hand girls are hearing, "You can do it all!" while on the other they are learning "but just don't take advanced math and science classes. They are too hard for you." When they believe this, they might self-select out of advanced classes and also become less likely to apply themselves when they are enrolled in these classes. This clearly serves to limit their academic and career potential.

Why is this still occurring in our current cultural climate, which also simultaneously praises girls' potential? There is ample research demonstrating how girls' beliefs serve to undermine their actual performance. The psychological principle of *stereotype threat* is helpful for understanding what happens when your daughter is exposed to negative messages about girls' abilities, especially in math and science. Stereotype threat occurs when you are told a stereotype about your particular group membership (for example, a teacher might say "As I hand you this exam, I just want to let you know that boys have always outscored girls on this test"). When this happens, you are more likely to do worse on the task than if you had not been reminded of the stereotype. For example, in one study, students were preparing to take a math test. The teacher said, "Boys typically get much better scores than girls in this test." This reminded girls of the stereotype that "girls are not good in math"; the stereotype was activated for them and they began to question whether or not it was true for them. As a result they did worse on the test than girls in another class who were told that both boys and girls do equally well on the test. This is significant: in studies involving classes where students are told that boys and girls are equally capable, there is no difference between boys' and girls' performance. Just suggesting the stereotype seems to trigger it in girls, and girls start to question themselves or even to believe the stereotype; this belief actually causes them to perform worse on that task![16]

In addition, girls can fall prey to stereotypes when the adults around them distort the research that reveals gender differences in boys' and girls' math and science abilities. Studies on group differences show that *as a group*, girls are slightly predisposed to and more comfortable with language and sequential detailed factual tasks. *As a group*, boys are slightly more predisposed to and more comfortable with problem solving and nonsequential visual and spatial tasks (visuospatial tasks involve things like looking at an image and being able to transform it into another image, working a three-dimensional puzzle, or reading a map; these are abilities often associated with skills needed for math and science fields). But what does this really mean for your daughter in particular? Not very much. Remember that these reports are based on scores when all girls are lumped into one group and measured against all boys lumped into a different group. The findings have nothing to do with your daughter's individual ability and can't be used to predict whether *she* will be successful in these areas. These findings are based on group averages. It is highly unfair to all students when these studies on group differences are used to discourage any one student from pursuing a particular area of interest.

Second, whatever abilities your daughter currently possesses can be improved, and any skill that doesn't come as naturally to her can be refined with training and practice. For example, if she is not strong in visuospatial skills, she can develop her abilities dramatically in a short time with training.[17] It is not something you "have" or "don't have"—it is something that can be developed with practice. This is true of any skill; your brain is shaped not only by your natural ability but also your experiences and beliefs about whether you will be good at it or not. The more you believe you can do something, the harder you will work at it; the harder you work, the better you will actually become; and the better your skill, the greater your confidence.[18] So your daughter can do math, science, and any other subject in school and she can do them well if she chooses to. It is our job to help her believe this despite what she might hear or observe from media, other students, or her teachers.

Resilience Strategies: What Can Parents Do?

- *Monitor and challenge stereotype talk in your home*. Think about the examples that your daughter might be exposed to: "Women are bad at directions," "Girls aren't good at reading maps," "Boys can't write poetry," "Go ask your Dad—I was never good at math," or even "Give your brother back his Legos!" (without considering that maybe she could have her own set!) Remember the studies on stereotype threat and how these messages can affect your daughter's performance.

- *Give her positive female role models*. Girls often lose interest in STEM fields because they receive the message that they don't "belong." Recent studies indicate that when girls are exposed to female role models who are working in STEM fields, they report more positive attitudes about these professions and have more motivation to pursue them as careers.[19] In another study, the researchers demonstrated that girls who viewed science textbooks with pictures of female scientists reported more positive attitudes about math and science careers than did girls who viewed traditional textbooks (that is, science books with pictures of male scientists only). Helping your daughter have personal contact with female scientists, engineers, and mathematicians can motivate her to see herself in these roles in the future.[20] It makes a big difference when she does not feel she has to limit her career aspirations solely on the basis of her gender.

DEVELOPING ACADEMIC RESILIENCE IN ALL GIRLS

Up to this point in the chapter, I have discussed resilience strategies for girls who are struggling in their pursuit of perfection and how this pursuit can actually serve to undermine their performance. I have just explored ways in which to challenge two gender stereotypes that can also limit girls' potential. How confusing for girls when they are bombarded with both the new expectations (*do it all, be perfect*) along with traditional gender prescriptions (*don't be too smart, you can't do math and science, and give up everything if a boyfriend comes along*)! No wonder that girls often become unsure of themselves and question their abilities as they reach adolescence! In the final section of this chapter, I will describe some strategies that all girls can use both to overcome the pressure for grades and perfection and also remain motivated to learn and achieve their potential. I will discuss and then dispel three common parenting myths from current culture: (1) you need to be grades-focused and praise your daughter about how smart she is, (2) you need to micromanage her academic career, and (3) multitasking is essential for getting it all done.

MYTH OF THE GRADES-FOCUSED MINDSET

Janet is the mother of Jada, an eighth-grader. Janet knows that Jada had a big test yesterday. She admits, "I asked her about the grade as soon as she came home from school. She said the grades hadn't been posted yet. Now I find myself checking PowerSchool (the school's online grade-management system) almost every hour to see if her grade has been posted. I just want her to do well so she can get into advanced classes next year in ninth grade. That's when the classes and grades really start to count."

If this scenario describes your typical reaction to your daughter's school performance, you are not alone. The teachers at my children's school encourage parents and students to check the grade-management site daily for grades and progress, and I know this is the case in schools across the country. It is hard not to evaluate each and every test or assignment score and to consider how each one affects *The Grade* for better or for worse.

Instead of a grades-focused approach, I ask that you consider an alternate outlook on your daughter's education, even if it feels as though you are swimming upstream against a grades/scores/numbers-obsessed culture. In fact, this approach might appear so countercultural that it seems idealistic at first glance. But hang in there and consider that there just might be another way of viewing your daughter's academic life.

If we want our daughters to learn that they are not defined by their grades or accomplishments, they need to learn to view all of life as a learning process and to see school as an opportunity to learn new information about the world. It can become a place where they can become curious about what they are being asked to learn and why, to think through problems, to solve complex challenges, and ultimately for building self-efficacy--her belief in her own ability to master new problems as they come her way.[21] Contrast the difference between this approach and the typical student attitude of studying just the material that is going to be tested or of worrying only about getting the right answer on an assignment even if she doesn't understand what she is learning. It is the difference between striving to be a good "test taker" versus becoming a curious, open-minded learner. Think about the change there would be if she actually approached assignments with a desire to *learn* instead of taking only those steps needed to make the highest grade possible. If girls feel intense pressure to always make the grade, they will continue to view the actual *learning* as optional.[22]

In the preceding example, instead of asking "What was your number grade on the test? How did that affect your overall grade in the class?" Janet could ask Jada questions like, "What are you learning in world history? What do you really think about the book you are reading? Why do you think educators believe it is important for students to know this material?" What if, as parents, we could learn to dial back our exclusive focus on grades and outcomes and instead focus more on the process of learning and mastery?[23]

At this point, you still might think I am living in a fantasy land, that I don't get how competitive it is in today's schools, that no one you know will ever get past a need to dwell on those all important numbers. Or you might be thinking, how nice it would be to have your daughter simply become interested in getting her grades up to speed. Either way, it is important for you to be aware of a strong line of research supporting the premise that a grades-focused approach does not necessarily lead to long-term success in school or in life. Rather than risking a lower grade or appearing as anything less than smart, students who are focused on making nothing less than an "A" actually learn to give up more easily, put in less effort over time, and avoid challenges more than those who are more focused on stretching themselves to actually learn something new. I will turn to this body of research and its implications for your daughter in the next section.

PROMOTING THE GROWTH MINDSET

Carol Dweck has dedicated a large part of her career to examining the mindset that students embrace when faced with academic tasks, and she has been able to dramatically and repeatedly demonstrate that it is the students who learn to embrace challenges, stretch themselves to learn something new, persist in the face of setbacks, and see *effort* as the path to mastery (not just whether they are naturally "smart") who have higher levels of actual achievement than do others. It is the students who *want to learn* (what she terms the *growth mindset*), not those who are heavily invested in their performance (the *fixed mindset*), who do best in school, career, and life.[24] Although this is not a phenomenon limited only to girls, the fixed mindset closely mirrors the pattern that many of today's girls develop in response to cultural pressures for high achievement.

For example, in several studies with fifth graders, Dweck's research team divided the children into two groups: one group received some puzzles and were told "You are so smart!" when they solved the puzzle successfully. The other group received the same puzzles but were praised for their efforts, not their intelligence or talent. When the researchers gave the children a set of harder puzzles, guess who did better in solving the new puzzles? The group that had been commended for their hard work and effort. The children who were told they were smart actually tried less and did worse and reported enjoying the challenging puzzles far less than did the other group. The children commended for effort were actually excited about the harder puzzles, kept working at them, and said they enjoyed the challenge.

The implications of this are profound, because these studies demonstrate that children who are repeatedly told they are "smart" actually put in less effort and can do worse on academic tasks compared with children who are praised for their *efforts*, not for their *accomplishments*.[25] People who are praised for their efforts learn to believe in themselves: *I tried hard and was successful, and with persistence I can keep learning, growing, and trying out new things. I don't have to be afraid of being judged because this is an area in which I can definitely improve through practice and experience.*

Therefore girls are most likely to excel when they believe that any skill—including all academic subjects—can be developed with effort. For example, I was pleased to get an e-mail from my daughter's math teacher one year stating that she appreciated Abby's improvement in learning her multiplication facts: she noted that her hard work was paying off for her, even though Abby had not yet made anything close to an "A" on this task. Praising her for effort will encourage her to keep learning and practicing until she has mastered these facts, while hearing "you're smart!" will do nothing in this regard. In fact, it might make things worse.

Here is another application of the benefits of the growth mindset. As I write this chapter, some graduate students in my counseling program are starting their practicum placements and actually counseling clients for the first time. This is an anxiety-provoking experience for most students; a lot of self-doubt and questioning goes on during these first few weeks, usually around themes like "I'm not good enough," "I don't have what it takes," or "I don't know enough to counsel anyone." This year I had a surprise. One of my students said in class, "I am trying my best to remember that I am not an *incompetent* counselor, I am just an *inexperienced* one." This jumped out at me as an example of Dweck's growth mindset: It is not whether she is a "good" or "bad" counselor; she just needs practice to get better, and she is being given the opportunity to learn and improve. As I discussed previously, instead of hearing "girls can't do math," girls need to hear "with effort and commitment, you can learn anything" and maybe "be patient; you just haven't learned this yet." When girls learn that their intelligence can expand with experience and learning, they actually do better on math tests and are more likely to say that they want to continue to study math or other subjects in the future. It is their commitment to improving their abilities that is most important.[26]

So how do you promote the growth mindset in your daughter? One significant influence you have is related to the way that you respond to her and praise her throughout her day. I will start with what you *don't* want to do.

What Not to Do

When your daughter brings home an "A," don't always say, "Wow! You are so smart!" or "You are so brilliant! I heard that that teacher is tough, but you get an 'A' every time!" The message she actually receives is *Oh no, if I don't get an A every time, they might not think I'm so smart anymore.* That response actually places a lot of pressure on her and keeps her dependent on your praise to feel good about herself. She may start to believe that her success is based on a permanent trait (being "smart") and that you are continuously judging her to see if it is still true. If she faces anything challenging in the future, she will be more likely to quit trying because it might reveal that she is really not so smart after all. Clearly this does not contribute to her confidence in facing new challenges.

What to Do

According to Dweck, here is what to say instead: "I like the effort you put into this." Praise her for her practice, hard work, study, persistence, use of good strategies, and improvement but not her actual grade or outcome (e.g., winning or losing). This is very different from telling her she is smart. In addition to reviewing the strategies she used that helped her to do well, also help her examine what she is learning from her mistakes so that she can learn to appreciate a challenge and do better next time (see Box 7.4). According to Dweck:

> Parents think they can hand children permanent confidence—like a gift—by praising their brains and talent. It doesn't work and in fact has the opposite effect. It makes children doubt themselves as soon as anything is hard or goes wrong. If parents want to give their children a gift, the best thing they can do is teach their children to love challenges, be intrigued by mistakes, enjoy effort, and keep on learning. That way, their children don't have to be slaves of praise. They will have a lifelong way to build and repair their own confidence.[27]

Levine also writes about Dweck's research and provides reassurance for those parents who feel that this type of encouragement might reflect a lowering of expectations. Instead, she says parents need to keep their standards high, just not focused on outcomes and performance but instead on effort and improvement.[28] This will help your daughter to learn the valuable lessons that come from making the effort to push through challenges. This type of encouragement will enable your daughter to stay resilient in the face of cultural pressures that demand perfection.

THE MYTH OF MICROMANAGING

I discussed this theme in Chapter Four, but it is especially important to revisit in our exploration of academic success. To prepare your daughter for the future, you are called upon to provide a delicate balance of support and challenge. Yes, you need to be there for her, support her endeavors, and check on her grades and progress. But you also don't want to be so involved that you hinder her growth in taking responsibility for her learning and her life. This will look different for every child, but it means handing her the primary reins for managing her academic career. In a nutshell, if you want her to feel confident and capable, she does not need you to manage her academic life. If you do everything for her, she will never learn to be responsible for herself. For example, this commitment to her growth means that you don't do her homework for her just because she ran out of time. You don't take the forgotten project or band instrument to school for her. You don't grill her about every assignment. In an age-appropriate manner, you back off and demonstrate that you trust her abilities. You show her that you believe she can do it for herself.

Remember that the ultimate goal is for your daughter to become independent, so that one day she will not need you to solve her every problem. Your goal is to provide opportunities so that she can learn she is indeed capable of handling challenges on her own—that she has what it takes to handle the demands of life. To achieve this goal, you also have to allow her to struggle and fail sometimes so that she can learn from mistakes. If you always rescue her, she won't have these opportunities. She will grow up to believe that you think she is unable to solve her own problems.[30] She won't know what it is like to fail, pick herself up, and try again. She can learn a lot more from her mistakes than from being constantly rescued from any pain or struggle. I know that this is difficult; I constantly have to fight my urge to manage things for my own children. As I have said repeatedly throughout the book, it helps to keep the big picture in mind: remember that what she needs most is not a problem-free life but to have the ability to effectively manage problems that will inevitably arise in her life.

THE MYTH OF MULTITASKING

The last area I will discuss as a general resilience strategy is related to the myth of multitasking. "Multitasking" has become a buzzword in our culture; it almost seems like a requirement for modern life. In fact, most mothers say they spend about half their waking hours doing two or more things at once.[31] Unfortunately research demonstrates that most of us think we are better at it than we actually are, especially when it comes to juggling electronic information. The brain is able to process and pay attention to only one thing at a time, so multitasking actually *reduces* productivity. According to the research of Clifford Nass, people who try to multitask between media—for example, watching TV while texting or jumping between e-mails and work tasks—actually perform very poorly in certain key skills: being able to filter out irrelevant information, keeping their memories organized, and switching from one task to another. In other words, compared with people who attempt one task at a time, they are more distracted by irrelevant information, less able to focus, and less accurate in what they are doing.[32] While we may think that we are getting a lot done, in reality multitasking adds, not subtracts, from the level of stress in our lives.

These findings are even more concerning when applied to our daughters, who are known for their frequent use of technology and multitasking as a way to balance their social and academic lives. One study of tween girls aged 8 to 12 found that those who multitasked by spending a lot of time watching TV and videos and using online communication were the most likely to feel less successful socially, to not feel "normal," to report sleeping less, and to say they had friends whom their parents saw as bad influences. In sum, the researchers concluded that multitasking harms the social and emotional development of girls because they are missing out on learning to pay attention and to have meaningful face-to-face communication.[33] Add this to the research cited previously showing that multitasking can also lead to poor analytic reasoning abilities (not being able to discern the most relevant information, pay attention to complete a task, adequately store new information in memory) and it is clear that multitasking can lead to poor outcomes for girls.

So what is the takeaway for parents? You might tend to praise her for her ability to do many things at once (e.g., switching between Snapchat, Facebook, listening to music, and texting her friends—all while doing her homework). Try to refrain from reinforcing this behavior. The reality is that she is actually stretching out her homework time and will be less likely to remember what she is learning, thereby experiencing more distraction and stress. If your daughter is staying up late at night on her computer, insisting that she is working on assignments for school, investigate how much time she is actually focusing on the assignment versus switching her screens back and forth between social media and her schoolwork (try the experiment suggested in Box 7.5). It may seem that she can do it all, but it is actually causing her to learn less and have less time for rest and sleep. Instead, help your daughter learn to focus fully on the task in front of her.[34]

Help her learn to focus on doing one thing at a time and being fully present with sustained attention for each activity. This idea is definitely countercultural, but research supports that it is the way our brains can work best.

CONCLUSION

It is my hope that you are now thinking about your daughter's academic success through a different lens. You can choose to transform

---

Box 7.5: AN EXPERIMENT FOR YOUR DAUGHTER TO TRY

Does the elimination of multitasking in your daughter's life seem like an impossible goal? Present it as an experiment for her to try for one week just to see what happens. For seven days, require that she spend a block of time turning off all social media (including her phone) and doing nothing but studying (no more than two hours, depending on her age). When she is done, she can reward herself with technology time.

At the end of the week, have her evaluate the results. Did she actually enjoy her social time more because she had completed her other tasks? Did she get her homework done more quickly? Did she feel that she understood it more?[35]

---

your view of her childhood and adolescence as a grueling race to meet certain one-size-fits-all standards. Her youth does not have to be hurried and stressful or steeped in peer pressure and conformity. You can both create an alternative vision for this developmental period as an exciting time for discovering herself and her passions and for seeing school as a place to learn new things about the world while mastering new challenges (see Box 7.6). If she is currently overburdened, take some steps to help her find ways to lighten her load. If she is underwhelmed, look for some areas that bring life and joy to her face when she talks about them. Help her discover some activities that light a spark within her—because she finds them fulfilling and meaningful and not because she is doing them out of obligation. To give you additional ideas, I will talk more about self-care, wellness, and coping resources in the next chapter.

Box 7.6: TRANSFORMING YOUR ACADEMIC SELF-CONCEPT

As a summary of many of the ideas in this chapter, consider sharing the following words of wisdom with your daughter. These are adapted from Lucie Hemmen's book *Parenting a Teen Girl: A Crash Course on Conflict, Communication and Connection With Your Daughter* (2012).

1. You are not your grade or your score. You are far more than your GPA, your test scores, or your sports record.
2. The ultimate point of school is not to earn high grades or be the top athlete; it is to learn and grow as a person.
3. As your parent, I value the effort you put into your work far more than your actual grade or sports performance.
4. I am excited when you learn new things about yourself and the world; these discoveries are more important than your grades or whether you win or lose.
5. There are many good colleges where you can thrive; you don't have to limit yourself to only a select few
6. It's okay not to be a superstar in everything. I expect you to do your best and to enjoy the process along the way.
7. I value your character far more than I value your grades or your achievements.
8. I love you for who you are, not because of your accomplishments. This is not dependent on your grades, your scores, or whether (or where) you go to college.

NOTES

1. Halpern, D. F. (2006) Girls and academic success: Changing patterns of academic achievement. In J. Worel & C. D. Goodheart (Eds.), *Handbook of girls' and women's psychological health* (pp. 272–282). New York: Oxford University Press.; Hill, C., Corbett, C., & St. Rose, A. (2010). *Why so few? Women in science, technology, engineering, and mathematics.* Washington, DC: The American Association of University Women (AAUW). Retrieved from http://www.aauw.org/files/2013/02/Why-So-Few-Women-in-Science-Technology-Engineering-and-Mathematics.pdf

2. Girls Inc. (2006). *The supergirl dilemma: Girls grapple with the mounting pressure of expectation.* New York: Author.

3. *Girls Life Magazine*, October/November issue, 2014. *Ace Life*, pp. 62–63.

4. Homayoun, A. (2012). *The myth of the perfect girl: Helping our daughters find authentic success and happiness in school and life.* New York: Penguin.

5. Mogel, W. (2010). *The blessing of a B minus: Using Jewish teachings to raise resilient teenagers.* New York: Scribner.

6. Hemmen, L. (2012). *Parenting a teen girl: Crash course on conflict, communication and connection with your teenage daughter.* Oakland, CA: New Harbinger.

7. Homayoun, A. (2012). *The myth of the perfect girl: Helping our daughters find authentic success and happiness in school and life.* New York: Penguin.

8. Homayoun, A. (2012). *The myth of the perfect girl: helping our daughters find authentic success and happiness in school and life* (p. 4). New York: Perigree Books.

9. Rosenfeld, A., & Wise, N. (2000). *Hyper-parenting: Are you hurting your child by trying too hard?* New York: St. Martin's.

10. The idea for using a tree metaphor came from Mogel, W. (2010). *The blessing of a B minus: Using Jewish teachings to raise resilient teenagers.* New York: Scribner.

11. Levine, M. (2012). *Teach your children well.* New York: HarperCollins.

12. Hemmen, L. (2012). *Parenting a teen girl: Crash course on conflict, communication and connection with your teenage daughter.* Oakland, CA: New Harbinger.

13. Homayoun, A. Myth of the perfect girl.

14. Hinkelman, L. (2012). *Girls without limits: Helping girls achieve health relationships, academic success, and interpersonal strength* (p. 100). Thousand Oaks, CA: Corwin.

15. Bogue, A. (2014). *9 ways we're screwing up our girls and how we can stop: A guide to helping girls reach their highest potential.* Dunham.

16. Good, C., Aronson, J., & Harder, J. A., (2008). Problems in the pipeline; Stereotype threat and women's achievement in high-level math courses. *Journal of Applied Developmental Psychology*, 29, 17–28.

17. Hill, C., Corbett, C., & St. Rose, A. (2010). *Why so few? Women in science, technology, engineering, and mathematics.* Washington, DC: The American Association of University Women (AAUW). Retrieved from http://www.aauw.org/files/2013/02/Why-So-Few-Women-in-Science-Technology-Engineering-and-Mathematics.pdf

19. Good, J. J., Woodzicka, J. A., & Wingfield, L. C. (2010). The effects of gender stereotypic and counter-stereotypic textbook images on science performance. *The Journal of Social Psychology*, 150(2), 132–147.

20. Ibid.

21. Dweck, C. S. (2006). *Mindset: The new psychology of success.* New York: Ballantine.

22. Homayoun, A. (2012). *The myth of the perfect girl: Helping our daughters find authentic success and happiness in school and life*. New York: Penguin; Deak, J. (2010) *How girls thrive*. Columbus, OH: Green Blanket Press.
23. Dweck, C. S. (2006). *Mindset: The new psychology of success*. New York: Ballantine.
24. Ibid.
25. Dweck, C. S. (2006). *Mindset: The new psychology of success*. New York: Ballantine.
26. Hill, C., Corbett, C., & St. Rose, A. (2010). *Why so few? Women in science, technology, engineering, and mathematics*. Washington, DC: The American Association of University Women (AAUW). Retrieved from http://www.aauw.org/files/2013/02/Why-So-Few-Women-in-Science-Technology-Engineering-and-Mathematics.pdf
27. Dweck, C. S. (2006). *Mindset: The new psychology of success*. New York: Ballantine.
28. Levine, M. (2012) Teach your Children Well. Harper Collins Publishers.
29. Dweck, C. S. (2006). *Mindset: The new psychology of success*. New York: Ballantine.
30. Bogue, A. (2014). *9 ways we're screwing up our girls and how we can stop: A guide to helping girls reach their highest potential*. Dunham.
31. Bianchi, S. M., Robinson, J. P., & Milkie, M. A. (2006). *Changing rhythms of American family life*. New York: Russell Sage Foundation.
32. Ophir, E., Nass, C., & Wagner, A. D. (2009). Cognitive control in media multitaskers. *Proceedings of the National Academy of Sciences of the United States of America*, 106(37), 15583–15587. doi: 10.1073/pnas.0903620106
33. Pea, R., Nass, C., Meheula, L., Rance, M., Kumar, A., Bamford, H., et al. (2012). Media use, face-to-face communication, media multitasking, and social well-being among 8- to 12-year-old girls. *Developmental Psychology* 48(2), 327–336.
34. Cohen-Sandler, R. (2006). *Stressed-out girls: Helping them thrive in the age of pressure*. New York: Penguin; Homayoun, A. (2012). *The myth of the perfect girl: Helping our daughters find authentic success and happiness in school and life*. New York: Penguin.
35. Homayoun, A. (2012). *Myth of the perfect girl: Helping our daughters find authentic success and happiness in school and life*. New York: Perigree/Penguin.

CHAPTER EIGHT

Resilience Dimension Five
Charting My Life Course

To this point, you have read a lot about the pressures your daughter will face regarding her appearance, the attention she receives, her acceptance by others, and her accomplishments. You have also learned many resilience strategies that will help her to swim upstream against these three specific pressures, which may undermine her self-worth. In this final chapter, I will turn to a very broad resilience dimension that has strong implications for every area of your daughter's life: her self-regulation skills. When your daughter is able to use these skills, she will be able to stay in control of her actions; that is, she will be able slow down in a given situation; become aware of her thoughts, emotions, and available options; and then plan her actions accordingly. She will not be a passive victim but rather an active agent in charting the direction of her life. Self-regulation is so important that, according to research, it is the one factor that is most predictive of a person's achievement, mental health, and social success. According to Laurence Steinberg, developing self-regulation should be the central task of adolescence, and promoting self-regulation in our children should be one of our primary goals as parents.[1]

Self-regulation is critical to resilience, yet is often hard to understand in practice. For this reason I will explain it through a focus on two skill sets: (1) problem-solving strategies and (2) coping skills. It is important for your daughter to have both sets of skills in order to engage in effective self-regulation. Problem solving helps her take effective action when she encounters a problem that she can actually do something about, while coping strategies are needed when she has to deal with a situation that she cannot actually change. Both of these skills are part of her ability to stop, gain awareness, think, and then plan a course of action (whether this involves a behavioral action, better regulation of her emotions, or changing the way she thinks or feels about a situation). The point is that she does have some sense of control; she does have choices. She doesn't have to give up and wait for someone else to solve her problem. She doesn't have to worry obsessively about the situation, ruminating over it incessantly with her friends. She also doesn't have to avoid the problem, turning instead to self-destructive methods like alcohol, drugs, food binges, or self-injury to numb her pain. When she believes that she has what it takes either to take action and solve a problem or to cope with the situation as it is, she is able to thrive—even in the midst of multiple stressors.

SKILL SET ONE: PROBLEM SOLVING

As your daughter encounters problems, you want her to learn how to solve them without always needing your assistance. As I have discussed throughout this book, your daughter will develop self-confidence when she learns to rely on *herself* to handle the difficulties that come her way. Remember that when you repeatedly rescue her from her problems, she actually learns to believe that she is incompetent and that you don't think she is capable of working things out for herself. You want to provide her with the tools she needs to think through a problem and come up with a plan of action. As also stated in previous chapters, girls tend to worry about problems, so that they are so caught up in the story that they aren't able to step back, evaluate the problem, and decide on what the best course of action needs to be in order to make the situation better. We all know from personal experience that when we worry about problems and avoid taking action on them, our procrastination can turn an initially small, manageable problem into an actual crisis. So your daughter needs to believe in her ability to take action when it is needed. She plays a large role in determining how things will turn out for her; she can learn to see that she is an active agent in her life rather than a passive victim.

There is a caveat to this, however, in that even though you want to promote your daughter's independence, you also want her to be able to recognize the difference between problems that she can solve completely on her own and those that are best handled by reaching out for help from trusted adults.[2] There are certainly times where it is appropriate and necessary for her to ask for adult support and guidance. Make sure that while you promote a problem-solving spirit in her, she also knows that asking for help is the smart thing to do when she feels that she is in over her head. Make sure she also knows that she can always come to you as a sounding board to help her talk through her problem and plans.

The steps for problem solving are fairly basic, but few of us take the time to map out our problems in a logical way. I have worked with many students and clients over the years who were surprised by how much these simple steps helped them think through a problem in order to come up with a plan of action. Problem-solving steps are as follows:

1. Acknowledge that this situation is difficult and that it would be helpful to use some problem-solving strategies to figure out what to do. Validate your daughter's feelings and let her know that you will be there to help her think the problem through and develop some possible solutions.
2. Problem definition. What exactly is the problem? What is contributing to the problem? What are the reasons that this is actually causing a problem? If there are multiple problems, what is the one that needs immediate attention?
3. Goal definition. What would be your ideal goal or outcome for this problem?
4. Solution generation. Brainstorm as many possible solutions as possible. Try to look at the problem from different perspectives. Be as creative as possible.
5. Evaluate possible solutions. After developing a list of possibilities, weigh the pros and cons of each option. What are the advantages and disadvantages of each? What are the potential outcomes for each possible solution?
6. Choose a solution. After looking at all the pros and cons, choose a solution based on how it fits with your goal/ideal outcome for this particular situation. What are the specific steps needed to act on the plan, and what are any barriers to completing them?
7. Evaluate the consequences. After you have tried out your solution, how did it go? What went well? How might it be done differently next time?

Although it is less detailed, an alternative model with a quick and easy mnemonic for remembering the steps is available from BanBossy.com. The organization suggests the following GIRL model:

G: Gather your choices: Brainstorm about possible choices you could make.
I : "I choose." Pick one choice and decide what you want to do.
R: Reasons are: Write the reasons for your choice.
L: List the outcomes: List all the things that could happen if you made this choice.

In addition to *solving a problem*, these same steps are also helpful for *decision making*:

1. What is the decision to be made?
2. Make a list of pros and cons for each option you are considering,
3. Evaluate your list and make a decision based on your analysis.

This is especially important when your daughter tends to make decisions based on what is most popular with her friends or when a decision is not thought out at all but is based solely on her feelings at the time. If you help her to practice these steps, she can learn to solve problems more easily and will feel in greater control of her life.

Frequently a girl's problems will be related to difficulties in her relationships. This is why, in addition to basic problem-solving steps, she may also need specific skills for solving relational problems. I talked about some of these in Chapter 6, and I will expand on them here. In the sections below, I provide steps for two areas in which many girls especially need education and practice: assertiveness (standing up for yourself without trampling on the rights of others; See Box 8.1) and conflict resolution (working through a conflict through active listening and negotiation; See Box 8.2).[3]

Box 8.1: ASSERTIVENESS SKILLS

I have adapted the following mnemonic from dialectical behavior therapy (developed by Marsha Linehan[4]), which provides an effective model for assertive communication using the mnemonic DEAR MAN.

- D: Describe. Describe the situation in a factual manner.
- E: Express. Express your feelings using "I" statements. "I feel ___ about ___."
- A: Assert. Ask clearly for what you want or do not want.
- R: Reinforce. Explain the benefits to the other person if he or she complies.
- M: Stay mindful. Keep your focus on what you want.
- A: Appear confident. Make eye contact and speak in a confident tone.
- N: Negotiate. Ask for feedback, offer alternative solutions, and be mindful of when to agree to disagree.

An example the use of this model:

Seventeen-year old Katelyn frequently felt powerless because she wasn't sure how to stand up for herself with her boyfriend. Because she feared that her boyfriend might get mad if she asked him for anything, she usually didn't speak up even when she disagreed with his plans. The next time she had a specific issue with her boyfriend, she tried the DEAR MAN strategy:

D: My curfew is now 10 p.m. and I really want to be home on time from now on so I won't be in trouble with my parents.
E: I feel frustrated because I have worked hard to get this new curfew time and you are always asking me to stay out later. I hate having my parents on my back all the time about being late and then grounding me for the next weekend.
A: If you are driving, I would like us to leave with plenty of time for me to get home so I don't get in trouble. If I am driving, I would like you to accept that I need to leave without arguing with me about it.
R: If this works, I think we will have a lot less fighting and a lot more fun when we are out together.
M: I know that you want me to be able to stay out even later, but this is about me not getting in trouble with a 10 p.m. curfew.
A: Looks him in the eye, stays calm.
N: What do you think? Can you help me get home on time tonight?

I have discussed throughout this book why it is so hard for some girls to speak up and tell a friend that she is angry or to assert her own opinion. When girls have been socialized to suppress anger and to do what it takes to preserve relationships, stepping out and risking a relationship is difficult. As her parent, encourage your daughter to speak up for herself and assert her needs as much as possible. As she learns to voice her needs effectively, she will be less likely to resort to aggression (harming others in the process) or to passivity (where she is hurt by silencing her thoughts and feelings). To encourage your daughter in this regard, I like this quote from the Ban Bossy organization:

Remember, it is not always easy to speak up but it's worth it. Girls are supposed to be confident but nice, ambitious but not selfish, successful but not conceited. The rules can be confusing and unfair. So not everyone is going to love it when you speak up. Trust your voice even when it feels like the world doesn't and stay close to friends and family who celebrate your strength.[6]

Rachel Simmons's five-step model of conflict resolution validates how important girls' relationships are to them while also encouraging girls to stand up for themselves. Help your daughter practice the following steps (I have included an example to make the steps easier to remember)[5]:

1. Affirm the positive aspects of the relationship ("Candace, I really liked going to your sleepover last weekend").
2. Avoid using the word "but" as you progress between steps. Use the word "and" instead.
3. Use an "I" statement: Define the problem and how you feel about it. Use the formula "I feel _____ when you _____." ("I am frustrated because you promised not to tell our friends about the problem I shared with you. You told me that you would keep it a secret.")
4. Include your contribution. Share whatever you did to make the problem bigger or worse ("I know I should have told you how I felt earlier instead of waiting until today to tell you how I feel.")
5. Ask how you can solve this together. Say what you need from the other person and also offer to do something yourself ("In the future, I would like you to avoid repeating things that I ask you to keep private between us. I will try not to drop such big problems on you in the future because I'm sure that this was probably hard for you to keep to yourself.")

SKILL SET TWO: ACTIVE COPING

What do we mean by active coping? In any stressful situation, we cope with the stress whether we are aware of it or not. Imagine you are worried about an upcoming project that seems insurmountable; you really question whether you can get it all done in time. You can choose to cope with the stress in a variety of ways, some healthy and some unhealthy, some that will make the situation better and some that will make it worse. For example, these are typical unhealthy (what are called "maladaptive") coping strategies that many people might employ in this situation:

• Procrastinate by doing other things unrelated to the project
• Because of procrastination, staying up late to complete the project at the last minute

- Drink more alcohol to soothe the stress
- Eat more sweets and junk food to numb the stress
- Spend time complaining about the project to anyone who will listen
- Distract oneself with mindless activities like watching TV or surfing social media
- Quitting or dropping out so as to avoid the stress

Note that most of these strategies may help you feel better in the short term but actually make the problem worse in the long run (the project doesn't get done, you experience only more stress, or you feel worse physically so you have less energy to devote to the task).

Active coping skills, on the other hand, refer to positive resources you can draw on when you find yourself in situations that can't be changed. You choose to change your *response* to the problem in ways that don't make the problem itself go away (e.g., the project is still due), but you make choices to help you feel *less stress in response to the situation*. In the previous example, there are many active coping responses that could have been used, such as the following:

- Viewing the deadline as a challenge and setting small goals to achieve each day
- Asking for help from colleagues
- Making time for exercise to lower stress and clear your mind
- Telling yourself just to do your best on the project in the time that's left
- Talking about your feelings with trusted friends
- Practicing deep breathing when your stress levels increase
- Leaving the situation for ten minutes to clear your mind and to refocus
- Eating a healthy diet and getting adequate sleep so you can function at your best
- Reminding yourself that your worth is not based on your performance on this project

As you can see, active coping is sometimes about making small behavioral changes to make the situation better, but many times the most effective response is a change in your thinking. Maybe nothing looks different to the outside world, but when you think about the situation differently, it makes all the difference to your outlook. This is important for your daughter to recognize: She needs to know that even when she is in highly stressful situations, she is always in control of how she reacts. She can take small steps to make the situation better for herself, and sometimes this will involve a decision to think about it differently. Ultimately it is her *reaction* that will determine the level of distress she will or will not experience.

Cognitive Restructuring: Changing Her Self-Talk

If your daughter learns that she can change the way she talks to herself, this skill alone will decrease her stress and increase her resilience dramatically. So she first needs to become aware of her self-talk. If you could peer inside her brain, what would your daughter's running internal dialogue sound like? What is her overall pattern of self-talk? Has she developed any patterns that are overly negative and that contribute to the level of stress she experiences? Does she tend to blame herself or other people when anything bad happens? Does she think she can influence how things turn out in her life, or does she believe she is a victim of fate? Does she see whatever happens as just a temporary bump in the road, or does she complain that it is the end of her life as she knows it? By examining these types of self-talk patterns, you can learn a lot about how she might be creating undue stress in her life.

Review the list of common thinking patterns presented in Box 8.3 (what mental health professionals call cognitive distortions) and try to see if any of them reflect the way your daughter typically talks to herself.

Steps for Changing Her Thinking

Help your daughter practice the following steps.

Step One

First, identify the *thought* that is causing you stress or worry. Does it contain a cognitive distortion (see Box 8.3)? Pay attention to the way that your thought about the event is causing you to be upset, not the event itself. In other words, your reaction to any situation is a result of your *interpretation* of that situation. Notice how this unfolds in the following example:

> *Three students have three completely different thoughts and feelings in reaction to the same event, demonstrating that it is the thought that leads to the resulting feeling, not the original event itself.*

Box 8.3: COMMON COGNITIVE DISTORTIONS ABOUT SELF, OTHERS, AND THE FUTURE[7]

- All-or-nothing thinking: You think of things in black-and-white categories, such as "all good" or "all bad" ("I messed up so I am a bad person").
- Mind reading: You assume that people are thinking negative things about you when you really have no evidence for this ("Those girls in the corner are whispering about me").
- Fortune telling: You predict that things are going to turn out badly when you don't have evidence for this ("I just know I am going to fail this test").
- "Should" statements: You criticize yourself based on how you think you "should" act or feel, based on unrealistic standards. ("I should be able to make all 'A's', no matter what").
- Discounting the positives, dwelling on the negatives: Despite any accomplishments or positive outcomes, you dwell only on the negative examples you can recall ("Even though I got an 'A' on my presentation and everyone seemed to like it, this one girl said it was 'Okay.' I wonder what she meant by that? Does she think I'm stupid? Did she make fun of my presentation behind my back?").
- Magnification or minimization: You either blow something way out of proportion or minimize its importance ("I wore the wrong shirt on spirit day! It was supposed to be the white one, not the gray one. Now everyone will always remember me as the idiot who wore the wrong shirt. I am too embarrassed to go back to school!").
- Labeling: Giving yourself a global label instead of recognizing that you made a mistake on a specific task ("I'm such a loser!! I forgot my binder!" vs. "I was in a rush this morning and I forgot my binder").

Once you have identified any of these tendencies toward distorted thinking patterns, you can help your daughter identify them as they play out in specific situations.

Event: The fire alarm goes off at school. Girl #1 thinks: We are all going to die! I am trapped in this building and can't get out! Feeling: Panic, terror.

Event: The fire alarm goes off at school. Girl #2 thinks: That annoying alarm again! Last time we had to stand outside for an hour before they turned it off. Feeling: Annoyed, irritated.

Event: The first alarm goes off at school. Girl #3 thinks: It's my lucky day! I have a major test that I didn't study for, and now we will probably miss it! Feeling: Relief, calm!

It is eye-opening when you realize that you have a choice in how you respond to a problem or event in your life. *You can choose to think about it differently.*

Step Two

Once you have identified *what* you are thinking about a situation (e.g., your friend doesn't talk to you before class: "Everyone at school thinks I am a loser!" or you made a D on a quiz: "I will never be able to pass middle school!"), the next step is to search for evidence to support whether the thought is realistic or true.

Some people find it helpful to compare this process to detective work. Suppose there are two detectives, a good one and a bad one. The good one looks for evidence and clues to figure out the truth before jumping to conclusions, while the bad one just blames the first "suspect" that comes to mind.[8] It is important to be able to sift through the available evidence like a good detective. Asking any of the following questions can help with this process:

1. Is my thinking extreme or overly self-critical? Am I falling into one of the cognitive distortions listed in Box 8.3?
2. Is there any evidence that this belief is true? Is my belief realistic?
3. What has happened in the past that might help me know if my present thought is true?
4. Am I 100 percent sure that this is true or that this will happen? If not, why not?
5. If this happened to a friend, would I think it was true?
6. Is there another way to think about it?
7. Is this belief helping me or harming me?
8. If this were true, what would be the best and the worst thing that might happen?
9. If it did happen, what could I do to cope with or handle it?
10. Would a good friend say this to me? What do I need to do to talk to myself in a more compassionate way like I might approach a friend with a similar problem?

After identifying the thought (step one) and then finding evidence to support that the negative thought is extreme or untrue (step two), the next step is to create a calm, helpful, logical, more balanced thought that is based on the reality of the situation.[9] One way your daughter can learn to do this is by imagining her negative thought as a "muck monster." She can learn to talk back to the "muck monster," thereby visualizing the negative thoughts as keeping her "stuck in the muck." She can be encouraged to dispute the negative thoughts (the "muck") and tell the "monster" the truth of what is really going on.[10]

> *Example of muck monster thought: No one will ever like me.*
> *Find evidence against the muck monster:*
>> *Q: What's another way of thinking about it?*
>> *A: I just moved here three months ago and these girls have been friends with each other since elementary school. They haven't had time to get to know me. Besides, if they are this mean, maybe I don't want to be friends with them either.*
>> *Q: What is the evidence for this belief?*
>> *A: It's true that some of the girls are making fun of me and that my boyfriend stopped calling me. It's true that this really hurts my feelings. But there is no evidence that no one will ever like me; I had lots of friends at my old school and there are lots of guys here who seem to want to talk to me.*
> *Talk back to the muck monster!*
>> *Q: Based on these answers, how can you tell the muck monster the truth by supplying a more realistic, helpful thought?*
>> *A: I can remember that I am a good friend and that people do like me when they have a chance to get to know me.*

In coming up with positive thoughts to replace negative thinking, some girls struggle because they are unsure of how to talk calmly and nicely to themselves. If your daughter is having trouble with positive thoughts, help her to develop a statement like one of the following:

1. A coping statement: Something that will inspire you to deal with the situation better ("*I will handle this. I just need to try my best*").
2. A positive self-statement: Something kind and positive about yourself ("*I am a good friend and I know it won't take long for the kids here to realize that*").

3. A realistic statement: Something that is actually based on the evidence you just collected ("*She is usually nice to me, so maybe there is a chance that she just didn't see me when I waved to her in the hallway*").

Self-Awareness for Parents: Monitoring Our Own Self-Talk

As emphasized throughout this book, our own attitudes and beliefs about ourselves make a big difference in how our daughters see themselves. You can say all of the right things, but unless you are applying these values in your own life, she will follow not your words but your footsteps. I encourage you to do the hard work of examining your own self-talk. How do you talk to yourself all day long? What is your own running dialogue? Is it full of criticism or of self-compassion? Our children are watching us every day and they do hear the derogatory comments we mumble aloud: ("I'm so stupid! I can't believe I am late again!!" "What a loser I am for forgetting to turn in that form!"). If we don't want our daughters to talk to themselves in this way, we can start to eliminate these types of statements that we so freely toss out about ourselves. Instead, we can accept that we are imperfect human beings and that we are not defined by how often we successfully master every challenge that we face. If we can't do this for ourselves, we will have great difficulty in teaching it to our daughters.

For example, if you get negative feedback from a supervisor (or partner, colleague, friend, etc.) about how you did on an assignment, how do you react? How would your self-talk sound? Do you take the feedback as a sign that you are a failure? Do you get mad at the person for being such a jerk? Or do you acknowledge your feelings about the feedback, then recognize that there are probably things you can learn from this that might help you do better next time? It is ironic to me that I recently got some negative feedback from colleagues about a chapter from this book. I was hurt and part of me wanted to be mad at them ("They are *so* wrong!! They don't know what they are talking about") and next I wanted to throw the manuscript in the trash ("They are *so* right! I am not capable of writing this book! I might as well quit!") But then, thankfully, I thought about it, realized that my thinking was extreme, and that a better explanation would be that my colleagues were just trying to help me improve. I was then able to turn my laptop on and start making edits based on the feedback they gave me. If you are reading this book now, it means I persisted and didn't listen to my initial negative self-talk.

The negative feedback from colleagues was just that—feedback on a writing project. It certainly did not need to define my value as a person or as a writer overall (a bad *writing day* does not equal a bad *person!*). I can take opportunities to share these types of experiences with my daughter. I want her to learn that (1) I am not perfect (okay, I think she already figured that one out!) and (2) I need to pay attention to my self-talk too, because it makes a big difference in how I feel and in my subsequent actions. I could say something like: *"I got a bad grade today—well, I don't get grades, but my two coworkers thought my writing didn't make much sense, so in a way it was a bad grade for me. At first I felt really badly about myself, but then I realized that I was thinking about it all wrong. They were just giving me some help so that my book could be better. Now I have to go back and do some editing so that I will end up with a better book. Sometimes this happens, and it's okay. I don't always get it right the first time")*. I want her to see that by first identifying her thoughts and then examining them, she can spot the flaws in her logic and then be better able to move forward.

More Coping Strategies: Regulating Her Emotions

Helping your daughter to learn cognitive restructuring skills to manage her *thinking* is critical, but she also needs to learn how to manage her *feelings*. Remember the discussion in Chapter Two, about the rapidly developing limbic system and how intense a girl's feelings become as she enters adolescence? So these emotion-based coping strategies are especially important for her to learn, practice, and use. I find that the most helpful way to help her with this is to teach skills drawn from dialectical behavior therapy (DBT), first introduced in Box 8.1—a counseling approach designed to help people manage their emotions in order to reduce their impulsive behaviors. These are basic skills that can help people gain awareness of what they are experiencing and keep their emotions from becoming too strong and overwhelming; it can also help them to tolerate painful feelings when they do arise. These DBT skills are termed *mindfulness, emotion regulation, and distress tolerance.*

Mindfulness Skills

Recall the discussion of mindfulness in Chapter Four, and how it can be applied to parenting? In this section, I will turn my focus to how mindfulness can help your daughter to more fully experience and better regulate her emotions. Unless she learns to practice becoming aware of what she is feeling and experiencing in the moment, it can be hard for her to know the most effective course of action she needs to take.

Becoming mindful helps people learn to pay attention to their emotions, thoughts, and physical experiences without necessarily trying to end them, numb them, or run away from them. When a person is mindful it means that she is in control of her attention; she has trained herself to pay attention to what is happening right in front of her and how she is responding to it. As she becomes more mindful in the present, she learns to see how her emotions come and go; they are not permanent fixtures but only feelings that are passing in and out of her awareness. As an example of this, think about a situation where you were highly upset on one day, but then, after waking up the next day, you found that the situation did not seem so bad. What happened? Nothing actually changed. You just found that your emotions were much less intense only a few hours later, even though you didn't actually do anything to change them. With mindfulness, your daughter can learn to pay attention to her emotions, recognize that they are only temporary, and realize that they can be tolerated. She doesn't have to run away from them. She doesn't have to act on every emotion she experiences. She can learn to just recognize that they are happening in the moment.[11]

Being present in the moment can't happen if you are plugged in, tuned out, or involved in multitasking. As we know, when girls are constantly checking their phones, listening to music, and doing multiple things at once, they are frequently unaware of what they are actually experiencing in the moment. At my university I am continually amazed at how oblivious students seem to be as they walk around campus. They are generally wearing earbuds and staring down at their phones as they walk. They walk into the street without even looking up. There have been many times when I have had to slam on my brakes to avoid hitting a student in the street—and the student never even looked up from his or her phone. I am sure you have had similar experiences. For your daughter to become effective at being mindful, she needs to have times when she is offline. As countercultural as it sounds, she needs to learn to be present in the moment, to know what she is experiencing in her present reality. This type of awareness isn't easy to cultivate, yet it is an effective skill that can be taught, and like any other skill, she can get better at it with practice. Here are two exercises you can try and then practice with your daughter (See Box 8.4).

Box 8.4: TWO MINDFULNESS EXERCISES

- Wordless watching
  Get in a comfortable place with no distractions. Practice mindfully watching your thoughts and feelings come and go as if they were on a conveyor belt. As an alternative image, some people like to imagine their thoughts and feelings floating on a leaf down a river. You can observe your thoughts and feelings as they float by. Just watch them come and go; you don't need to judge them, wish they weren't there, or force them to stop. They are your thoughts and feelings, and you can learn to pay closer attention to them through this exercise[12].

- One mindfully
  This is a skill that helps us banish multitasking and instead approach a task with "one mind"—by focusing on just one thing at a time. As an exercise in doing things with one mind, practice focusing your attention on the task at hand, whether this is brushing your hair, brushing your teeth, or eating a sandwich. Do one thing at a time, and keep your mind focused only on what you are doing. When your mind starts to wander, bring it back to focusing only on the task at hand. Complete the task with your full attention.

Another way to practice a mindful approach is by focusing fully on what you are eating. How often do you eat without paying attention, just inhaling your food while you are doing many other things? It is helpful to practice mindful eating using the following steps.

- Mindful Eating

Try this with your daughter (supplies needed: One chocolate kiss candy for each of you).

1. Hold a chocolate kiss in your hand. What does it feel like? Take a moment to smell it, to touch the foil, to pay attention to the look and feel of the candy. What thoughts are you experiencing? Do you have any urge to eat the candy?
2. Now mindfully and slowly unwrap the candy, keeping your attention on the crinkles in the foil, the unwrapping process, and the feel of the chocolate inside. Now hold the kiss in your hand for at least thirty seconds. Smell the chocolate. Does it smell different now that it has been unwrapped? What are you noticing about the wrapper and the chocolate?

3. Now take a moment to decide whether you want to eat the chocolate. Is this what you are hungry for right now? If not, put it aside (In case you are thinking that this is a joke, I have done this exercise in many workshops and believe it or not, I have seen some people decide not to eat their candy and to place it back on the table!)

4. If you have chosen to eat it, slowly take a small bite of the chocolate. Don't swallow it right away. Feel the chocolate on your tongue, roll it around, and notice how the flavor is released in your mouth. Savor the flavor for a moment. Then swallow the bite of chocolate. Notice the sensation of swallowing and whatever flavor remains in your mouth. What feelings does the taste of the chocolate evoke? What memories are associated with the taste of chocolate for you?

5. Decide what you want to do next. Make a decision as to whether you are going to eat the rest of the kiss in one bite or take small bites in order to extend the experience. Why are you making this decision? Regardless of your decision, pay full attention to the taste and feel of the chocolate and fully enjoy the experience of eating one chocolate kiss.

6. How was this experiment in mindful eating different from the way you would normally approach eating a piece of candy? Could slowing down and paying full attention to your food cause you to approach your eating in a different way?[13]

Regulating Emotion

Emotion regulation strategies are just what they sound like: skills used to reduce or regulate our emotions so that they do not become too intense or feel like they are out of control. The best way to learn how to do this is to become more aware of situations that trigger emotional reactions, learn ways of releasing these emotions through identifying them and expressing them, and reduce vulnerability to strong emotional reactions in the first place.

Some specific skills for the regulation of emotions include the following[14]:

1. *Teach your daughter to identify the trigger of the emotion.* What actually happened prior to the emotional reaction? What was the triggering event?

2. *Assist her to observe and describe her emotions.* Let her know that it is good to speak openly about her feelings. Encourage her to find a safe place to express how she is feeling, whether this is with a trusted person or in a journal.

3. *When she is having a strong emotional reaction, help her to examine any associated physical changes.* Instead of becoming embarrassed about her emotions, help her respond to any negative or uncomfortable feelings with understanding and self-compassion. For example, help her to recognize that her anger is a normal feeling but is best expressed when she first notices it, so that it does not become an angry outburst, causing her to regret the consequences of her actions.[15]

4. *An important aspect of emotional regulation is not only to express strong emotions appropriately but also to decrease the likelihood that she will have intense emotional reactions in the first place.* She can reduce her vulnerability to strong emotions by practicing self-care. For girls, self-care usually means getting enough sleep, engaging in exercise, and eating a balanced diet. It also means taking time to discover what it is that brings her enjoyment and fulfillment (I will discuss this more in a later section). For now, sleep, exercise, and nutrition are highlighted in the following paragraphs.

Sleep

Why is sleep so important in reducing your daughter's vulnerability to stress and intense emotional reactions? According to the National Sleep Foundation, up to 70 percent of girls get less than 8 hours of sleep on an average school night, even though the recommendations are for adolescents to get between 8.5 to 9.25 hours of sleep per night.[16] Because you are a parent, you have likely already experienced the effects of sleep deprivation during your child's infancy, so I don't need to overemphasize its negative effects. You already know how lack of sleep can lead to concentration problems, decreased problem-solving ability, irritability, poor memory, and that feeling of walking around in a fog. For preteens and adolescents it can lead to additional problems; for example, making it more likely that their academic performance will suffer, exacerbating their acne and skin problems, increasing their susceptibility to illness, and even making them more likely to gain weight (because they may be eating more unhealthy foods, like sugary treats and fried foods).[17]

After living through many sleepless nights with my children when they were young, I often say that sleep is *not* overrated! Now that I am able to sleep more, I look back on those years and realize how detrimental the sleep deprivation became to my physical and mental health. And these same problems are often occurring in our daughters, even though they don't recognize what is going on; they don't understand that much of the distress they are experiencing stems from their lack of sleep. As an adult, I now know very well why I was feeling so foggy and couldn't concentrate; but adolescents don't yet have this perspective.

Unfortunately it is not easy to deal with this problem. During the week, preteens and adolescents tend to stay up late completing homework assignments; then on the weekends, they want to stay up late with their friends. Moreover, at this time there is also a basic biological shift in their brains. Adolescent brains secrete melatonin (the hormone that helps us get to sleep) later in the day, so your daughter really may not feel sleepy until late at night once she reaches her teen years. She is actually wired to stay up later and sleep later the next day. This biological need is in sharp contrast to her school schedule, which requires that she get to school early, even though she, like many adolescents, is sleep-deprived and walking around like a zombie. This predisposition toward staying up late is something that can't be changed, but there are things that you can do to encourage your daughter to get to sleep a little earlier (especially if she is struggling with memory problems, emotional outbursts, and impaired academic performance).

- Make sleep a priority, even if that means letting go of some activities. Set appropriate and consistent bedtimes for yourself and your children.
- Create a sleep-supportive environment at night: Help your daughter create a routine that teaches her body that it's time for bed. Do the same thing every night. This might involve dimming the lights prior to bedtime, controlling the temperature (not too hot or cold), having her take a warm bath or shower, and letting her read or listen to soothing music.
- Turn off all media at least thirty minutes to an hour before bedtime. There is evidence that the light from electronic devices actually suppresses melatonin production, therefore interfering with the ability to sleep.
- In addition to turning off media, require that your daughter keep her electronics off at night (and, as I suggested in Chapter One, even require that she leave them with you for the night and not in her room). Up to 72 percent of parents say that their children between ages 6 and 17 have at least one electronic device in their bedrooms at night while sleeping, and those who leave these devices on at night get thirty minutes less sleep per school night than do those who don't leave them on. That's 2.5 hours of sleep per week that your daughter could be losing!

- If she is worried or stressed about all she has to do, have her record her worries and fears in a journal. In this way she can process her emotions throughout the day so that they are not bottled up at bedtime, and she can also write out her to-do list before bed. Once she gets it on paper, she will be less likely to lie awake worrying about it.
- Encourage her not to eat heavy meals or exercise right before bed; both can interfere with sleep.[18]

Exercise

Why is exercise important in reducing your daughter's vulnerability to stress and intense emotions? For one, exercise is among the best stress reducers that your daughter can employ, given that it causes the body to release endorphins and calming brain chemicals that relieve stress and fear. In addition to the well-known physical benefits of exercise, we also know that girls who are physically active perform better academically and have higher self-esteem than girls who are not active.[19]

Despite the benefits of exercise, research shows a decline in physical activity from childhood into adolescence, particularly for girls. There are many reasons for this. When girls feel bad about their changing bodies and appearance, they are less motivated to exercise or participate in group activities involving physical activity. As they begin to shrink back from exercising, they may begin to feel even worse about their bodies and experience lower self-esteem. This can become a self-defeating cycle for many girls.

The evidence is clear: although not every girl wants to be an athlete, your daughter *does* need to make physical activity part of her life in order to relieve stress and feel her best. Remember that traditional sports are not for everyone, but exercise can be as simple as taking a walk, roller blading, chasing after a younger sibling, or even dancing around the house. One caveat: Keep in mind what we discussed in Chapter Five regarding exercise: it should be done as part of caring for her mind and body—helping her improve her mood, stamina, and concentration. It's not just about how it makes her *look*; it's for how it makes her *feel*.

Nutrition

Why is nutrition important for the management of emotion? Our bodies need a steady supply of energy in order to handle stressors well. When we are not eating well or drinking enough water, not only do our bodies suffer but our moods and ability to think can also become compromised. Although the basics of a healthy diet are beyond the scope of this chapter, it is important that your daughter be aware of the connection between what she eats and how she feels. Sometimes she just may not realize that her positive food choices (e.g., eating breakfast, eating whole foods that will give her lasting energy) will affect her mood and her ability to cope. For example, if she eats a lot of simple sugars and consumes a lot of caffeine, she will experience frequent energy bursts followed by crashes in energy, leading to irritability. She may love the brief rush of energy that comes from her frappuccino paired with a doughnut, yet fail to recognize that this sugary food/drink combination makes her feel bad a few hours later. Help her to notice the mind-body connection that comes from feeding her body well. Some ideas:

- Parents are the role models when it comes to nutrition. If we don't eat well, our children probably won't do so either. Even though there are a lot of outside influences on what your children eat, you remain the primary influence over what food is in the house and how it is consumed. Be mindful of your role as a model for good nutrition.
- As reviewed in Chapter Five, dieting should be discouraged. Promoting nutrition is about a healthy lifestyle that encourages positive health and wellness. Don't encourage her to restrict calories. Instead, encourage her to eat plenty of whole grains, brightly colored fresh fruits and vegetables, lean meats, and high-calcium dairy products. It's also important to drink plenty of water.
- Be mindful of her caffeine intake. Too much caffeine can interfere with sleep and may also lead to energy highs and crashes. Encourage her to limit her caffeine consumption six to eight hours before bedtime.
- Encourage her to eat when she is hungry and stop when she is full. Help her get her emotional needs met in ways other than by consuming food. This is easier for her if she is already getting adequate nutrition; if her body is well fed, she will be less drawn to bingeing on food in an effort to cope with stress.[20]

To summarize, as your daughter learns to regulate her emotions, she will become more aware of how her emotions are affecting her and will be better able to manage her reactions to stressful situations. As she does this, she can learn to recognize that she does have control over how she reacts to her emotional experiences and that she can actually change her emotional responses; they no longer have to control her.

Distress-Tolerance Skills

Distress tolerance is the ability to cope with emotional pain ("distress") in situations that cannot be changed, at least in the present moment.[21] These are the skills needed to accept a situation as it is, even if it is difficult, and to self-soothe in the moment until a crisis (or what is perceived of as a crisis) is over. Distress tolerance can help your daughter to cope with a difficult situation without making things worse. Here is a sampling of distress-tolerance strategies that your daughter can learn:

Observe your breath. When you are anxious, you tend to breathe too fast, which can result in dizziness and even greater anxiety. Instead, encourage your daughter to practice deep breathing throughout the day and especially when she is feeling stress.

> *Deep breathing exercise.* Begin taking several slow, deep breaths, taking air in through the nose, pausing at the top, and breathing out through the mouth. As you breathe in, your abdomen should extend and expand, and it should deflate as you exhale. Pause for several seconds before you take another breath. Notice how relaxed you are becoming as you pay attention to your breathing.

Use muscle relaxation. A great way to learn to relax in a stressful situation is to progressively tense the muscle groups throughout the body and then release the tension. A full description of progressive muscle relaxation is beyond the scope of this chapter, but if your daughter is tense and anxious much of the time, it can be very effective for producing a sense of relaxation.

> *Exercise: Here is an exercise for a brief version of progressive muscle relaxation: Take a big breath, lift up your shoulders, tense all muscles in your body, make a fist with your hands, wrinkle up your face to make a grimace, then silently say word "relax" and allow your whole body to go limp like a rag doll.[22] An additional resource you can consult is www.amsa.org/healingthehealer/musclerelaxation.cfm*

Use visualization. When you are in a distressing situation, take a mini-vacation. First select a beautiful place (either real or imagined) where you could feel peaceful and there is no stress. For some people, this might be an image of the ocean, mountains, or meadow, while for others it could be an image of people they love or a sacred place they have visited (for assistance with this, see **www.Kidsrelaxation.com/?cat=15**). Regardless of the image, it is important to have an image you can draw upon that brings you peace.

> *Exercise: Take yourself away from the stressful situation for a moment by focusing on your personal tranquil picture any time you need to escape the stress of the moment. Stay there in your mind for a few moments, then return when you are ready.*

Improve the moment in one small way. When you are stuck in a distressing situation, try to accept the situation but also do at least one small thing to improve it for yourself.

> *Exercise: The next time you find yourself in a stressful situation, like being caught in traffic or running late for school, make a conscious effort to take a small step toward making the situation better for yourself. This could be as simple as taking a break, walking away, saying a prayer, or telling yourself "I can handle this!"*

Use self-soothing strategies. Your daughter needs some strategies that provide some soothing and self-care when she is feeling down or having a difficult time. These are things that she can provide for herself, so she doesn't have to rely on others when she is in distress. Try to help her think of things that make her feel better by naming a few that relate to each of the five senses.

> *Exercise: Identify some self-soothing strategies; try to think of at least one for each of the five senses. Remember the ones listed here are only suggestions; your list might look very different.*
>
> *Vision: Do I feel better when I look at art, nature, photos of my family or friends?*
>
> *Hearing: Do I feel better when I listen to soft music or sounds of a waterfall?*
>
> *Smell: Do I feel better when I smell scented candles or aromatherapy oils?*
>
> *Taste: Do I feel better when I taste certain flavors from drinks or foods, like herbal teas or chocolates?*
>
> *Touch: Do I feel better when I touch soft objects, like a favorite blanket or velvet pillows?*

Here is an example of several ways in which your daughter could incorporate these strategies:

> *Frances learned that she tended to avoid her painful feelings and was frightened when she exploded in anger at her parents and siblings. When she learned about*

some of these new distress-tolerance skills, she was willing to try them to make things better for herself. She liked the idea of trying to improve the moment in a small way, because many times her problems occurred at home and she could not change the overall situation. However she could do little things like take some deep breaths in her room, visualize a peaceful place, hold her soft pillow, and listen to a soothing song. She also learned to write about her feelings in her journal in order to sort through the stress she was experiencing. When she felt distress at school, she chose to take deep breaths, leave the class to get a drink of water or to go to the bathroom, or change her thoughts to more positive ones.

What Type of Coping Strategy Is Needed?

Another way to think about coping skills is to match them to the kind of emotion your daughter is experiencing. For some emotions, like anger, a release of energy is needed. For other feelings, like sadness and loneliness, perhaps soothing strategies are more effective. It is important for your daughter to think about how she can develop a few strategies for each category so that she will be prepared for whatever situation arises.

Here are five questions that you may find helpful in selecting which coping skill will be the most helpful in a particular situation:

1. Do I need to do something fun?
2. Do I need to do something that releases energy?
3. Do I need to do something soothing and relaxing?
4. Do I need to talk to someone?
5. Do I need to change the way I am thinking about the situation?[23]

To explore these questions further, see Box 8.5.

Coping Through Spirituality, Gratitude, and Compassion

A final aspect of coping involves three characteristics found in girls who are resilient. Resilient girls possess (1) a strong sense of spirituality involving meaning and life purpose, (2) gratitude, and (3) compassion and a passion for service to others. Before discussing these areas, I want to note that your family's spiritual beliefs and how you choose to promote them in your children are highly personal issues that are best explored as a family and within your faith community. The purpose here is not to tell you *what* to teach your daughter but rather to highlight how important

> **Box 8.5: MY COPING SKILLS PLAN**
>
> ---
>
> Complete this activity with your daughter to help her develop coping strategies for each category listed below.
>
> - **Do something fun**. What do I like to do for fun? What do I need in order to do it? When will I do it? How often? (These are things I do because I like them, not because I have to do them.)
> - **Do something to release energy and stay healthy**. What are some things I can do to be more physically healthy? Is there anything I need to do to practice better self-care (sleep, nutrition, exercise)? When can I do these things? How often will I do them?
> - **Do something soothing and relaxing**. What do I like to do to relax? List three things. What do I need in order to engage in more relaxing activities/events? When will I do these things? How often?
> - **Increase social support**: Who makes up my network of support right now? Whom can I call when I am having a problem? Who is someone that I trust will be there for me? What is my plan for spending more time with supportive people?
> - **Change the way you think about it**: Do I typically think about problems in a negative, self-defeating way? How can I change this? See also information on cognitive restructuring, discussed earlier.

these family discussions are to your daughter's wellness and her ability to cope.

Nurture Spirituality. Spirituality is a core aspect of a person's overall well-being. This is a broad term, but here I describe it as encompassing personal, private beliefs that enhance your life, give you a sense of meaning and purpose, provide you with the core values that you choose to live by, provide an anchor from which you can make your decisions, bring you comfort during difficult challenges, and leave you with hope and optimism about the future. For many people, spirituality includes an awareness of God's presence in their lives. For others, it is viewed as an awareness of a being or force that transcends the material aspects of life and gives them a deep sense of wholeness and connection with others.[24] If a girl draws her sense of meaning from her spiritual beliefs, she will find less need to focus on appearance, attention, or accomplishments as she searches for happiness or life satisfaction. Viewing life from a spiritual perspective helps her to see that she is part of something larger than herself and her own problems. This helps her to cultivate a sense of gratitude for the good things she has, so that she begins to focus less on what she perceives is lacking in her life. It also helps her in her quest to find meaning and purpose. Help her to imagine the kind of life she wants to lead and whether her current life is in tune with that vision. It is important for your daughter to periodically examine what her life is all about: *Why am I running so fast and feeling so burned out?* or *Why did I stop running or trying? Where do I want to end up?* [25] As she focuses on her spiritual beliefs, how she finds meaning, and what her life purpose is about, your daughter will be better able to stave off cultural pressures to seek her worth through her appearance, the attention she can attract, and her accomplishments.

Cultivate Gratitude. As reflected in national surveys, gratitude in young people is on the decline; in those surveys, a significant number of people say that even when they do express gratitude, it is usually for self-serving reasons.[26] Despite this national trend, parents should work to cultivate a sense of gratitude in their children; there is evidence that people who are grateful are most likely to have a sense of meaning in their lives, are more optimistic about the future, and have more confidence in themselves; they are more likely to feel that they have what it takes to meet the demands of life.[27] Gratitude is not related to the accumulation of material possessions; there are many examples of children from highly wealthy families who feel that they don't have anything to be thankful for. On the other hand, there are children living in poverty who display high levels of gratitude.

When your daughter learns to be grateful for what she has (and in turn thanks others for their kindnesses and gifts to her), she learns to look for the good in a situation and is able to think more positively about life. Here are two gratitude practices you can encourage:

1. *Encourage her to keep a gratitude journal.* If she can write down her top ten things she is grateful for each day, she will start noticing all of the blessings in her life.
2. *Model gratefulness for her*: Make gratitude a regular part of your conversations with your children. Share with them the things you are grateful for (not only the things you want to complain about). Thank others for their kindnesses when your children are around. Encourage them to do the same.

Encourage Compassion and Service. When your daughter is grateful for what she has, it is easier for her to have a desire to give to others. Help her to cultivate a desire to give to others without the expectation of anything in return (what Homayoun terms "selfless service"). This is far different from the required community service projects that girls have to complete as school projects in many schools today. These projects are often viewed as obligations, as one more thing to check off on college applications, rather than because girls truly want to make a difference in others' lives. Ginsberg writes that contributing to one's community is an ideal ingredient that builds resilience: it helps girls see beyond themselves and their own problems and pulls together the important "three C's": *competence* (learning new things by engaging in service projects); *connection* (feeling connected with one's neighborhood, school, community, and beyond); and *confidence* (building a sense of purpose and mastery).[28] Encourage your daughter to become involved in service projects that make a difference in her community and her world. This not only contributes to selflessness and gratitude but also builds leadership, confidence, and connections with positive mentors and peers.

As a final exercise, help your daughter to learn some goal-setting skills that can help her move closer to the life she wants for herself. Help her imagine her dreams through a wide lens and then help her hone in on some specific steps she can start taking now in order to make her dream a reality (see Box 8.6).

Box 8.6: TURNING YOUR DREAMS INTO A PLAN[29]

1. In one paragraph, write out your dream. What is your big bold vision?
2. Translate that dream into at least one definable, achievable goal. What can you do in the next year on your way to your dream?
3. Break your goal into steps. What specifically needs to happen? Make a list.
4. Rate each step as to where it falls into the following risk zones:
   a. Comfort zone: This step would be easy to do.
   b. Low-risk zone: This step makes me a little nervous but not terrified.
   c. High-risk zone: This step would be so hard for me to do that it's even hard for me to imagine trying.
5. After you evaluate your steps in terms of how risky they feel to you, circle your first step. What will you do first?

CONCLUSION

In this final chapter I have focused in on the idea that your daughter does not have to feel that she is being tossed about by the waves of her tumultuous childhood and adolescence. You can empower her to see that she can indeed chart her life course; she does have choices in how she responds to cultural pressures and life stressors. She can learn to recognize situations in which she can use problem-solving skills to change things for the better. She can also learn to recognize those times when she might not be able to change the situation, but that she can make an active choice in how to respond to it. These are times when she can employ the coping skills already reviewed, such as changing her self-talk, using mindfulness, regulating her emotions, or using distress-tolerance strategies. In addition to front-line coping skills, we also zoomed out to see the benefits when she considers the bigger picture, seeing her problems from a different perspective that encompasses spirituality, gratitude, service, and setting goals for the future. When she develops a sense of meaning and purpose, this helps her see beyond her worries over a hot-sexy-thin-beautiful appearance, gaining attention through popularity and romantic relationships, and accumulating a long list of accomplishments. It broadens her view so she can see that she is much more than her appearance, her acceptance, and her accomplishments; she is part of something bigger than herself and her current concerns. When she recognizes her purpose, this helps her to prioritize and make decisions that might not be popular in the moment, but will instead enable her to swim upstream toward a more positive, fulfilling future.

NOTES

1. Sternberg, L. 2014 *Age of opportunity: Lessons from the new science of adolescence.* New York: Houghton Mifflin Harcourt.
2. Levine, M. (2012). *Teach your children well.* New York: HarperCollins.
3. Kennard, B. D., Clarke, G., N., Weersing, V. R., Asarnow, J. R., Shamseddeen, W., Porta, G, . . . & Brent D. A. (2009). Effective components for TORDIA cognitive behavioral therapy for adolescent depression: Preliminary findings. *Journal of Consulting and Clinical Psychology,* 77, 1033–1041.
4. Linehan, M. M. (2014). *Dialectical behavior therapy skills training manual* (2nd ed.). New York: Guilford.
5. Adapted from Simmons, R. (2002). *Odd girl out.* Orlando, FL: Harcourt.
6. BanBossy.com (2014)
7. Adapted from Beck, J. (1995). *Cognitive therapy: Basics and beyond.* New York: Guilford; Burns, D. (1999). *Feeling good: The new mood therapy.* New York: William Morrow.

8. Gillham, J. E., & Chaplin, T. M. (2011). Preventing girls' depression during the transition to adolescence. In T. J. Strauman, P. R. Costanzo, & J. Garber (Eds.), *Depression in adolescent girls: Science and prevention* (pp. 275–317). New York: Guilford.

9. Rapee, R. M., Wignall, A., Spence, S. H., Cobham, V., & Lyneham, H. (2008). *Helping your anxious child: A Step by step guide for parents.* Oakland, CA: New Harbinger.

10. Stark, K. D., Streusand, W., Krumholz, L. S., & Patel, P. (2010). Cognitive behavioral therapy for depression The ACTION treatment program for girls. In J. K. Weisz & A. E. Kazdin (Eds.), *Evidence-based psychotherapies for children and adolescents* (pp. 93–109). New York: Guilford.

11. Linehan, M. M. (2014). *Dialectical behavior skills training manual* (2nd ed.). New York: Guilford; Kabat-Zinn J. (2011). *Mindfulness for beginners: Reclaiming the present moment—and your life.* Louisville, CO: Sounds True Press.

12. Safer, D. L., Telch, C. F., & Chen, E. Y. (2009). *Dialectical behavior therapy for binge eating and bulimia.* New York: Guilford.

13. Adapted from Safer, D. L., Telch, C. F., & Chen, E. Y. (2009). *Dialectical behavior therapy for binge eating and bulimia.* New York: Guilford.

14. Skills drawn from Linehan, 2014; Miller, A. L., Rathaus, J. H., & Linehan, M. M. (2007). *Dialectical behavior therapy with suicidal adolescents.* New York: Guilford.

15. Miller, A. L., Rathaus, J. H., & Linehan, M. M. (2007). *Dialectical behavior therapy with suicidal adolescents.* New York: Guilford.

16. National Sleep Foundation, 2014. *Sleep and teens.* Available at www.sleepfoundation.org/ask-the-expert/sleep-and-teens-biology-andbehavior

17. Ibid.

18. Ibid.

19. DeBate, R. D., Gabriel, P. K., Zwald, M., Huberty, J., & Zhang, Y. (2009). Changes in psychosocial factors and physical activity frequency among third-to-eighth-grade girls who participated in a developmentally focused youth sport program: A preliminary study. *Journal of School Health, 79,* 474–484.

20. Ginsburg, K. (2011). *Building resilience in children and teens: giving kids roots and wings.* Elk Grove Village, IL: American Academy of Pediatrics.

21. Linehan, M. M. (2014). *Dialectical behavior skills training manual* (2nd ed.). New York: Guilford.

22. Jacobson, E. (1938). *Progressive relaxation* (2nd ed.). Chicago: University of Chicago Press; Anxiety BC. Available at www.anxietybc.com/parenting/how-to-do-progressive-muscle-relaxation.

23. Stark, K. D., Hargrave, J., Hersh, B., Greenberg, M., Herren, J., & Fisher, M. (2008). Treatment of childhood depression: The action treatment program. In J.R.Z. Abela & B. L. Hankin (Eds.), *Handbook of depression in children and adolescents* (pp. 224–249). New York: Guillford; Stark, K. D., Streusand, W., Krumholz, L. S., & Partel, P. (2010). Cognitive behavioral therapy for depression: The ACTION treatment program for girls. In J. K. Weisz & A. E. Kazdin (Eds.), *Evidence-based psychotherapies for children and adolescents* (pp. 93–109). New York: Guilford; Stark, K.D.J., Hauser, M., Simpson, J., Schnoebelen, S., Glenn, R., & Molnoar, J. (2006). Depressive disorders during childhood and adolescence. In E. J. Mash & R. A. Barkley (Eds.), *Treatment of childhood disorders* (pp. 336–410). New York: Guilford.

24. Myers, J., & Sweeney, T. J. (Eds.).(2005). *Counseling for wellness: Theory, research, and practice.* Alexandra, VA: American Counseling Association Publications;

Homayoun, A. (2012). *Myth of the perfect girl: Helping our daughters find authentic success and happiness in school and life*. New York: Perigree/Penguin; Newsome, S., Waldo, M., & Gruszka, C. (2012). Mindfulness group work: Preventing stress and increasing self-compassion among helping professionals in training. *Journal For Specialists In Group Work, 37*(4), 297–311. doi:10.1080/01933922.2012.690832

25. Homayoun, A. (2012). *Myth of the perfect girl: Helping our daughters find authentic success and happiness in school and life*. New York: Perigree/Penguin.

26. John Templeton Foundation Survey (2012). Available at http://www.templeton.org/who-we-are/media-room/in-the-news/how-grateful-are-americans-about-the-results-of-the-jtf-funded-gra

27. Ibid.

28. Ginsberg, K, (2011). *Building resilience in children and teens: Giving kids roots and wings*. Elk Grove Village, IL: American Academy of Pediatrics.

29. Exercise adapted from BanBossy.com

CONCLUSIONS

I started the book with a bleak portrait of current girl culture. No matter a girl's age, she is already being bombarded daily with expectations as to what she needs to do to be successful, to fit in, and to be acceptable. She is told that she is not okay unless she is thin-beautiful-hot-and-sexy. She reasons *this* must be the formula for success. But then she also hears that she should attract as much attention as possible, whether in real life or online. She learns that she should be famous, be sought after by males, be adored through social media. So she might start to run after that goal too. But wait! That's not enough. She has to pursue those standards, yes, but to really become successful, she has to accrue a long list of accomplishments, including grades, athletics, extracurriculars. And so she keeps running, exhausting herself, pursuing validation that she is indeed worthwhile. What gets lost in all of this is a sense of who she truly is apart from these cultural expectations. These standards are not her own; she has adopted them because she isn't aware that she has any choice in the matter. She believes that this is her standard of worth. The problem is that because she can never meet these standards (who could?), she is always left with a feeling of emptiness, of never being good enough. When she learns that her sense of worth is based on external standards—her appearance, acceptance, and accomplishments—she will believe that she can never measure up.

In Part One of this book you learned a lot about these three cultural standards—appearance, acceptance, and accomplishments. I also talked about the ways in which they are perpetuated through the media and that, as a result, the more time girls spend with media, the more likely they will be to adopt these standards as their own. I discussed the tremendous developmental changes that girls go through during childhood and adolescence and how these can result in stressors that mount up over time. I also explored what happens when these pressures and stressors become too much for girls to manage, resulting in mental health problems like depression, anxiety, eating disorders, self-injury, substance abuse, and relationship violence.

Once armed with this information, in Part Two of the book you were first asked to make conscious decisions about your parenting in light of what you learned in Part One. You had an opportunity to clarify what you want for your daughter—to develop a vision for your family and your daughter's future. I talked about how you can start to parent from your inner core instead of being caught up in current cultural trends. The discussion then turned to resilience skills for your daughter. We looked at how you can help her build her inner strength so that she does not center her identity around her appearance, attention, and accomplishments. Hopefully, with your guidance she will now be empowered to believe the following:

"I am more than how I look. It is just one part of me."
"I am more than how much attention I can get online and in real life."
"I am more than my accomplishments. My success as a person is based on far more than just a list of achievements."

Although each chapter provides specific strategies, there are several broad themes that cut across the resilience dimensions reviewed throughout the book:

- To be resilient, your daughter needs to develop an authentic self. She needs to create an identity that is not defined merely by what others want for her. If she is to stand up for herself when others are pressuring her to do things that go against her values, she needs to know who she is and what she stands for. Staying true to herself within her relationships, she can learn to be close to others and respect their needs while also asserting her own thoughts and feelings.
- To be resilient, your daughter needs a sense of wellness and balance. With your help, she can learn to appreciate herself for her strengths in all life areas. She can develop a sense of balance so that she does not have to focus excessively on any one dimension. She is a *multidimensional* being, and it is important for her to believe that she is valued for all of who she is and not just for what the culture seems to prioritize for girls.
- Related to balance is a third essential theme for resilience: her need for your unconditional approval and love. She needs to know that she is loved and accepted by you just because of who she is. As I said in Chapter

Four, she needs to know that if you had to choose a child out of all of the children in the world, you would still choose her as your own. Let her know that you love her unconditionally and that you like her. This cultivates her resilience more than anything else you can do.

A final theme emphasized throughout is self-awareness. This book was really all about helping you and your daughter know that you have the power to choose. If you are aware of cultural trends, you can make decisions as to whether you want to follow them. As her parent, you can decide what you believe is best for your daughter. You don't have to follow the culture. Likewise, your daughter can gain awareness that she has choices too. Remember that she will have a lot of questions as she grows older, and she will be looking to the culture for many of the answers. But you are now more aware of the kinds of answers she will receive as she does this. Left unchecked, she will follow these expectations because that is all she hears on a daily basis. It makes sense that most girls will believe there are just no other options.

I hope that you will now have learned ways whereby you can help your daughter to see that there *are* other options and that, just like you, she can opt in or out of cultural trends. You can make a significant difference in helping her discover that there are alternatives to deriving her worth from her attractiveness, her ability to gain attention, and from accruing a long list of accomplishments. I truly believe that it is parents who can play the most crucial role in helping their daughters to swim upstream rather than just floating along in the toxic cultural tide.

I hope it is indeed empowering for you to know that *you* can make a lasting difference, and as a result, it is also my hope that this book has inspired you to take action. Remember my challenge from the Introduction: Because these cultural expectations and trends are new, we don't fully know about their long-term effects on our daughters. As never before, girls are under cultural pressure and stress, and while many are surviving, we need more girls who can actually thrive in spite of current culture. To make this happen, we have to make conscious countercultural decisions that protect and nurture our daughters' resilience. Since you have read this book, you should now feel better prepared to take on this challenge and to teach your daughter to do the same. It is not easy, but it will be well worth the effort as you make positive choices to promote your daughter's optimal health and well-being. The call to action is here: parents, it's time for us to swim upstream.

RECOMMENDED RESOURCES

BOOKS ON GENERAL PARENTING

Allen, J., & Allen, C. W. (2009). *Escaping the endless adolescence*. New York: Ballantine Books.

Elkind, D. (2006). *The hurried child—25th anniversary edition*. Boston: De Capo.

Ginsburg K. R. (2011). *Building resilience in children and teens: Giving kids roots and wings*. Elk Grove Village, IL: American Academy of Pediatrics.

Levine, M. (2012). *Teach your children well*. New York: HarperCollins.

Mogel, W. (2008). *The blessing of a skinned knee: Using Jewish teachings to raise resilient children*. New York: Scribner.

Senior, J. (2014). *All joy and no fun: The paradox of modern parenthood*. New York: HarperCollins.

Taffel, R. (2005). *Childhood unbound: The powerful new parenting approach that gives our 21st century kids the authority, love, and listening they need to thrive*. New York: The Free Press.

BOOKS ON PARENTING GIRLS

Deak, J. (2003). *Girls will be girls: Raising confident and courageous daughters*. New York: Hyperion.

Greenspan-Goldberg, A. (2011). *What do you expect? She's a teenager!: A hope and happiness guide for moms with daughters ages 11–19*. Napierville, IL: Sourcebooks.

Hemmen, L. (2012). *Parenting a teen girl: Crash course on conflict, communication, and connection with your teenage daughter*. Oakland, CA: New Harbinger.

Hinkelman, L. (2013). *Girls without limits: Helping girls achieve healthy relationships, academic successes, and interpersonal strength*. Thousand Oaks, CA: Corwin.

Masarie, K. (2009). *Raising our daughters: The ultimate guide for healthy girls and thriving families*. Portland, OR: Family Empowerment Network.

BOOKS ON GIRLS AND ACADEMIC SUCCESS

Cohen-Sandler, R. (2006). *Stressed-out girls: Helping them thrive in the age of pressure*. New York: Penguin.

Donaldson-Pressman, S., Jackson, R., & Pressman, R. (2014). *The learning habit: A groundbreaking approach to homework and parenting that helps our children succeed in school and life*. New York: Penguin.

Dweck, C. (2006). *Mindset: The new psychology of success.* New York: Ballantine.

Homayoun, 2012 *Myth of the perfect girl: Helping our daughters find authentic success and happiness in school and life.* New York: Perigree.

Mogel, W. (2011). *The blessing of a B minus: Using Jewish teachings to raise resilient teenagers.* New York: Scribner.

BOOKS ON THE SEXUALIZATION OF GIRLHOOD

American Psychological Association (2007). *Report of the APA task force on the sexualization of girls.* Washington, DC: Author.

Bogue, A. (2014). *9 ways we're screwing up our girls and how we can stop. A guide to helping girls reach their highest potential.* Dunham.

Lamb, S., & Brown, L. M. (2006). *Packaging girlhood: Rescuing our daughters from marketers' schemes.* New York: St. Martin's Griffin.

Levin, D. E., & Kilbourne, J. (2008). *So sexy so soon: The new sexualized childhood and what parents can do to protect their kids.* New York: Ballantine.

Sax, L. (2010). *Girls on the edge: The four factors driving the new crisis for girls.* New York: Basic Books

BOOKS TO PROMOTE BODY ACCEPTANCE

Neumark Sztainer, D. (1995). *I'm like, SO fat: Helping teens make healthy eating choices about eating and exercise in a weight obsessed world.* New York: Guilford.

Silverman, R. (2010). *Good girls don't get fat: How weight obsession is messing up our girls and how we can help them thrive despite it.* New York: Harlequin.

BOOKS ABOUT TECHNOLOGY AND MEDIA

American Academy of Pediatrics (2013). *Policy statement on children, adolescents, and the media.* Available at www.pediatrics.aappublications.org/content/132/5/958.full?sid=f31bfb76-437f40c0-8101-267c2d1cc581

Steiner-Adair, C. (2013). *The big disconnect: Protecting childhood and family relationships in the digital age.* New York: HarperCollins.

PUBERTY AND ADOLESCENT BRAIN DEVELOPMENT

Greenspan, L., & Deardorff, J. (2014). *The new puberty: How to navigate early development in today's girls.* New York: Rodale.

Natterson, C. (2013). *The care and keeping of you 2: The body book for older girls.* Middleton, WI: American Girl Library.

Schaefer, V. (2012). *The care and keeping of you: The body book for younger girls.* Middleton, WI: American Girl Library.

Steinberg, L. (2014). *Age of opportunity: Lessons from the new science of adolescence.* Eamon Dolan/Houghton Mifflin Harcourt.

BOOKS ON RELATIONAL AGGRESSION

Dellasega, C., & Nixon, C. (2003) *12 strategies that will end female bullying: Girl wars.* New York: Simon & Schuster.

Simmons, R. (2002). *Odd Girl Out.* Orlando, FL: Harcourt.

Simmons, R. (2009). *The curse of the good girl: Raising authentic girls with courage and confidence*. New York: Penguin.

Wiseman, R. (2009). *Queen Bees and Wannabes: Helping your daughter survive cliques, gossip, boyfriends, and the new realities of girl world*. New York: Harmony.

RECOMMENDED ONLINE RESOURCES

Girls and Depression

http://helpguide.org/mental/depression_teen_teenagers.htm#.Tlum9Sh4xPM.email

HELPGUIDE.org gives tips and tools so that teens can better cope with depression.

http://kidshealth.org/teen/your_mind/mental_health/depression.html#

Kidshealth.org gives an overview of what depression looks like in teenagers and provides information on how to get help.

http://www.about-teen-depression.com/teen-depression.html This site addresses teenage depression symptoms, signs, screening tools, and risk factors.

http://www.nimh.nih.gov/health/publications/women-and-depression-discovering-hope/how-does-depression-affect-adolescent-girls.shtml

The National Institute of Mental Health describes how depression disproportionately affects adolescent girls.

Girls and Anxiety

http://www.adaa.org/living-with-anxiety/children

The Anxiety and Depression Association of America's information page on anxiety in children and teens contains statistics on anxiety disorders in children, information on anxiety disorders, tips for parents and caregivers, and links to several resources.

http://www.anxietybc.com/parent/index.php

The purpose of the AnxietyBC website is to inform parents and young people of the various ways excess anxiety can express itself and to provide individuals with effective strategies to begin to address anxiety. The website contains information, programs and videos on various topics related to anxiety and related disorders, and it contains a section geared specifically to teens.

http://www.aacap.org/AACAP/Families_and_Youth/Resource_Centers/Anxiety_Disordr_Resource_Center/Your_Adolescent_Anxiety_and_Avoidant_Disorders.aspx

The American Academy of Child & Adolescent Psychiatry's Anxiety Disorder Resource Center contains information on recognizing the signs of anxiety, provides information on anxiety, panic, and phobias; it also discusses the causes and consequences, and gives advice on how to respond and treat anxiety in young people.

http://kidshealth.org/parent/positive/talk/anxiety_disorders.html#

KidsHealth's parent's page on anxiety disorders contains information on the distinction between normal and disordered anxiety, causes of anxiety, signs and symptoms, and treatment options.

Girls and Substance Abuse

http://beta.samhsa.gov/about-us/who-we-are/offices-centers/csat

http://findtreatment.samhsa.gov/TreatmentLocator/faces/quickSearch.jspx

Substance Abuse & Mental Health Services Administration's Center for Substance Abuse Treatment homepage and substance abuse treatment facility locator service.

http://www.casacolumbia.org

CASAColumbia assesses what works in prevention, treatment and substance abuse management and encourages every individual and institution to take responsibility to reduce these health problems. The site contains specific information on addiction, prevention, and treatment.

http://www.girlsinc.org

Girls Inc. Friendly PEERsuasion develops girls' skills to resist pressure to use harmful substances, such as drugs, alcohol, tobacco, and household chemicals. After learning healthy ways to manage stress and to deflect peer, media, and other pressures that contribute to substance use, girls become peer educators (PEERsuaders) for younger girls. Friendly PEERsuasion, for girls ages 11 to 14, targets the years during which girls begin to more fully experience and respond to influence and pressure from their peers.

http://www.crchealth.com/troubled-teenagers/teenage-substane-abuse/adolescent-substance-abuse/

The Adolescent Substance Abuse Knowledge Base contains statistics, signs and symptoms of drug use, information for parents of teens, and additional resources.

Girls and Eating Disorders

http://NationalEatingDisorders.org

The National Eating Disorders Association (NEDA) is a nonprofit organization dedicated to supporting individuals and families affected by eating disorders. The site provides a wealth of information regarding prevention and treatment, including downloadable handouts for students, parents, loved ones, and educators.

www.anad.org

The National Association of Anorexia and Associated Disorders provides resources intended to help prevent and alleviate the problems associated with eating disorders, especially including anorexia nervosa, bulimia nervosa, and binge eating disorder.

http://www.dove.us/Our-Mission/Real-Beauty/default.aspx

http://www.dove.us/Our-Mission/Girls-Self-Esteem/default.aspx

The Dove campaign for real beauty site features educational videos and information to help promote body acceptance and self-esteem.

Girls and Self-Injury

http://www.crpsib.com

The Cornell Research Program on Self Injurious Behavior in Adolescents and Young Adults is a research project at the Cornell University Family Life Development Center. The website provides links and resources for understanding, detecting, treating, and preventing self-injurious behavior (SIB) in adolescents and young adults. The CRPSIB team has also developed factsheets and web-based presentations about several therapies commonly used to treat self-injury.

http://www.selfinjury.com

The Self Abuse Finally Ends (SAFE) Alternatives treatment approach is a nationally recognized approach, a professional network, and an educational research base committed to helping people achieve an end to self-injurious behavior. The website provides general information and resources for professionals and clients, information on how to find a therapist, and a store to purchase resources.

http://www.selfinjuryfoundation.org/

This foundation aims to provide funding for education, advocacy, support, and research for self-injurers. It contains information about self-injury and resources for self-injurers, parents, friends, medical professionals, schools, clergy, and crisis staff. There are also directions for those individuals interested in volunteering or donating to the Self-Injury Foundation.

Girls and Sexual Violence

http://www.NCTSN.org

The purpose of the National Child Traumatic Stress Network is to improve access to services for traumatized children, their families, and communities throughout the United States. According to its stated vision, the network provides resources to raise public awareness of the scope and serious impact of child traumatic stress, to advance a broad range of effective services and interventions by creating trauma-informed developmentally and culturally appropriate programs and to work with established systems of care to ensure that there is a comprehensive trauma-informed continuum of accessible care for traumatized children.

http://www.seekingsafety.org

Because so many adolescent survivors of sexual violence cope with their feelings through using alcohol and other drugs, the Seeking Safety program was developed for adolescents with PTSD and comorbid substance use. It is an evidence-based and widely-used group model that focuses on establishing safety in all life areas.

http://www.cdc.gov/ViolencePrevention/sexualviolence/index.htm

IThe National Center for Injury Prevention and Control (NCIPC) site provides facts and statistics regarding sexual violence, provides links to relevant research, describes effective prevention and training programs for professionals, and lists links to resources for survivors.

http://www.rainn.org/

Rape, Abuse & Incest National Network (RAINN) is currently the nation's largest anti-sexual assault organization. RAINN created and operates the National Sexual Assault Hotline and National Sexual Assault Online Hotline (800.656.HOPE and Rainn.org) in partnership with over 1,100 local rape crisis centers across the country. RAINN also carries out programs to prevent sexual assault, help victims, and ensure that rapists are brought to justice.

Girls and Dating Abuse

http://vetoviolence.org/datingmatters/index.html

Dating Matters is a no-cost, sixty-minute online training program designed to help educators, youth-serving organizations, and others working with teens to understand the risk factors and warning signs associated with adolescent dating violence. The training covers adolescent dating violence and its consequences, information on how to identify risk factors for dating violence, strategies for communicating with adolescents about the importance of healthy relationships, and provides resources to prevent dating violence.

http://www.break-the-cycle.org

Break the Cycle provides honest, practical help and information for teens and young adults. From learning the warning signs of abuse to safety planning to navigating the legal system, they provide young people and those who advocate for them the tools they need to live safer, healthier lives. The website includes a Dating Violence 101 section with definitions, warning signs, an interactive teen power and control wheel, statistics, and legal information.

http://www.loveisrespect.org/

Love is Respect is a program of Break the Cycle. The website contains relationship quizzes, information on various topics, including emotional/verbal abuse, stalking, physical abuse, sexual abuse, financial abuse, digital abuse, and abuse within LGBTQ relationships, and free downloadable materials. The website also contains contact information for Love is Respect's peer support advocates who are available through chat, text, and telephone.

http://www.cdc.gov/violenceprevention/intimatepartnerviolence/teen_dating_violence.html

The Centers for Disease Control and Prevention (CDC) Teen Dating Violence information page contains information on the definition, prevalence, consequences, and causes of teen dating violence, as well as links to fact sheets, studies, print, online and video resources, and hotlines.

Girls and Health
http://Girlshealth.gov

This site, created by the US Department of Health and Human Services' Office of Women's Health, offers girls ages ten to sixteen information on their health and well-being. Among included topics are relationships, puberty, health, nutrition, and exercise.

http://www.nimh.nih.gov/health/publications/the-teen-brain-still-under-construction

Interesting article from the National Institute of Mental Health on brain science and how this research affects our understanding of the developing teenage brain.

http://www.newmovesonline.com

This innovative site is dedicated to the New Moves program, a school-based physical education program aimed at improving body image and self-image in adolescent girls. New Moves strives to provide an environment in which girls feel comfortable being physically active, regardless of their size, shape, or skill level.

Girls and Relationships
Resources for General Healthy Relationships
http://www.hhs.gov/ash/oah/adolescent-health-topics/healthy-relationships/

This site from the Office of Adolescent Health is intended to provide parents and individuals who work with teens with resources regarding friendships, dating, bullying, dating violence, and other topics related to adolescent relationships.

Resources Specific to Same-Sex Relationships

http://community.pflag.org/document.doc?id=495

Our Daughters and Sons: Questions and Answers for Parents of Lesbian, Gay, Bisexual, and Transgender Youth and Adults. Available at

https://docs.google.com/a/pflag.org/file/d/0Bz_Rb69kZTYDbTl2dmhWTFc4MGc/preview?pli=1.

Be Yourself: Questions and Answers for Lesbian, Gay, Bisexual, Transgender, Queer, and Questioning Youth.

Girls and Leadership

http://BanBossy.com

Sponsored in part by Lean In.com and the Girl Scouts, the Ban Bossy website contains resources for girls, parents, and troop leaders. The site contains excellent suggestions and handouts for activities to promote girls' ability to speak up and take on leadership roles in their communities.

https://girlscouts.org/research

Girl Scouts Research Institute provides information about their latest research and evaluation projects and information from outside sources on issues that affect girls ages five to seventeen.

Girls and Media Literacy

http://www.mediaed.org/Handouts/DeconstructinganAd.pdf

Visit this page from the Media Education Foundation to learn specific steps for deconstructing a print advertisement.

http://mediasmarts.ca

Media Smarts is Canada's center for digital and media literacy. It is a clearinghouse of research and resources that promote critical thinking skills needed for media literacy in children and youth.

http://www.nationaleatingdisorders.org/get-involved/media-watchdog

Visit this site from the National Eating Disorders Organization to view their Media Watchdog program. This program works to improve media messages about size, weight, and beauty by encouraging viewers to become advocates for change. On this site, you and your daughter can support current Watchdog actions and notify NEDA about praise or protestworthy ads. The page also contains helpful links to other media literacy resources.